D1600507

UHI

*The Making of
a University*

UHI

The Making of a University

by

Graham Hills and Robin Lingard

DUNEDIN ACADEMIC PRESS
Edinburgh

Published by
Dunedin Academic Press Ltd
Hudson House
8 Albany Street
Edinburgh EH1 3QB
Scotland

ISBN 1 903765 42 0

British Library Cataloguing in Publication Data
A catalogue record for this book is available from the British Library

Design and pre-press production by Makar Publishing Production
Cover design by Mark Blackadder
Printed in Great Britain by Cromwell Press

This book is dedicated to the memory of
Sir Robert Cowan (1932–1993),
whose vision and personal commitment,
as Chairman of the Highlands and Islands Development Board
and of Highlands and Islands Enterprise,
laid the foundations for the creation of UHI.

Contents

List of Illustrations

List of Abbreviations

AAC	Academic Advisory Committee
CATS	Colleges of Advanced Technology
FE	Further Education
HE	Higher Education
HEFC	Higher Education Funding Council
HEI	Higher Education Institution
HICN	Highlands and Islands College Network
HIDB	Highlands and Islands Development Board
HIE	Highlands and Islands Enterprise
HNC	Higher National Certificate
HND	Higher National Diploma
HRC	Highlands Regional Council
ICT	Information and communications technology
ISDN	Integrated Systems Digital Network
IT	Information technology
LANs	Local Area Networks
LECs	Local Enterprise Companies
OU	Open University
QAA	Quality Assurance Agency
RITTS	Regional Innovation and Technology Transfer Strategy
SHEFC	Scottish Higher Education Funding Council
SISTERS	Special Institutes of Science, Technology, Engineering and Research
UGC	University Grants Committee
WANs	Wide Area Networks
UHI	University of the Highlands and Islands
UHIMI	University of the Highlands and Islands Millennium Institute

Introduction

Although the narrative element of this book extends to the summer of 2003, the symbolic ending of the story it seeks to tell might be dated more appropriately to Thursday 26 April 2001.

That evening some 25 people gathered for dinner in a country house hotel near Inverness. They had all played a role, at some point during the previous decade, in the project to create a new university in the Highlands and Islands of Scotland – UHI. The task was still unfinished and might not be completed for some years yet, but for all of them it was a time to recognise progress and to celebrate achievement. We hope that our book, initially conceived mainly as a record of events in which the authors were themselves engaged during that decade, will be seen to have the same positive purpose.

At the same time, it would be less than honest to pretend that over those ten years the UHI Project enjoyed an unbroken record of internal agreement and external support, that every detail of UHI's current state corresponds to the aspirations of its initial backers or that there is at present a single, shared vision of how the institution should operate ten years hence. Given the complexity of the concept, the large number of people from different backgrounds engaged in trying to realise it and the geographical distances it spans, the problems which have been encountered and overcome should also be an integral part of the story.

Our aim has been to put UHI's problems in a wider context, hoping that the account may offer some lessons to others engaged in seeking to develop new regional universities. For this reason we have also sought, throughout the book, to place the project within the theoretical and institutional framework of higher education which applied at the time – and which those who first planned UHI sought to influence and challenge.

But we are also conscious of the unavoidable limitations of trying to present such a narrative as history. For a start, we ourselves were profoundly involved in events up to 1997, but only peripherally thereafter.

Although we have spoken widely to those who played key roles in the later progress of UHI, what is recorded is inevitably projected through our own consciousness. In striving to avoid bias, we have also tried to avoid the trap of bland reporting.

We have also had to face up to a fundamental handicap in the recording of events so soon after they have occurred. It is the contribution – positive or negative – of people that shapes a project, yet there can be points in such an account when to attribute a role or an action to an individual still active in the community and known to many of the potential readers might appear either sycophantic or vindictive. On the other hand, there is no virtue in ignoring what is already on the public record. We have tried to strike a balance between naming individuals among the *dramatis personae* and presenting events as the outcome of corporate decisions. This may have led to some blurring of the story line. Later historians will no doubt remedy this fault, as well as correcting our own myopia.

In the larger scheme of things, it is the recognition of achievement which unites a group in a common cause and inspires them to finish the task. Our wish – as individuals and as authors – is for UHI to succeed, both for itself and for the region which it was designed to reflect and to serve. We have therefore rounded off the narrative with our personal summary of the lessons we feel might be learned from the progress of the UHI Project to date and with some thoughts on the way ahead, both for Scottish higher education in general and for UHI in particular.

The confidence we feel in UHI's ultimate success is an echo of the words of Sir Robert Cowan, Chairman of Highlands and Islands Enterprise when the UHI Project was launched: "We have a new and real opportunity to create a Highland university of a different kind."

The opportunity is still there, but so much has already been done.

Graham Hills and Robin Lingard
July 2003

Preface

This is both a narrative account of the efforts to found a small new university in the Highlands and Islands of Scotland and a commentary on the problems of seeking to innovate within the British system of higher education.

Scattered over a dozen, in most cases tiny, campuses, UHI – as yet a university-in-waiting – represents the response to the information and communications technology (ICT) revolution by a large but sparsely populated area of Britain, its extremities not far short of the distance between the north and south of France. History may regard the foundation of the new university as remarkable not just in its novel attitudes, which will eventually become commonplace, but rather in its timing. A region looking for a way to regenerate its economy and its culture began to search precisely at the time when the means to do so, effectively and inexpensively, came rushing over the horizon.

Because the new communication systems discount both place and time, earlier insuperable obstacles of distance and remoteness have suddenly dissolved. It is not too fanciful to say that, at a stroke, the Internet has democratised knowledge as well as the privileges of locality, history and splendour, provided only that people everywhere learn to use and exploit the new technologies. It was to achieve this single goal, and the economic benefits stemming from it, that the idea of a networked system of university colleges to reach all of the Highlands and all of the Islands was conceived and put in train.

And with the technology came new attitudes – to knowledge, to learning, to training, to education, and to the management of dispersed sites – which themselves were made possible by that technology. A new learning paradigm effectively suggested itself. The taming of the knowledge base by the infinite memory and instant accessibility of the Internet and the World Wide Web had the potential to turn traditional education on its head. The massive, passive teaching experience of the crowded auditorium could give way to the personalised learning experience of a new kind of student, now less concerned to memorise and regurgitate second or third hand information and more concerned to develop the aptitudes of exposition and application of all kinds of knowledge.

The hope was that the drudgery of rote learning would give way to the motivation of discovery. The avalanche of new knowledge would be fended off to make way for the human experience of interaction between the teacher and the pupil. The doing and the being would then be on a par with the knowing, the philosophic basis, no less, of the once renowned Scottish system of education.

Thus in this freshly-created university for the modern age it was planned that the new technology and the new learning paradigm should go hand-in-hand, bringing benefits as much to individual students as to the communities throughout the region. So the efforts to found the University of the Highlands and Islands (UHI) were not about creating a chip off an old block but rather about the planting, perhaps a little after the style of Summerhill School, of a mustard seed in the most fertile of soils. Summerhill was the dream child of A S Neil, an educational idealist who believed that pupils learned more by doing what they wanted to do rather than what they were told to do. He was a pioneer of the belief that education at all levels is an emotional rather than a mechanical process. It is enough here to recall that for all its success it was effectively ridiculed and ostracised. The old teaching paradigm was not to be altered.

At a more specific level, the ideas and objectives which launched the UHI Project can be translated into four main themes, which run through the narrative of the book and which remain central to the future of this ambitious venture. They are, in some order of priority, as follows:

(1) UHI, was seen first as a catalyst of economic development. If the region was to prosper, it would need to find its own path to modernisation which would sustain a life style, a younger population and new industries appropriate to the region. This required new ideas, new faces (not only of students) and above all new technologies.

(2) At the same time UHI was seen not just as a marginal extension of existing systems of higher education but rather as a new kind of university made possible by the new learning technologies endeavouring everywhere to displace the old. It was deeply felt that the ICT revolution and UHI should go arm in arm.

(3) To make the most of scarce resources it was thought sensible as well as necessary that higher education (HE) and further education (FE) should be taught and learned under the same roof. Successive binary lines in tertiary education as a whole had always been a source of friction and it was considered that UHI should embrace both, by

deliberate horizontal and vertical integration of courses and facilities, wherever it was fruitful to do so.

(4) Because UHI would be in direct competition for its undergraduate clientele with other, established universities, it was considered essential to develop a distinctive element in the curriculum, designed to attract full-time higher education students from outside the region – indeed, from far beyond the UK. Ideally, these courses would be linked directly to the culture, history and spectacularly different natural environment of the Highlands and Islands, thus offering the double attraction of being able to study a subject while living in the very special community which it had helped to shape. While two-thirds of the student body, of all ages, might be residents of the region, it would be this externally-recruited group that would bring new life to the region – and, potentially, new sources of income to the infant institution.

The effort to found UHI was therefore recognised as an attempt at a bold educational experiment, but one with essentially practical objectives. Its success would have implications for all universities. Its failure would be one more in a long list of efforts to disturb an essentially conservative school of thought, summed up in the phrase that more or new always means worse.

That, anyway, was the idea. The reality is, of course, always different and requires the reconciliation of the content of knowledge to its context. This book then is, at one level, a cautionary tale of what might be done in the realm of higher education, given the freedom and will to do it. To its founders it represented almost a clean sheet of paper. No one could have asked for more.

Acknowledgements

The authors acknowledge with gratitude the financial support towards the costs of publishing this book by The Carnegie Trust for the Universities of Scotland, Highlands and Islands Enterprise, Highlands Council and the UHI Millennium Institute.

PART I
Visions and Aspirations

CHAPTER 1

The Historical Background

The emergence of Europe from its 'dark ages' can be traced by the sequential foundation of its universities. First Bologna in 1088 and then Paris (1150), Oxford (1167) and Cambridge (1209), followed by a flood of centres of learning and civilisation which in northern Italy would define the Renaissance. In Scotland, St Andrews (1411) was followed by Glasgow (1451), Aberdeen (1495) and Edinburgh (1582). In Ireland, Trinity Dublin (1592) completed the pattern. There was then a pause when not much happened to British higher education over the succeeding three hundred years. London (1826) finally saw the light when, in the early 1800s, two Scotsmen descended on England – one, the poet Thomas Campbell, to found the 'Godless' University of London and the other, Dr George Birkbeck, to found the London Mechanics Institution, the forerunner of the great civic universities. By the mid 1800s English universities in the continental sense of the word were sprouting everywhere. No city or town could regard itself as arrived without a university to add to its cathedral, town hall and play house.

The universities before 1800 had been largely religious foundations. They prepared priests for the ministry but also students of medicine and law. After 1800 emergent universities were secular in nature. They were devoted to knowledge in its widest sense and not least to scientific knowledge which would come to dominate all other kinds of knowledge.

The growth of the universities in Britain was far from even. It is noteworthy that despite Scotland's relatively small population – compared with England only 10% – it would, for centuries, boast four universities to England's two. All would be small by present numbers but whereas the two English universities would remain almost to the present day as religious foundations in practice and thought, the four Scottish universities would be largely secular and much more open to science and systematic knowledge in general. Thus, the Scottish Enlightenment found its reflection not in England but in France and in the United States.

It was from Scotland that the United States took most of its principles and a sizeable part of its constitution. There was an atmosphere of utility in Scotland which also took root in the United States. Harvard, Princeton and many other colleges were founded by Scots. Most noticeably, the Liberal Arts Colleges, which would become the backbone of higher education in North America, would be modelled on the broad, philosophy based curricula of the ancient Scottish universities.

John Henry Newman's defence of Oxford as a place of gentlemanly knowledge (in *The Idea of a University*) found no resonance in either Scotland or the United States. One result of this was an aspiration shared by both countries that the way to success should be open for any boy with ambition to climb the academic ladder or otherwise to be educated and trained to the level of his capacity. Not surprisingly Edinburgh earned a reputation as the Athens of the North and Glasgow its pre-eminence as the starting block of the Industrial Revolution.

There would be other differences between the universities of England and Scotland which would also manifest themselves until the present day. All four Scottish universities were firmly rooted in their localities, in their cities and in their communities. Their students invariably came from local families. These localities took a keen interest in their universities. With the later exception of St Andrews, they were universities of their regions, not simply in their regions. The same could not be said of the universities of Oxford, Cambridge, London and many other English cities. They were in but not of their regions and disputes between town and gown persisted until recent times. Only now are English universities seen as vital assets of their localities, potential engines of progress, catalysts of the knowledge economy, and successful industries in their own right.

This difference in attitude towards useful learning on the one hand and mere scholarship on the other would also be reflected in what was taught, and how it was taught, in the universities of the two countries. Practical subjects such as medicine, law and engineering flourished in Scotland. The medical schools of Edinburgh, Glasgow and Aberdeen were renowned. The British Empire was built, it was said, by Scottish engineers. Moreover, the methods of teaching and learning would also differ greatly. Until recent times, higher education in Scotland was broadly based and taught in a more discursive philosophic vein. Degree courses lasted longer in Scotland than in England, and still do, although not as long as in continental Europe.

But above all else, university education in Scotland was seen as desirable and a proper goal for all Scots, be they the sons of the gentry or of crofters. The social pyramid was low and reinforced, as such, by a democratic attitude to learning and advancement, the so-called democratic intellect. The result of this was that in Scotland education mattered. Schooling would be even more important and the status of the teacher high. Proportionately many more young people would go to university, and they still do.

In these circumstances, the four ancient Scottish universities developed slowly but surely out of their mediaeval traditions. The number of students remained small, ie hundreds rather than thousands, but they produced a large number of gifted scholars, authoritative works and inventions. Adam Smith's *The Wealth of Nations*, David Hume's *A Treatise of Human Nature*, James Clerk Maxwell's *Electromagnetic Theory of Light* and Alan Turing's *The Possibility of a Computing Machine* would be triumphs enough to justify the educational prowess of such a small country.

However, in the northern mainland of Scotland (the Highlands) and in the islands (especially those to the west) the regard for education and scholarship took a different course. The primarily oral culture of the Celts encouraged music, poetry, song and dance, but during Scotland's renaissance these Gaelic-Celtic regions entered a period of repression and decline. The Gaels therefore remained cut off by language, culture and politics alike. While this sturdy independence preserved the separateness of their traditions, it left them ill fitted to play a significant part in the modern scholarship which became the staple of universities everywhere. Above all, they had no university of their own through which to sustain their heritage.

The concept of a university in the far North did attract forward-looking thinkers. As early as 1653 Sir Thomas Urquhart put forward his own plans for a university in Cromarty (see Figure 1). Now known to most only from shipping forecasts, Cromarty was once, as were many other towns along the Moray Firth, a prosperous community trading with the Baltic States and erecting fine buildings. But the last battle fought on British soil, on Culloden Moor in 1746, not only defeated the Stuart cause. It led to a revenge by the English and their lowland Scots allies which all but stamped out the Highlands, their language and their way of life.

Once the clearances began in earnest, Highland Scots emigrated en masse to Canada, Australia, New Zealand and elsewhere in the Old Commonwealth. However, for those who remained in the Highlands and in the island groups around the rugged shores, the love of learning kept alive the tradition of centuries. As in many rural areas across the world, the more remote and poor the

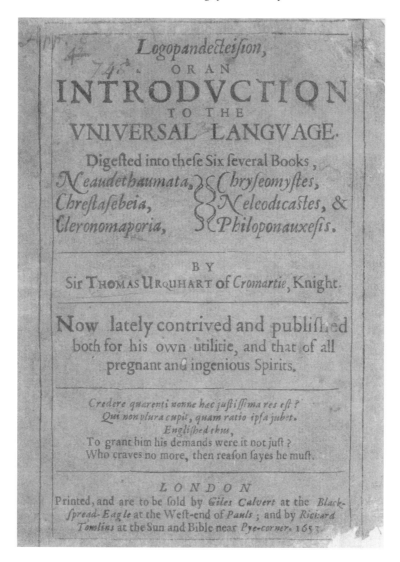

Figure 1 – The title page of Sir Thomas Urquhart's 1653 volume wherein he made the following declaration (Book 6, paragraphs 20 and 21): "I would have encouraged likewise men of Literature, and exquisite spirits for invention, to converse with us for the better civilising of the country, and accomodating it with a variety of good, whether honest, pleasant or profitable: by virtue whereof, the professors af all sciences, liberal disciplines, arts active or factive, mechanic trades, and whatever concerns either virtue or learning practical or theoretic, had been cherished for fixing their abode in [Cromarty] . . . I had also procured the residence of men of prime faculties for bodily exercise . . . and what else might any way conduce to the accomplishment of either body or mind, enriching of men in their fortunes or promoving them to deserved honours." *(Photograph courtesy of the Trustees of the National Library of Scotland)*

locality, the greater was and is the aspiration to do well at school and beyond. There is a legend, both in Scotland and the United States, of the way to the top as paraphrased by the *lad o' pairts* or the bell-boy to president. Humble origins are not an obstacle and there is no class-based envy towards those who succeed.

Even today, in the Outer Hebrides the proportion of students entering higher education in Edinburgh, Glasgow and elsewhere is significantly above the Scottish average and much higher than the average for the UK. Yet there is a snag. The young people who proceeded successfully from, say, Nicholson's Academy in Stornoway to Glasgow University seldom returned to their homes. Until quite recently, there were few jobs available to retain them, to challenge their intellects or to utilise their newly acquired qualifications and skills. It was a one-way journey for most and a source of hurt for those, parents or friends, who remained behind.

The result has been a steady drain of young people from the Highlands and Islands of Scotland to the Lowland Belt and beyond. A fascinating feature of this brain drain is that it was able to continue unabated, for at least two hundred years, from the same population. Still these young people migrated and still they reflected the good education they had received. Evidently, education and intellect are not genetic factors in which the academically inclined are fractionally distilled away from their origins. Rather, the Highlands and Islands have presented a continuing stream of young people well educated and keen to progress because it was the ethos of this part of Scotland for them to do so.

Nevertheless, the continued loss of a region's young people is a serious handicap at any time. In times of great change, this is doubly so because it is the young who are most likely to accommodate the latest changes in technology and in social attitudes. The depopulation of remote areas and especially those dependent on agriculture has been common throughout Europe. Indeed, getting people off the land and into urban society is generally seen as a necessary first step for all industrialising nations.

Suddenly, however, that is not the necessity it once was. Across most of the region depopulation is now being stemmed by better communications, by the rise of tourism as a major industry and by a preference for life styles that can only be found in rural settings.

It was these changes in demographic and economic factors which gave rise in recent decades to the idea of a University of the Highlands and Islands which is the subject of this book.

CHAPTER 2

Early Proposals for a University

It was as long ago as the 1830s that the people of the Highlands began to formulate ideas for a university of their own. Throughout the autumn and early winter of 1833 a series of discussions took place in Inverness, the main population centre of the region, on the benefits which an institution of higher learning could bring to the town. On Monday, January 27, 1834, these discussions were crystallised publicly for the first time at a meeting of the town council where: "a subject was broached of great importance to the town. The Provost averred to the advantage which the North of Scotland and particularly the town of Inverness would derive from the establishment of a college or university in Inverness for teaching the higher branches of education and conferring degrees."

The committee set up by Inverness Town Council at that historic meeting worked against a background of unprecedented popular expectation – the Great Reform Act massively extending the franchise had been passed through Parliament less than two years previously – but also in a situation where many other public concerns had higher priority than universities. Contiguous with the widening campaign for a university or higher college (the terms were used interchangeably) was the beginning of a movement aimed at introducing a Gaelic Chair into one of the existing Scottish universities.

By the mid-1830s, then, Inverness's campaign for a university was well-defined. It had supporters in London, Edinburgh, in the House of Commons and in councils throughout the Highlands – although in Inverness itself the Town Council on 18 May 1835 "reserved for further consideration" its committee's communication in respect of "the endowment of a college in Inverness".

In the next phase of the Highlands' long struggle for a university, it was the politics and administration of Aberdeen's two colleges which appeared to offer an opportunity for progress. By mid-October 1837, the government commission which was visiting the Scottish universities "with a view to their reform and improvement" was sitting in Aberdeen. One of the key matters which it had under discussion was the prospect of uniting King's and Marischal colleges into one university.

The Inverness lobby saw their opportunity and advanced the view that "the educational interests of the country would be best advanced, not by sinking one of the colleges or keeping both as at present in Aberdeen, but by transferring one of them to a central situation such as Inverness".

From Highland MP's, the Inverness proponents complained, there was not "a syllable in support of such a proposal, in a way to show that they were very serious in recommending it". But the real problem, as argued in Aberdeen, was that their endowments were connected with a college in Aberdeen and could not be transferred to Inverness. In Inverness, it was argued that an Act of Parliament could alter the bequests and "change the destination of these endowments to King's College, Inverness". Fort George was also considered as a location. It is still there, unchanged, though at the time it was also being considered as a jail. Meetings were held to examine ways of raising the upset price of £9,000 for land. The merging of the ground and buildings of the Academy in Inverness was also mooted as a basis for the new college at a time when it was thought the many schools to be built by Dr Bell's bequest could meet needs in the burgh.

In the event, the Government supported neither the Aberdeen merger nor an Inverness establishment. However, although the 1830's campaign for a Highland University did not achieve its desired objective, it had two useful consequences.

The first was that some clear arguments had been advanced in favour of a university in the Highlands and these were to be aired again both when King's and Marischal were finally merged in 1860 and, rather briefly, at the time of J S Blackie's involvement in the Highland campaign for land reform in the 1880s.

John Stuart Blackie is recalled in this text not just because he was involved in the financial tug-of-war between Aberdeen and Inverness. He was at the centre of the debate as to where Scottish higher education itself was going in the nineteenth century. He was a strong supporter of the humanist view of higher education and took the line which would surface later when Lindsay founded Keele University, the first attempt in Britain to establish a Liberal Arts university. What Blackie said at the time could have been said at any moment in the life of UHI.

> My cry is for learning in the widest and most comprehensive sense of
> the word; not for Greek and Latin learning only, but for Icelandic and

Sanscrit; for the history of the beautiful forms of art and of great social revolutions, as well as of Greek particles and Latin pronouns. What Scotland wants, and what Scotland, I feel assured, will at no distant period produce, is not now editions of trite Greek plays already edited so often and tortured so critically, . . . on the contrary, we demand a scholarship with a large human soul and a pregnant social significance, which shall not seek with a studious feebleness to avoid, but rather with generous vigour to find contact with, all the great intellectual and social movements of the age.

The second consequence of this early attempt to create a Highland university was that one of the proponents of the 1830's campaign, Provost John Fraser of Inverness, took his educational campaigning to pastures new where he was to meet with success. By 1840, ex-Provost Fraser, then living in Sherbrooke, Lower Canada, was a key figure in the ultimately successful campaign for a college in Kingston, Ontario. That institution, Queen's University, is now one of North America's leading universities and retains a strong interest in the Scottish origins of its founders.

With the exception of a further abortive initiative in 1848 (when the Inverness Royal Academy's Minute book contains details of a proposal to combine the funds and assets of the Mackintosh Fund, of Dr Bell's Institution and of Inverness Academy to provide a college in Inverness with the power of granting degrees), the case for a university in the North received only limited attention for the next 100 or so years. However, the cause could still provoke eloquence. The author Hugh Gunn, in *The Distribution of University Centres in Britain: a plea for the Highlands of Scotland*, published in Glasgow in 1931, wrote:

> The main defect in Scotland is not in the quality but the distribution of its university facilities. It is almost pathetic to think that no further provision has been made for the Northern two thirds of Scotland since the establishment in 1494 of Aberdeen University which began with fewer than twenty students and no buildings.

In the post-war world after 1945, with the economy of the Highlands being boosted by the major investment in hydro-electric power schemes and the prospect of mains electricity for even the most remote communities, thoughts turned again to a university. The *Inverness Courier* of 13 December 1946 contained a letter from Mr G H Pritchard of Beauly encouraging the creation of a Council Committee to develop a university proposal with Lochiel of Lochiel as Convenor. This followed a letter from the Inverness Town Clerk in November to the Scottish Home Department making representation to the Secretary of State to consider favourably Inverness as a suitable location for the proposed foundation of a Fifth University in Scotland. The letter went on to highlight the absence of "higher and technical facilities", the particularly high proportion of students per head of population undertaking such studies elsewhere, together with the economic impact caused by students having to leave the Highlands to enrol at existing universities in Scotland or England.

In the early 1960s the subject of achieving a university was much in evidence in the records of the day. The Royal Burgh of Inverness re-kindled this topic at a meeting in March 1961 and again in 1964.

In the latter meeting it was recorded: "let us emphasise again that to create a new university in Inverness would be the means of bringing to the Highlands a large and thriving industry on a scale which otherwise would be quite impossible. It has been decided to invite representative citizens to identify themselves with the setting up of a new university in the vicinity of Inverness. It is of paramount importance that this representation should be as wide and influential as possible."

A later meeting at the Town House makes particular reference to the establishment of a library for the university. But by now Inverness was deeply engaged in its last major attempt to remedy the educational deficit in the North by attracting a traditional university to its own bounds.

CHAPTER 3

The Robbins Report and the Battle of Stirling

The change in Britain's grudging attitude to education at all levels, but to higher education in particular, was brought about by one of the social earthquakes that marked Britain's post-war emergence as a small and relatively poor country. Socialist ideals for universal medical care (the National Health Service, 1948), greatly increased secondary education (the Butler Education Act, 1947), massive investment in housing (MacMillan, 1956) and the nationalisation of dying industries (1940s and 1960s) eventually focused on higher education. In 1961 Professor Lionel Robbins (of the London School of Economics) was invited to chair a Royal Commission into the future of higher education. Its final recommendations, the Robbins Report, could be summarised in one phrase, the proposal that "higher education should be available to every citizen that could benefit from it". Such a recommendation would survive all its detractors. At the same time it would mark a step-function change in the financing of higher education. It would have all manner of other implications for education itself.

The premise was clear. Britain's workforce was under-educated and under-trained. The 20th century was demanding more knowledge and more advanced skills. The way forward was to expand higher education by creating more universities.

The response of the Higher Education establishment itself to this sudden movement was predictably chilling. It could be summed up in another phrase widely current at the time, namely, "More means worse". The existing universities, especially the ancient universities, were not keen to share and thereby dilute their privileged position. Even those that had been lately ennobled, such as the satellite colleges of London University, could only sulk.

Lionel Robbins himself became a pariah in the higher echelons of British university life but his report was accepted. The recommendation – which in 1964 became an Act of Parliament – was to create another seven universities in England. Scotland got overlooked, accidentally one must presume, and it required a second Act of Parliament to remove the oversight. Eventually an entirely new university was created close to the small town of Stirling in one of Scotland's most beautiful localities.

Implications for the Highlands

The effect this would have on the Highlands was dramatic. It dashed the hopes of Inverness of becoming a university town equivalent (or nearly so) to Aberdeen, Bristol or Southampton. If only for historical interest it is important to recollect how this surprising decision came about. It is also important to understand the profound consequences of the particular ways in which the Robbins recommendations were interpreted and implemented.

Robbins was in no doubt that Britain needed to have more and better universities. Being an economist, he was also well aware of the costs and of the conflict between State funding and university freedoms. The benign reign of the University Grants Committee would be threatened as the fraction of university income from the Treasury grew to exceed 50%. The crossing of this frontier would, by law, activate the interest of the National Audit Office. The question of whether students should pay towards their education would be set aside for later consideration. The large questions of general accountability now to be engaged were blithely ignored, by both government and academia. The simplistic decision was taken just to extrapolate the existing system and to hope for the best.

Because of the influence of Oxbridge, in the persons and in the background of higher education in the 1960s, a single template emerged of the desirable university of the future. First of all it would have a campus, preferably leafy and with vistas. The importing of the American campus was a mistaken view of part of the supposed magic which would later be attached to places like Silicon Valley or Route 128. The fact that universities had for centuries been civic in character and that all existing universities were centred on cities was overlooked, for two reasons. The first was that the cities of Oxford and Cambridge presented themselves as charming rural backwaters. The corollary of this was an arcadian belief in the virtues of countryside for living in and raising families. Britain's dark Satanic mills were not going to produce another Jerusalem, certainly not a university of Jerusalem.

These criteria, when applied to Scotland, would lead inexorably to Stirling as the place for Scotland's only Robbins's university. Lord Robbins, as he then became, would fittingly become its first Chancellor.

Thus Lancaster, York, Sussex, Warwick and the rest would become parked in out-of-the-way locations, nevertheless close to schools and amenities suited for the dons of the future. Several of them saw themselves as embryonic Oxbridges and boasted feeble copies of collegiate life.

There would be other much more sinister repercussions of the Oxbridge interpretation of the Robbins proposals. That peculiarity of English higher education, the specialised single Honours degree would also become the norm. Its academic character and values would lead to a clutch of Oxbridge clones. The CATS, the then designated Colleges of Advanced Technology, the pride of the industrial cities of Britain were, on the tail of Robbins, also given university status. They at once began a process of gentrification, of acquiring liberal studies and even the arts in their repertoires. Academic drift was seen as the way to enhanced reputations, greater incomes and a better social status. One last desperate attempt to improve Britain's flagging technology by instead designating the CATS as SISTERS, Special Institutes of Science, Technology, Engineering and Research, was vetoed by the older universities.

Twenty-five years on would see all the polytechnics brought safely on board the great galleon of higher education embodying a single model of a British university.

The Defeat of Inverness

This long digression into the antics of the 1960s is essential to this narrative and to the understanding of how and why the case for a Robbins University of the Highlands at Inverness foundered. With it went the last opportunity in Britain for a fully funded state university to be created from scratch.

When the case of a Robbins's university in Scotland had been finally if tardily argued through the Westminster Parliament, the door was opened for formal applications to be made on behalf of aspiring towns and their communities. Inverness was not the only contestant. Dumfries had a strong case dating back to the 1800s when a rich endowment by an extraordinary patron, Elizabeth Crichton, was vetoed by the other universities (*plus ça change* etc) and diverted to create – as it was then termed – a lunatic asylum.

Another eminent previous seat of government, Falkirk, was thought by many to be most likely to succeed. The most active protagonists, those on behalf of the new town of Cumbernauld, were of course dismissed as parvenus. In the extensive notes and memoranda describing these episodes of Scottish politics, now disclosed under the thirty year rule, it is not difficult to discern that from the beginning it was in the minds of the officials that Stirling should prevail.

The criteria in favour of Stirling included reasonably good access, agreeable housing (in neighbouring Bridge of Allan) for potential staff, good schools and above all a magnificent campus in the shadow of the Wallace Monument and likely to be gifted by the local authorities including the local health board. This was the time for discarding Victorian buildings and concentrating on new build. No other contender could offer the same opportunities. It was a field day for architects and concrete.

The single criterion telling against Stirling and one that could easily have trumped it out of existence, was that it would be yet another university in the Lowland Belt. The Dundee half of the St Andrews' axis had broken free, the Royal College of Science and Technology in Glasgow and the Heriot Watt College in Edinburgh had already acquired university status. An eighth university within fifty miles of the others was hard to accept, especially by Dumfries and Inverness. As noted earlier, both towns would make charming university centres. Both yearned for the privilege. In the end both were denied. But by whom?

It is interesting to note that the University Grants Committee (UGC) nominated its own group of inspectors to recommend to the main committee in London the winner of the Scottish contest. Again it is easy to read into the minutes and memos, recurring statements suggesting that not only was Scotland too far away from London for comfort but that Inverness and Dumfries were impossibly distant from anywhere. Having squeezed all but one of the UGC visitations into one day, it was left for the foraging party to contemplate the further 150 miles to Inverness. An overnight stay at Perth did nothing to assuage the doubts and the UGC entourage took the greater part of the next morning to reach Inverness by what is now called the scenic route and therefore in a slightly queasy condition.

A large gathering of the different factions representing the Highlands was there to greet them. There was a big lunch, too many speeches (some in Gaelic) and an abortive – and militarily challenged – attempt to look over the still functioning barracks of the Cameron Highlanders with a view to their reuse as student accommodation. The visit did not go well. The visitors returned to civilisation and recommended Stirling. That was the end of the Highlands' best efforts to achieve the university they had worked hard for and for so long.

Even then there was a sting in the tail. It transpired that one of the main reasons for preferring Stirling, the gifting of the beautiful campus-to-be, turned out not to be a gift at all. Yet another Act of Parliament was required to raise the £500,000 to buy the land and then Stirling University was legally born.

Beyond Robbins

To run ahead of the main story line, it is worth recording at this point that the establishment of Stirling was to be the last time a university in Britain would be generously endowed with land, buildings, residences, libraries and laboratories of the kind looked for in a traditional university of the Oxbridge kind. In the 70s and 80s, successive British governments ran out of money. The watchwords were now consolidation and economies. Increasingly smaller grants were made for capital projects and equipment. Eventually both sources dried up. During this time the UGC's loose rein gave way to direct rule by the Department of Education and its various successors. Year after year the Treasury exacted savings on a differential basis. Some universities grew richer. Most got poorer.

The forty or so universities following the Robbins's expansion grew slowly to accommodate demand. Some were fined for growing too quickly. By 1992 the number had expanded again when the polytechnics and their Scottish counterparts (the central institutions) came on board. The same unsuccessful efforts were made to repel boarders but by 2000 Britain boasted over one hundred universities, slightly more than the number surrounding one city in the United States famous for its universities – namely Boston, Massachusetts.

CHAPTER 4

The Changing Highlands

The timing of the Battle of Stirling, with its rejection of Inverness as too remote and obscure for the site for Scotland's newest university, can now be seen as a fine example of historical irony. For in the following year a major step was taken in the steady and continuing conversion of the Highlands from a backward, problem area "on the nation's conscience" into one of the most modern and confident rural regions in Europe.

As background to this part of the narrative, the map at Figure 2 shows Scotland and its principal centres of population, the histogram at Figure 3 shows the population density of countries and regions across Europe and the map at Figure 4 gives some sense of the distance between the extremities of the Highlands and Islands region.

The Role of HIDB

The establishment in 1965 of the Highlands and Islands Development Board (HIDB), as an agency dedicated to the social and economic regeneration of both the mainland Highlands and the adjacent areas of Argyll and the Western and Northern Isles, was the culmination of years of debate about how – or indeed whether – to try to bring an area representing one sixth of the UK land-mass into line with the growing prosperity of the rest of the nation. The war-time initiative to bring hydro-electric power to the area had already provided not only a welcome stimulus to employment throughout the late 1940s and 1950s but also the social benefits of mains electricity in even the most remote communities. The Hydro Board's obligation to provide a service throughout the region meant that it was able to report with some pride in 1961 that 91% of potential consumers were already connected to its system.

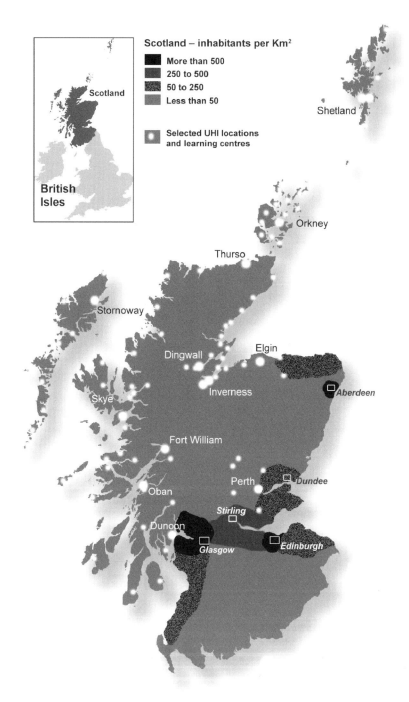

Figure 2 – Scotland's main areas of population in relation to the UHI learning centres.

Into this changing context the HIDB brought a number of powerful assets:

- wide and integrated geographical remit.
- A recognition, from its founding Act, that in fragile rural communities economic progress and social development had to move in parallel.
- A budget large enough to make a difference.
- A licence to innovate and experiment, which in turn attracted high quality staff both to its Inverness headquarters and to its local offices.

This is not the place to give a considered view of the record and achievements of HIDB during its two and a half decades of operation. It did much excellent work, yet it was never without its critics, some of its experimental schemes went spectacularly wrong and at times it seemed blissfully insensitive to the natural heritage which made its region so special.

But on even the most critical assessment the HIDB brought to its area three lasting benefits which should perhaps be seen as its main achievements and which were material to the eventual relaunch of the university project.

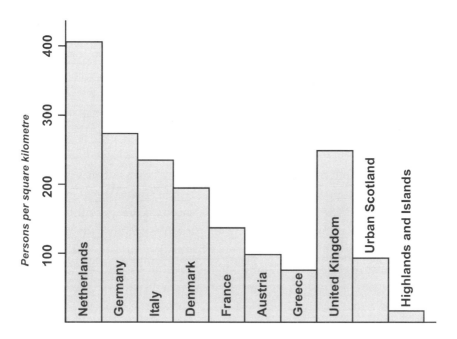

Figure 3 – Histogram of population densities across Europe.

Figure 4 – Map of Scotland superimposed on that of France.

The first benefit was that it helped to rebuild the confidence of individuals and communities across the Highlands and Islands. Seeing new initiatives and new forms of support reaching out to them, they came to believe that their region had a future as secure and attractive as that of any other part of Scotland or the UK. More than that, through HIDB's encouragement of cultural as well as economic development (including in particular support for the Gaelic language) they were helped to rediscover what made their corner of Europe so special and so worthy of care and pride. The second benefit was that HIDB proved the case for treating the region differently. Solutions dreamed up in London or Edinburgh rarely worked in Inverness, let alone in Benbecula or Fetlar. History, geography and culture were as important as economics in shaping development on the ground. Without a sensitivity to those factors and to the diversity of what might appear to the outsider an undifferentiated wilderness, progress would have been resisted. Instead, progress became the community's goal. The third benefit (perhaps not seen as such by all) was that through its geographical coverage HIDB converted the "Highland problem" into a "Highlands and Islands solution". In other words, it was able to draw together the positive strengths of different traditions from as far apart as Arran and Shetland and to do so in a way which sought to balance their interests against the centripetal influence of Inverness.

It can be argued that the HIDB arrived in the nick of time. The 1961 Census had shown the population of the Highlands and Islands at its nadir – some 320,000 people now inhabited an area that had supported 430,000 a century earlier. By 1971, helped by the efforts of HIDB and by the changing perception of the region's future, the long downward trend had stopped and gone into reverse, with the Census that year measuring a population growth of some 10,000 over the decade. This was to be the start of a much more significant renaissance.

Over the 30 years from 1961 the population of the Highlands and Islands grew by over 50,000, equivalent to a new town the size of Inverness. The contrast with the rest of Scotland tells its own story. Between 1981 and 1991 the Highlands and Islands population increased by 2.6% while Scotland's population as a whole fell by 3.4%. Something very special was happening in the North.

Oil and Electronics

An important new factor was North Sea oil. Although it was Aberdeen rather than Inverness that became the centre of Scotland's oil boom, the economy of the Highlands and Islands enjoyed a massive direct boost from the early 1970s through the construction and operation of huge platform fabrication yards, major oil terminals, sea and air supply bases. With this investment and employment came indirect benefits of equal significance, both through increased spending in local economies and through Government-backed investment in the infrastructure of roads, bridges, ferries and airports. For example, road improvements brought down the average driving time between Inverness and the Central Belt of Scotland from seven hours to three hours. Thus the modernisation of the Highlands in the twenty years after 1964 annulled much of the reasoning behind the preference for Stirling over Inverness as a university town.

Arguably, that process was completed in the late 1980s by strategic investment in the even newer technology of data communications. An imaginative deal between the HIDB and British Telecom secured not only the upgrading of the region's existing telephone system but in addition the installation of a new network incorporating BT's latest Integrated Systems Digital Network (ISDN) technology, enabling greater volumes of data to be transmitted at higher speeds. At the time, this standard of technology was only just becoming available in the world's major cities and its installation in the Highlands and Islands was seen as symbolic of the ability of remote rural areas to use digital technology to equalise the terms of trade across the globe. Unlike some previous Highland initiatives, this one turned out to have benefits even greater than were initially claimed. The initial target for HIDB's investment was that it should create 500 jobs in the Highlands and Islands over ten years, both in new enterprises based on computing and data transfer and through diversification and expansion of existing firms. In fact, by early in the year 2000, ten years after the new network was completed, the recorded jobs total had passed the 2,000 mark and was still rising.

Hope Springs Eternal

Although after 1964 the group of supporters that had championed the prospect of a university at Inverness quickly dispersed, the cause of learning was not defeated. Indeed, the region's educational infrastructure shared in and contributed to the economic and social renaissance. The Technical Colleges at Inverness and Thurso underwent a major expansion, the latter linked closely to the needs of the experimental nuclear power facilities at Dounreay. In Skye, a very different kind of educational initiative was launched. Thanks to the vision, work and generosity of a small band of dedicated people, an old farmstead on the south-west peninsula of Sleat was turned into a college dedicated to teaching entirely through the medium of the Gaelic language. Sabhal Mòr Ostaig became a place of pilgrimage not just for the people of the Highlands and Islands but also for the global diaspora. It also proved to be a key factor in bringing Gaelic back into the mainstream of the region's culture and – through publishing and television in particular – of its economic life.

With these developments and the parallel strengthening of the further education base in the Western Isles, Orkney and Shetland, the Highlands and Islands had become equipped with the kind of vocational underpinning its modern economy needed. Yet for higher education the region continued to depend chiefly on sending people away. For those who could not leave the area there was now a wider range of options, including the extra-mural facilities of Aberdeen University (which had long seen the Highlands as its hinterland) and the new and flexible techniques of open and distance learning championed by the Open University, but the dissatisfaction with the absence of a "home base" for higher education grew again as surrounding prosperity increased.

There remained a stubborn belief that it was the responsibility of government, and especially of central government in Whitehall, to continue to minister to the educational needs of the entire country. This, at any rate, was the view of the town council of Inverness. It had digested its disappointment at failing to secure a Robbins university and once again turned its attention to the desirability of a Highland University. A sponsoring committee was set up in 1970 and it commissioned PA Management Consultants to look again at the prospects of a university campus in or near Inverness.

The brief for the consultants was essentially a rerun of the application to the Robbins committee some six years earlier. The sponsors – and thus the consultants – had in mind an orthodox university similar to St Andrews and of roughly equal size. The economic advantages to the town and the region were obvious – e.g. using spare lodging accommodation outside the holiday season. The cost saving of not transporting Highland students to Edinburgh or Glasgow was also held to be a significant factor. Inverness was seen as a potential centre of research (and excellence) in such fields as ecology, social and economic studies and fish farming.

Principal power brokers, such as the London-based University Grants Committee (UGC), were canvassed and gave their guarded support. In Inverness, at least, the prospect for new universities was held to be good, if only because it was believed that if the existing universities "grew beyond a certain size and grew at too fast a rate" then educational standards would suffer, as in the event they probably did.

The concluding lines of the consultants' report were: "We are equally confident that the benefits to the Highlands from a university could make this the most important contribution to the development of the Highlands of the decade." No mention was made of the contribution the town or the region itself might make by way of its own investment in this attractive project. That was not in the thinking of the times.

So it was left for the UGC to make the first move. Of course, it did nothing of the sort.

Another Grand Plan

The consultants were paid, but their report gathered dust on a shelf for a further five years. Then in November 1975 the HIDB arranged a further seminar in Inverness on the case for a university in the Highlands. It was addressed by Dr Farquhar MacIntosh, then Rector of the Royal High School of Edinburgh and Convenor of the Education Sub-committee of the Highlands and Islands Development Consultative Council, who outlined the recommendations of his committee as a three-stage process.

He proposed that the three stages should be:

- the progressive upgrading of Inverness Technical College;
- the gradual establishment of specialised out-centres located wherever appropriate throughout the area;
- the eventual amalgamation of all these institutions to form a federal university or 'polyversity' for the Highlands.

Delegates agreed the following resolution:

> that this seminar of educationalists together with industry represen-
> tatives of the Highlands and Islands Development Board, industry and
> regional and Island authorities, held in Drumossie Hotel, Inverness on
> 14 November 1975, resolved to recommend to the Highlands and
> Islands Development Board that a working party be formed consisting
> of representatives from the Board, regional and Island Authorities and
> Industry to consider and advise on the need and the means of achieving
> an expansion and improvement of higher education facilities in the
> Highlands and Islands as population increases and demand for
> improved educational facilities emerges: the working party to have full
> regard to both oil and non-oil areas and needs, and in all their deliber-
> ations the working party to be advised by educationalists from within
> and outwith the Board's area.

Once more, the plan proved premature. It would take a further fifteen years of progress, both in the regional economy and in the concept of higher education, before Farquhar MacIntosh's forward-looking ideas could be translated into a renewed campaign for a Highlands and Islands university.

PART II
Developing a Blueprint

CHAPTER 5

New Concepts and New Hopes

If any year marked the watershed between regretting the absence of a university in the Highlands and Islands and taking positive action to fill the gap, it was 1990. At that time there was no single, concerted plan or vision. Instead, a number of separate initiatives were launched by different organisations and individuals. It was as if patience with the *status quo* had at last given out.

The timing also reflected a period of growing confidence about the region and its future. The HIDB had fought off the threat of abolition or of absorption into the Glasgow-based Scottish Development Agency (SDA). Instead, both bodies were to be transformed, simultaneously taking on the functions and staff of the Training Agency and decentralising these and their original responsibilities to a network of Local Enterprise Companies (LECs). When these changes became formal, in April 1991, HIDB would be renamed Highlands and Islands Enterprise (HIE), with the SDA becoming Scottish Enterprise.

The Stirling Connection

It was HIDB – and specifically Sir Robert Cowan as HIDB's Chairman – which launched one of a group of separate initiatives to bring higher education to the region.

In the autumn of 1990 Sir Robert opened a dialogue with the Principal of Stirling University, Professor John Forty, about "ways in which the University might extend its work into the Highlands and Islands". The choice of Stirling rather than Aberdeen for this approach was perhaps unexpected, given the long tradition of young people from the Highlands and Islands looking to Aberdeen

University for their higher education courses. On the other hand, as the younger university, Stirling was more likely to be looking to expand further. There was also more than a hint that Stirling "owed something" to the Highlands for having beaten Inverness for the Government's favour in 1964.

At a meeting in October 1990, Professor Forty and his colleagues set out for HIDB a number of options for collaborative developments. These included:

- Delivery of higher degrees by distance learning to those continuing in full-time employment.
- Franchised access and undergraduate courses accredited by the university at one or more of the Highland FE colleges. (On this model, after due training and induction, locally-based staff could be recognised as approved teachers to work in collaboration with staff from Stirling.)
- Vocational training courses relevant to the industries of the Highlands.
- Research programmes targeted at Highland issues.
- Establishment by Stirling of local learning centres within the region.
- Use of interactive TV across the new ISDN Network.

It was noted that "in due course [the university] would see the establishment of a Highlands campus as a sensible objective."

The meeting produced a broad consensus that the second option – university-accredited access and undergraduate courses delivered at Highland colleges by local staff – came closest to HIDB's aim of starting to develop a higher education capability within the region. Sir Robert suggested that Stirling should approach Inverness and Thurso Colleges (but starting with Inverness as the larger FE institution) to see if a collaborative relationship could be developed on that basis. He also hinted that for the longer term a Stirling University campus within the Highlands might be an attractive prospect to HIDB – especially if it turned out to be a natural growth from collaboration with existing colleges.

A Shetland Perspective

Meanwhile, proposals for an entirely different approach to the development of higher education were emerging in Shetland. Oil-related development had brought prosperity and low unemployment to the islands, but by 1990 doubts were being expressed about the longer term future of the Sullom Voe oil terminal. The Shetland Islands Council had therefore initiated thinking about ways of strengthening its traditional economic base and of diversifying into other sectors.

One project which had quickly secured public and private sector support was a brand new college, dedicated to the training and research needs of the Shetland fishing industry but also capable of attracting students to Shetland from the rest of Scotland and beyond. From this vision grew the reality of the grandly named North Atlantic Fisheries College, in an impressive new building in Scalloway. In due course, it would be a great success.

The Council was well aware of the continuing claims of Inverness to host a University of the Highlands. To the traditional wariness of the Northern Isles about the dominance of Inverness was now added a determination to ensure that Shetland's colleges (both the planned new fisheries college and the local authority's own Shetland College of Further Education) were not sidelined in higher education developments. A position paper on a Highlands and Islands University was produced in 1990 and updated in 1991 by John Robertson of the Council's Research and Development Department.

His recommendation was for a "federal" university to serve the Highlands and Islands, not based on a single campus in Inverness but built on the foundation of the numerous FE colleges and research establishments scattered across the region. Such a university could make use of the region's new electronic communications networks to enable students to gain access to its courses wherever they lived. In the period before it gained full degree-giving status it might seek a validation agreement with existing universities committed to the region. Its market would include both young and adult students, its curriculum should be relevant to the needs and characteristics of the region (particularly marine science) and one of its benefits should be to help overcome any residual image of the Highlands and Islands as offering nothing more than "sheep, fish, peat and rain". John Robertson emphasised the need to invest the university concept with the region's own quality image: "Imagine the colourful brochure the HIU could produce, extolling the virtues of such locations as Shetland, Orkney, Western Isles or Caithness. There can be a direct appeal to offer the student a 'quality of life' experience alongside academic growth." Proposing in his 1991 paper a gathering of all the interested parties to brainstorm the idea and create a unified proposal, he noted that: "Many of the required structures and processes are already in place. If an 'all-singing, all-dancing' complete University was not the aim, but rather an embryonic one that could be allowed to grow to meet demand, then the first seeds could be sown in 1992."

Deus Ex Machina?

The third of these initiatives was the most unexpected, in many ways the most improbable – and yet arguably the most influential as a spur to action. Out of the blue, a property developer named Dr Samir Mattar unveiled plans in the autumn of 1990 for a major project at Milton of Leys on the southern outskirts of Inverness. Even for a fast-growing town this was to be a development on the grand scale – 1,250 high quality houses, a bottling plant for spring water, a hotel and two golf courses. The location was equally impressive, on high ground just off the A9 trunk road to Perth, at the point where the north-bound traveller has a first sight of Inverness and its back-drop of mountains and firths. What made Dr Mattar's proposal even more special was his offer to include a university in his development plans.

Not surprisingly, views about the motive behind Dr Mattar's offer were polarised. He himself, a long term resident in the UK but originally from Palestine, said that he felt Inverness and the Highlands had the potential to become "the Switzerland of the North", not just in tourism but also in the development of high technology industries such as pharmaceuticals. For this role the Highlands had the scenery, the clean air and the pure water – but it lacked any higher education establishment to supply good quality graduates and to undertake research work. He wanted to help fill that gap.

A number of influential figures in the area felt this was too good an offer to miss and allied themselves with his proposals, even though they were more an aspiration than a detailed project. Others, however, saw the offer of a university as an extreme case of the "planning gain" proposals beloved of property developers, whereby objections to an otherwise unacceptable project are reduced or overcome by being packaged with another development of benefit to the community.

For the more cynical observers, too little was being said about how the running costs of such a university could be financed, even if its premises were ever built. Was it to become part of the mainstream of public higher education, for which the Scottish Office showed no enthusiasm, or was it to be a private university on the model of the University of Buckingham, for which there was little instinctive sympathy in the north of Scotland?

The Three Models

These three initiatives, developed separately but all proposed initially during 1990, each advocated a different route towards the creation of the future university. The proposed collaboration with Stirling could be characterised as the colonising model, in which an existing university franchised its courses and skills into a "host" in a new geographical area, with the long term objective of creating an independent academic entity. The concept emerging in Shetland (with strong support from Orkney) was based on developing the existing but scattered tertiary education infrastructure of the whole Highlands and Islands area, by upgrading and networking its capability, to build an integrated institution of university status – the evolutionary model. Dr Mattar's proposal (which existed only as a broad outline) was for a brand new institution, independent from the start and designed to meet the region's wider economic needs. This might be described as the custom-built model. Two of the three models followed 1960s thinking, in assuming that a University of the Highlands (preferably located in Inverness) was the answer to the higher education needs of the Highlands and Islands as a whole. Only the Shetland proposal, from a distinctive geographical perspective, envisaged a fully decentralised solution which would deserve the title of the University of the Highlands and Islands.

Choosing the right option – or combination of options – for such an important element in the future of a whole region would not be an easy task.

CHAPTER 6

The Council Takes the Initiative

The Highland Regional Council was only responsible for the mainland parts of the region, not for the island groups, but its size and influence gave considerable weight to the view it would reach on the best way to make a reality of the various plans for a university.

In 1990, in so far as it favoured any of these models, the Council was perhaps most attracted to a custom-built university in Inverness, for which it had provisionally designated a site to the east of the town. However, there was also support in the Council for options which would assist Inverness and Thurso Colleges (then still under local authority control) to develop into higher education institutions. It now found itself, as a planning authority, with a pressing need to respond to the specific proposals tabled by Dr Mattar. Clarification of policy towards the various options for a university therefore became an urgent requirement.

Following consideration of a thirty-eight page report on the options by its Development Department, the Council sought further evidence as a basis for the development of recommendations. Thus the Council wrote formally in April 1991 to the eight Scottish universities, to Napier Polytechnic and Robert Gordon's Institute of Technology and to the Open University, seeking their views on the concept of a university in the Highlands and on the role they might play in assisting its establishment. The preamble to the letter gave a clear indication of the model the Council had by then come to favour:

> Highland Regional Council support the concept of establishing a Highland University, ideally with a collegiate structure embracing existing higher (sic) education establishments in the region, in particular Inverness and Thurso Colleges and Sabhal Mòr Ostaig in Skye.

The letter asked for indications of whether advisory support might be offered towards the creation of such an institution, for information on existing courses or facilities which might be relevant to the establishment of a new university and for views on the benefits it might be expected to bring to the region. Almost all the responses were broadly positive. The clear exception was the University of Glasgow, which felt that, with a government statement on higher education imminent, "this is not a matter on which we feel able to express a view at the present time."

At the very least, the other institutions were happy to provide advice. Those showing the greatest readiness to go further, with specific support aimed at helping create a new university for the Highlands, were Stirling University (linking its response to its emerging academic collaboration with Inverness College), Heriot-Watt University (making reference to its existing commitment to delivering higher education in Orkney), the Open University (including a personal expression of interest in the project from its Vice Chancellor) and Napier Polytechnic. Indeed, Napier had already submitted an expression of interest in helping to create "Napier Polytechnic, Inverness" in a document sent to the Highland Council in January 1991 by its Principal, Professor Bill Turmeau – himself an Orcadian.

With a general election in prospect, the Highland Council also sought views on the university project from all the Scottish political parties. The Scottish Liberal Democrats and the Scottish National Party were unreservedly enthusiastic, while the Labour Party offered sympathetic encouragement. Scottish Conservatives, as the party in power which might have to do something about it, were personally cool at the level of their President, Michael Hirst, but provided a surprisingly positive response from their Education Policy Committee. All the parties seemed to favour the evolutionary approach of building on the foundation provided by the region's existing tertiary education colleges, though the SNP in particular urged that the colleges in the island groups should also be included and that the active support of the Islands Councils should be sought by the Highland Council.

Creation of the Advisory Group

Encouraged by these responses, in June 1991 the Highland Regional Council first established its own Steering Group, tasked with taking forward the university concept. Then in September 1991 – by which time the Mattar proposal had been turned down on planning grounds which had nothing to do with higher education – the Council established a Highlands and Islands

University Advisory Group. Its role was to widen the range of partners working together to the common goal – which had now become, as the Group's title implied, a university to serve the whole of the Highlands and Islands.

Those additional partners were, initially, Highlands and Islands Enterprise, together with local representatives of the Scottish Council Development and Industry (SCDI) and the Confederation of British Industry (CBI) and the Principals of Inverness College and Thurso College. Subsequently, representation was added from other Highlands and Islands local authorities and from Sabhal Mòr Ostaig. As if to emphasise the strategic role of the Advisory Group (and certainly reflecting his own personal commitment to the cause), Sir Robert Cowan himself acted as the representative of HIE. The Chair of the Advisory Group was taken by Councillor Val MacIver, already a tireless campaigner for the university project in her other Council roles as Chairman of the Education Committee and Chairman of the Inverness College Board.

At the first meeting of the Advisory Group, on 3 September 1991, it was agreed that they should appoint an Academic Adviser to assist and guide them in their work. There was strong support for the proposal by Sir Robert Cowan that this post should be offered to Sir Graham Hills, who had recently retired as Principal of Strathclyde University.

CHAPTER 7

The Changing Face of Higher Education

The Highland Regional Council was faced with a pressing need to reconsider the case for a university – but had the wider context of higher education become any more favourable towards the establishment of a new institution between 1964 and 1990?

In one sense, the odds still remained heavily stacked against the Highlands. The overwhelming obstacle to the creation of any new institution of higher education was the absence of any endowment. Universities are expensive institutions to build and to run. In previous times the absence of endowment would have meant that further progress was simply impossible. But two new considerations had entered the argument by 1990.

- There was an increasing awareness that the new economies would be knowledge economies, that somehow or other high level education and, even more so, high level training would increasingly be an essential element to modern revitalised economies everywhere.
- There was a recognition that the economic multiplier of academic activity was high. In the 1980s Professor McNicol of Strathclyde University had made an intensive study of this factor and concluded that the multiplier was not far short of three. He showed that even as a stand-alone entity a university is good business and a very good long-term business. A University of Inverness or a University of the Highlands and Islands enrolling, say a thousand students, would represent an annual business turn-over of £20 million. Surely something could be built on this projected income stream?

The Impact of ICT

To this was added another aspect, the most important of all. Estimates of the nature, the costs, the economics and the investments attending a university invariably stem from considerations of existing universities. However, already by the early 1990s, it was evident that the information and communications technology (ICT) revolution was going to change all businesses, especially knowledge businesses of which the universities would be a significant part.

Among the new developments would be the instantaneous on-line and off-line information transfer, most of it in vivid formats such as to challenge and outgun traditional methods of education. There would be video-conferencing and much improved telephony. Suddenly, mere distance became immaterial. It was as easy to chat 10,000 miles away as with the person next door.

Maybe knowledge as information would itself undergo a sea change of values. Certainly it would be as easy to access in the Outer Hebrides as in Los Angeles. Already a number of Scottish island communities were experimenting in the use of computers for collaborative learning. Immediately, then, the wisdom of even attempting to create a traditional university was challenged. Not only might there be 'out there' a new kind of university, but it might be much cheaper as well as much better. Moreover, whereas the older universities might well wish to embrace the new technologies they would find it more difficult to do so. Perhaps a new university with a clean sheet of paper in front of it was the best opportunity for the Highlands and Islands. The prescience of having installed a new communications network could not have a better reward.

On these assumptions, it was thought to be possible to create not only a new university but a new kind of university, astonishingly modern and therefore attractive to many kinds of students. Because it would reduce the importance of large libraries, large laboratories and the costs of most of the other overheads of existing universities, it now mattered less where its buildings were or how large they were.

To the more forward-looking observers of the higher education scene it was becoming clear that two – and only two – factors would drive the undergraduate activities universities of the future:

- immediate access to all data-bases by all students, and;
- concerted programmes of student-centred learning involving extensive student-student contact, tutorials, case-studies, projects and other self development exercises.

A New Perspective on Learning

The thinking of those contemplating the new university harked back to earlier initiatives to reform higher education in the UK, such as "Education for Capability" and "Realising our Potential". A year or so after the UHI team had mapped out its future, UNESCO published a report on "Education for the Twenty-first Century". Among its recommendations was the need to recognise three pillars of education in the future, namely:

- learning to know;
- learning to do;
- learning to be.

It was the last two, they averred, that would most help to build citizens for the future. Of course, for centuries the main business of the universities had been largely confined to learning to know.

As the planning process continued, there emerged gradually the possibility of a new university which would satisfy generations of educational idealists, of would-be reformers of a monolithic educational system more concerned to replicate itself than to prepare students for future lives of employment and self-satisfaction. At the same time such a university would better serve the interests of industry, creating new business, new jobs and new wealth. Central to this new vision would be a number of vital pedagogic reforms.

- Student-centred learning would be made easier by reducing the burden of traditional rote learning of facts and other material to be memorised as the basis for later examination.
- The time and effort so released by these more efficient procedures could then be used to make possible more face-to-face encounters between staff and students. The way would be open for more staff-intensive instruction of skills, some manual, some intellectual and some social. There would be a greater chance for students to develop their personalities.
- The exploding knowledge base, painfully evident in bursting libraries and their exhausted budgets, would be tamed by the use of electronic delivery, initially characterised as 'just-in-time' rather than 'just-in-case' but later evolving into 'just-for-you' procedures as personal learning experiences came to exploit the full potential of the Internet.
- There would be more opportunity to marry education and training, to bridge the unwanted gap between hand and brain.

It looked an exciting and not very expensive future, but one only possible for those universities prepared to jettison their pasts.

Crumbling Barriers

Finally, to complement the impact of ICT and the flowering of new pedagogic concepts, the institutional environment for a new university was changing rapidly. In particular, there had been a progressive breaking down of some (but only some) of the traditional barriers separating UK higher education from other forms of post-school learning.

The Open University had already begun a quiet revolution, effectively democratising higher education by simplifying and improving access to degree courses and by the introduction of credit-based learning to the UK. Aspects of this new formula were picked up by many of the more traditional institutions, recognising the importance of new markets. In the early 1990s the remaining polytechnics were on the point of achieving full university status, giving Scotland alone five new universities with a strong vocational bias – Napier, Robert Gordon's, Abertay, Paisley and Glasgow Caledonian. Across the UK, the percentage of school-leavers going into further education had continued to rise, as had the average age of those taking degree courses, reflecting the growth of adult participation in higher education.

Within the further education sector, colleges were showing a fresh confidence and ambition, reflected in Government plans to take them out of local authority control. In most colleges the logical stepping stones to degree-level higher education (Higher National Certificates and Diplomas) were now available across a range of subjects – though a survey carried out in the Highlands in the early 1990s showed many gaps in this sub-degree provision. An increasing number of colleges were entering into franchise, access and other articulation arrangements with local universities which enabled their students to move on smoothly to degree courses, often without having to leave their original place of study. Higher education no longer required going to where the university was. In many circumstances, the university would come to you.

Yet, as the pending transformation of the polytechnics showed, the cachet of the university title was still keenly sought – and closely guarded.

CHAPTER 8

The Hills Investigation

All these elements in the changing higher education scene were in the mind of Sir Graham Hills in the autumn of 1991 as he took on the task of acting as Academic Adviser to the Highlands and Islands University Advisory Group.

He had been Principal and Vice-Chancellor of the University of Strathclyde in Glasgow from 1980-1991. He brought with him to that post experience of flexible credit based courses and financial devolution gained from periods at Southampton University and two universities in the United States. In 1990, he had written a brief for a new university to be founded in Lanarkshire, following the closure of Ravenscraig Steel Works. That brief was also prepared from a clean sheet of paper, but with Strathclyde University in mind. As things turned out the competition to deliver this new university was won by St Andrews University. For reasons not known, the project foundered and this plan for a new kind of university was still-born.

The Roving Commission

The post of Academic Adviser to the Steering Group carried with it a clear and immediate task. It was summed up in the familiar question put to Graham Hills when he was approached on behalf of the Steering Group by Sir Robert Cowan of HIE: "Was it possible to visualise a thriving university in the Highlands? And if so, what form should it take?" It offered another clean sheet of paper, which is all a reformer can hope for.

A draft study brief had been prepared by the Highland Regional Council as early as July 1991, covering the main organisational options ("stand-alone", collegiate or satellite), but the remit actually given to Graham Hills in his contract from HIE in late November 1991 allowed him essentially a free hand. The guidance he was given included, significantly, the following: "An important part of the project will be your assessment of the existing educational infrastructure of the area in a series of visits to local institutions and other relevant parties . . . "

Following initial meetings with HIE and the Steering Group on 9 and 10 December, Graham Hills started his travels. By the end of February, when he compiled his initial report, he had visited Inverness College and Thurso College on the Highland mainland, Sabhal Mòr Ostaig in Skye, Shetland College, Lews Castle College in the Western Isles, and the Further Education unit at Kirkwall Grammar School in Orkney. Outside the region, he had met and discussed the concept of a university for the Highlands and Islands with the principals of the Open University, Heriot Watt University, the Universities of Edinburgh, Stirling and Aberdeen, and Napier Polytechnic.

Among the Highlands and Islands colleges he found two contradictory reactions to his visit. The first was an assertion of independence. In the case of Inverness, Thurso and Lews Castle they were looking forward to the prospect of freedom from local authority control. Sabhal Mòr Ostaig, already an independent institution, was very conscious of its primary allegiance to the Gaelic-speaking community. Orkney and Shetland were traditionally wary of anything that might imply control from Inverness. However, the second reaction was a recognition of vulnerability and of the need for partnerships.

Indeed, some partnerships were already forming – but, since they had as their purpose the local provision of higher education, they necessarily all involved institutions outside the Highlands and Islands. The talks between Stirling University and Inverness College, initially prompted by HIDB, had advanced to the point of a formal Academic Association, coming into force from the beginning of 1992 and supported financially by HIE. Thurso College was beginning to work closely with Robert Gordon's Institute of Technology in Aberdeen and Sabhal Mòr Ostaig had forged links with Aberdeen University. A different form of co-operation could be found in Orkney, where Heriot-Watt University had established a research centre and a base for post-graduate studies in marine resources, attracted by the clean waters of Scapa Flow and encouraged by the Orkney Islands Council. However, Graham Hills marshalled a number of key arguments to suggest to the Highlands and Islands colleges (and to Moray College, which was outside the formal bounds of the region but had expressed interest in his remit) that their best course towards a higher education future might lie in a partnership with each other, rather than in individual partnerships with established universities.

"All for One and One for All"

In essence, what Graham Hills put to the colleges was the case for the evolutionary, federal model of a university proposed first in Shetland, in which all the existing colleges and research institutions of the Highlands and Islands would come together to form, over time, the region's own higher education institution. But he added to this concept some angles of his own.

The first concerned the approach to learning which the new institution might embrace. Given the changes in pedagogy which ICT made possible, he felt the region might aim for a single ladder of attainment, with seamless progression from school, to college, to university and to research. He also argued that there was the opportunity for the Highlands and Islands university to distinguish itself in a crowded market place by offering a different type of degree.

The model he advocated was itself not new. It was based on the old Scottish academic tradition of a first, general degree, of the kind widely accepted as the outcome of most courses of liberal arts or liberal sciences. Such an approach emphasises the necessary marriage between breadth and depth, the latter emerging as the defining characteristic of graduate schools and particularly of professional training for medicine, law, science, engineering and other specialist activities. In this model such Englishisms as A-levels, Honours Degrees and low-grade doctoral programmes would be banished in favour of the Scottish tradition of breadth and the Continental tradition of thoroughness. He argued that these would eventually be the desirable characteristics of the British universities of the future – and that the Highlands and Islands might as well be there first.

The second "Hills angle" concerned the link between study and place of study. Why should a university in the far north of Scotland be the preferred place for students to study in these new ways? He argued that the answer lies outside every institution in the region – namely the scenery of mountains, rivers, rocky coasts, moorland wilderness and the small communities that farm, croft and preserve these natural assets. These are potentially what marketeers call a unique selling point – attracting university students studying in other places and in other countries to enrol in excellent courses enriched still further by a Highlands and Islands experience dedicated to the enhancement of the individual and located in small towns and communities where the individual still counts.

This romantic view of why students opt to study in one place rather than another is crucial to any attempt to establish universities in small communities and remote areas. One of the consequences of the new conformity of university studies and standards is that all now offer the same attractive new courses. In a world where one lecture theatre is much like any other and even professors uncannily resemble each other, the choice then comes down to the academic pecking order and the quality of the surroundings. It is in this latter aspect that the University of the Highlands and Islands could expect to score. One of the reasons why so many students studying in Scotland opt for a small university in the tiny town of St Andrews is that the location is charming and secure. Its small population engenders a spirit of camaraderie not found elsewhere. Of course, the academic prowess of St Andrews is an equally important factor but that is the product of its first-rate staff which it is open to any foundation to emulate.

Two other factors enter these considerations. The first is size – the belief that the mega universities have to be self-defeating entities as long as individuals, personalities and emotional relationships are important to higher education. The second is that the broadly based foundation courses advocated for UHI are close to those of the hugely successful undergraduate courses of the United States. If there is to be a common thread through the global university village, this is it.

So this view of marketing UHI world-wide was fundamental to Graham Hills' third, very practical set of arguments. Like all other universities a Highlands and Islands university would rely on student numbers for its income and viability. From the beginning it was recognised that many indigenous students would continue to prefer to study elsewhere, in circumstances quite different from their own. Everything would therefore depend on recruiting into the Highlands students from elsewhere and preferably from countries with very different cultures and environments. For as well as contributing to cultural diversity, overseas students and especially those paying full-cost fees would play an essential part in the new university's search for financial stability. The income from this cohort of students, probably studying for three semesters a year, would, when added to the marginal fees of UK students, make it possible to run and continuously to invest in a new university. This appeared to be the only financial basis on which the new university could be built, given that never again would government fund a new university from scratch.

These financial considerations then led Graham Hills back to the vital role of the existing colleges. For where would the money come from to create the new university? There was only one answer. The colleges already thriving in the region had buildings and even campuses of a sort. These would have to be the sufficient basis on which to build another layer, this time of higher education.

The Reaction of the Colleges

Each of the colleges visited by Graham Hills was taken in turn through these arguments and asked, not persuaded, if they would join further joint work on the concept. All were keen but cautious. Some clearly had other options they might prefer to pursue. Inverness College and Moray College were arguably large enough to go it alone, the former fortified by its association with Stirling. Both Inverness and Moray were already considerably larger than Aberdeen when it was founded (with ten students) or St Andrews in its hey day (with less than one thousand students). However, there was a feeling that, taken together, the colleges and the region's research institutions might represent collectively a potential resource for higher education significant enough to command attention and support from Highland Regional Council and Highland and Islands Enterprise. They might even attract the interest and consent of the Scottish Office which would during this vital period set about incorporating and effectively owning all of Scotland's FE colleges.

There remained two managerial aspects of the envisaged university which Graham Hills was convinced it was essential to confront at the outset. Failure to be absolutely clear about this could have serious consequences.

The first was the relationship of the independent colleges and research institutions to the over arching body which would represent the existence of one university rather than several university colleges. The obvious relationship was a federal collegiate one. Federal systems and their governance are well understood. They bring peace and organisation to any collection of like interests. Joining a federation is voluntary and good behaviour can be anticipated. The collegiate aspect is to ensure that as far as possible all members enjoy equal status. The small can be expected to be protected by rules which govern all, large and small.

This is the basis of the system of Oxford and Cambridge colleges. Some of these are large and rich. Others are small and (relatively) poor. But they live together and speak with one voice when that is necessary. There is another inherent principle governing the behaviour of sensible federations and that is subsidiarity. As much as can be done at the local college level should be done at that level. The centre representing the University as a whole should be small.

To exaggerate only a little, the best federations have a "polo-mint" structure, in the belief that central forces tend to grow spontaneously and need to be continually pruned.

The second aspect that needed to be settled at the start was the nature of the interface between the older FE components and the new HE components. In Britain, these interfaces always give rise to problems. They resemble class barriers with self-appointed guardians of the kind which once regulated the traffic between universities and the polytechnics. It was the cause of much ill-will, supposedly dissolved by the act of unification which made most of the institutes of higher education into universities. But the removal of one binary line led to the magnification of another, namely that between the now united HE and the newly incorporated FE colleges. They would be separately funded and the border between them patrolled to prevent academic drift from FE to HE.

Academic drift has been a great worry to successive British governments. Because HE is funded at a higher level than FE, drift from FE to HE incurs extra costs which the Treasury will always resist. It also adds to the problem of insufficient and inadequate training in essential skills. Skills have only recently been recognised as at least as important as knowledge. Many, lamenting the disappearance of apprenticeships, would say more so. It did not follow that FE alone was the custodian of skills but simply that Britain was in danger of foregoing skilled professional practitioners in favour of largely unskilled and academically biased social scientists and economists.

In short, FE needs protection from HE because the one frequently devours the other, sometimes for base reasons of increasing student numbers and enlarging the university's income. Because the barrier between FE and HE is wasteful of effort and wrong in its implications, it would be more sensible to remove it. This would allow a more easy progression of students into areas of value to them.

Flexible, credit-based modular courses automatically allow for this free flow of people. Student progression is not inhibited and diversity encouraged. From the outset, therefore, Graham Hills recommended that the new university should seek to ignore the interface between FE and HE. A seamless robe of progression from Highers to certificates, diplomas, first degrees and further degrees was all that was needed. That too was accepted by the Highlands and Islands colleges as a desirable characteristic of the new university.

What the Universities Said

The two universities closest to the Highlands, Aberdeen and Stirling, viewed the new proposals with understandable suspicion. For centuries, it might be said that Aberdeen has regarded the Highlands as its hinterland. Ferries to the Northern Isles sailed from Aberdeen. Until the 1970s it had been the natural university for Highland students to turn to. Although there had never been any thought of the mountain going to Mahomet, Aberdeen had slowly but steadily established itself as the provider of extra mural education in the region.

Aberdeen was particularly proud to be pioneering, in the rural Highlands and the Northern Isles, an electronic remote learning system called the White Board so that students, singly or in classes, could exchange writing and diagrams as well as telephonic conversations with their tutor. The director of this aspect of the University's work clearly did not welcome the thought of a new-comer intruding into his empire. The University's less-than-enthusiastic response to the UHI concept was probably influenced in part by this perspective.

Certainly Aberdeen was, on the wider scene, going through a difficult period. The possibility of its merger with Robert Gordon's College, later to become a university in its own right, had left scars on both partners and it was in no mood to collaborate in the new venture. In the end, it was Robert Gordon's University that became the more helpful, if arms-length, supporter of the new university. So for the time being the Aberdeen connection did not prosper.

Stirling University was of course already deeply involved in the out-reach of higher education into the Highlands. It had forged its close link with Inverness College at a time when most universities were seeking junior partners or collaborators so as to strengthen their own position and their student number base. Well understood articulation agreements allowed further education colleges to offer degree bearing courses – generally to the level of the General or Ordinary Degree. These would be validated by the parent university which would then happily, though not necessarily, invite the students on such courses to spend their third year in a university stream. Arrangements of this kind were in place between the college and the university to cover a small range of popular courses in, for example, business studies, business technology and social sciences.

As a result, neither Inverness College nor Stirling University was enthusiastic about the possibility of a new, independent university eventually embracing the college. Because this was not an immediate issue, Graham Hills concluded that Stirling should be encouraged to continue its pioneering work, particularly if it did not preclude the involvement of Inverness College in other enterprises. It would be true to say that Stirling seemed to envisage a long-term relationship with Inverness College and that it was happy, on these terms, to assist the embryonic university.

Of the other universities approached, the Heriot-Watt University responded particularly generously. They felt that the experience gained with their outstation in Orkney, as the base for a Masters Course, validated many of the concepts Graham Hills was proposing. They – and especially their students – were enthusiastic supporters of the Highlands and Islands as a place to learn and to grow at the same time. Napier University, perhaps because it was so young itself, also reacted positively. Its principal, Bill Turmeau, as well as being an Orcadian, had been a pioneering "up-start" for most of his career. He had been the strongest supporter of the Mattar proposals and was no less so for the idea of developing a collegiate university in the region. The Open University, which might have seen the new institution as a threat to their own market, proved instead to be staunch supporters of the concept and a ready source of assistance for turning it into reality.

As for the larger, more established universities in Scotland, there was the predictable wait-and-see attitude to new, risky ventures. Not many were condescending and most offered help in kind.

Of course, what people will say in public and what they believe behind the scenes may be quite different. During the early stages of the foundation of UHI, news of its vision and mission reached distant parts. Visitors came from several countries but mainly the USA. One such visitor, unable to locate where the new university actually was, made an innocent request to the distinguished principal of a distinguished older Scottish university. His reply was short and simple. "Don't bother. It will never come to anything," the visitor later laughingly informed his hosts in Inverness.

But by and large the university community welcomed the new development. Many universities, in the person of their Principal, President or senior staff welcomed the newness of the vision and wished it success. There was no doubt that at least some of that welcome derived from a historic regard for Scotland and its Highlands and its well earned respect for education.

The Barail Conference

The final element of guidance for Graham Hills in formulating his conclusions was provided by a perfectly timed event which took place on the island of Skye two weeks before he was to deliver his report to the Advisory Group. The centre for Highlands and Islands Policy Studies (better known under its Gaelic title of Barail) had organised a major conference for 18 and 19 June 1992, on the topic of "A University for the Highlands and Islands – Prospects and Possibilities". The imminence of the Hills Report was widely known and it was felt timely to open up some of the key issues to public debate and press comment before everything was cut and dried.

Together with speakers from the Faroes and from Ireland, Sir Robert Cowan of HIE, Councillor Valerie MacIver of the Highland Regional Council and Councillor Howie Firth of the Orkney Islands Council set out their vision of what a university could do for the region – and their views on what kind of university would best fit the bill. The convergence of ideas, both from the speakers and from the audience, was striking. The call was for an institution which reflected the values and priorities of its own community but was open to the wider world, and for a university which, while keeping faith with the past, embraced all that was best in modern technology. There was also a strong consensus that it would have to be the kind of university which could "be present" in all the main centres of population across the region.

Sir Robert Cowan, with the intensity of a man whose health was by then failing, set out a powerful series of arguments about the benefits a university could bring to the region for which he had worked so hard. Although Sir Graham Hills also spoke, he was necessarily constrained in what he could say by the confidential status of his report at that time. It was therefore the conclusions of Sir Robert's presentation which most stirred the imagination of delegates and stayed in their minds. It is appropriate to record them here.

> We have a new and real opportunity to create a Highland university of a different kind, because a new market is opening up as access to a university is being widened, and because new models of what a university is means that they can be much less capital intensive. A Highland University could thus become affordable.
>
> There will be huge economic and other benefits. A new university will not be like a manufacturing inward investment project where the jobs are relatively confined and tangible. I would liken it more to a blood transfusion to the whole area. Benefits would spread to all parts of our society and these benefits would only partly be quantifiable, by the rather pedestrian techniques of the economists who will have to evaluate the expenditure involved.
>
> We will however maximise these benefits only if we break the mould. We have to eschew conventional thinking. We have to aim for something radically different and of supremely high quality.
>
> Secondly we must aim to blur the distinction that has too long existed between education and training. This is a kind of snobbery which is out of place in the world beyond 1992.
>
> We must be outward looking and concentrate on building links with the outside world rather than becoming introspective and concerned only with Highland affairs.
>
> The University must be widely accessible to new sectors of our population, flexible in format and delivery – and here our new information technology capability will be an important factor.
>
> I hope I have said enough to demonstrate why I think we should have a Highlands and Islands University – and quickly.

Commitment to Action

The Hills Report

Armed with the strong consensus from the Barail Conference and from his widespread discussions with the region's colleges and the higher education sector, Sir Graham Hills presented his final report to the Highlands and Islands University Advisory Group at their meeting on 29 June 1992.

It was in every sense a positive endorsement of the feasibility and desirability of creating a university of the Highlands and Islands, on a new model. His advice was that circumstances and events now offered an ideal window of opportunity to the region. The call to take action, in partnership with others, was clear and compelling. He estimated that the new university might be inaugurated as early as 1998.

Because of what it contained and what flowed from it, the document is reproduced in full at Appendix I. Here it is perhaps enough to quote some particularly significant sections from the report's Executive Summary, whose words have continued to reverberate throughout the UHI story.

> A wide range of interests has been canvassed from which it is evident that there is considerable support for the systematic extension of higher education within the Highlands and Islands region. The cultural and economical value of further and higher education and of training is widely recognised and held to be a key factor in sustaining cultural values and in regenerating the economy.
>
> The opportunity to create a new university is seen to be attractive, especially if [it] can embrace the most modern educational attitudes, procedures and technologies. The model most favoured is that of a

distributed network of independent colleges linked to a small administrative hub. The new university would then be a federal, collegiate university, not unlike Oxbridge, but in distance terms more like the much larger University of California.

The main authority of the new university, especially its central administrative and academic authority, would then derive from the collective will of the constituent university colleges, in the form of a committee or senate of their individual Principals.

It would be a deliberate policy of the new university to blur the present distinction between education and training. It would therefore seek to provide courses offering coherent mixtures of vocational and non-vocational studies and at levels ranging from foundation studies to the honours degree.

In its steady state the new university could aspire to a student population of 5,000 full time equivalent students, at least a half being part-time mature students, many from outwith the Highlands. The direct economic benefit of such a student population would annually be £20 million.

The Advisory Group's Response

The Advisory Group accepted the report with enthusiasm. They committed themselves not just to the concept but also to the practical steps Graham Hills recommended towards the creation of a University of the Highlands and Islands (henceforward UHI, to both friends and enemies). These included the establishment of the first provisional operational structure for the new institution, including an Academic Advisory Committee and a Project Task Force, led by a University Steering Group which should include all the key supporting agencies and, building on the foundations of the existing Advisory Group, should "to oversee the launch and growth of the new university".

Graham Hills suggested that by about the end of 1993 it would be appropriate to add to these a fourth body – a group of Patrons, people committed to the region and prominent in their own field, who would act as friends and supporters of UHI and "lend it some of their distinction until it could repay them with its own".

It is interesting that the question of how to fund such an ambitious enterprise as a new university had little airing in the Advisory Group's discussions – and indeed that the final report contained no overall estimate of the financial commitment implied by UHI.

In retrospect, this may seem cavalier. At the time, it reflected a sense among the key partners that the formula chosen to achieve a long-standing regional goal seemed right and that there was nothing to lose in pursuing it with all vigour in the hope that the necessary resources would be found. The characteristics of the UHI solution, to be built on the foundations of an existing educational and electronic infrastructure, also offered the real hope that it would be significantly cheaper than all previous models proposed within the region.

Graham Hills himself had pointed out that government money now 'followed' the student, so that the evolutionary approach, building on the existing student base of the participating colleges, was the logical way to build up operational income for higher education activities. Capital funding, he suggested, might come from a combination of commercial mortgages, Scottish Office investment, European Community programmes and external fund-raising. In the short term, the only unavoidable expenditure would flow from the need to establish the Project Task Force and, from it, the "planning secretariat" at the hub of the new institution, for which he estimated annual running costs of around £250,000.

Having funded the initial study, HIE and the Highland Regional Council were readily able to agree to meet the further costs (initially expected to be largely in kind) of setting up a small project team which would be responsible for beginning to implement his recommendations – and also of retaining Graham Hills himself as Academic Adviser to the UHI Project An early task for the project team would be to commission formal financial projections, but for the present it was enough for the Advisory Group to endorse the conclusion of the Hills Report that UHI was a feasible concept and to release it to the press and to the wider community for them to reach their own views.

The Wider Response

As their response to the Barail Conference had suggested would be the case, on the whole the Highland media were highly positive in their view of the Hills Report and of the university concept it recommended. The more usual cynicism about major and potentially expensive initiatives in the Highlands and Islands was markedly absent.

However, there were also dissenting views. Even within the region, some worthies feigned – or really felt – incredulity that the Highlands and Islands could aspire to any such thing as a new university, particularly one which was to be based on "the local tech". In defence of their negative attitudes, it was only fair to suppose that anything they would recognise as a normal university, with professors, faculties, libraries and auditoria, was nowhere on the horizon. Questions asked in public were of the kind – "Where is the campus to be?" or "Will there be a law school or a medical school?" There were also early rumblings of a campaign to centre everything in Inverness, reverting to the more conventional (and understandable) plans of the 1960s.

Indeed, part of the problem was to convince the wider public that a university which was to be so heavily based on ICT could be anything other than a second-rate (and second hand) experience for its students. Stressing the remarkable new possibilities of utilising computing and telecommunications to do things in a completely different (but still effective) way simply encouraged some people to think that UHI was to be no more than a Highland branch of the Open University. Others suggested that university life at UHI would mean solitary, kilted scholars at the end of a distant glen staring perpetually at their television sets.

The question that followed – "What kind of an education could that be?" – was difficult to answer without explaining what the emerging new learning paradigm was trying to achieve. This was not a "win-win" position. If UHI was that modern, it would not be respectable. If it was not modern at all it could not be justified. There was evidently a lot of winning of hearts and minds to be done.

Outside the Highlands, where the Hills Report became the vehicle of many discussions, some of a general nature and others relating to particular universities, the reaction was more mixed. Among the journalists, Olga Wojtas of the *Times Higher Education Supplement* had kept an eye on the project from the beginning and was sympathetically critical. More generally there was an air of disbelief that such a radical experiment could take place independently of the mainstream of higher education – and in such a "remote" corner of the realm. The determination to be different evoked of course a variety of negative responses for those who were instinctively conservative about all things.

By this time the now enlarged cohort of Scottish Universities had formed a Committee of Scottish Higher Education Principals (COSHEP). As this got under way, one of its first tasks was to respond to the UHI proposal. It gave a cautious welcome but there were mutterings that, given the financial difficulties of the existing universities, another mouth at the table was hardly to be welcomed. Ironically, the pressure of the ICT revolution would soon force most of them to consider some if not all of the new learning methodologies then being championed by their tiny challenger.

Potentially far more worrying was the silence with which the Hills report was greeted in the Scottish Office. A Conservative Government had recently been returned to power once more at the General Election and both the Secretary of State for Scotland (Ian Lang) and his Education Minister (Lord James Douglas Hamilton) were early recipients of the report, sent by the Chairman of the Advisory Group. For the present, however, there was no formal response and behind the scenes officials would do little more than express polite interest in Sir Graham's findings while referring pointedly to the accumulated strength and excellence of Scotland's existing universities.

But none of this could dampen – at least for the present – the growing commitment of so many agencies and individuals across the region to make UHI a reality. Exactly how and when were questions it would take longer to answer.

PART III

The World Outside UHI

CHAPTER 10

New Paradigms

Early Supporters

The novelty of the UHI proposals and the realities of its financial position spurred on its proponents to consider the many new ways in which it might earn its reputation as well as earning its living. Fundamental questions of what course materials would need to be created, as well as borrowed, of what kind of academics would best serve the new kind of university and of what kind of students it would wish to attract, took on new significance.

Whilst these issues were being debated and long before they were settled, it was clear that for many existing academics two criteria of success were already present: (1) that UHI was prepared to be both bold and new and (2) that it was to be in a place already precious in many peoples' minds. Scholars, professors and other professionals familiar with the Highlands and Islands wrote in to express their interest and offer their support. A surprising number of them were leaders within their subjects, Fellows of the Royal Society or otherwise successful in their lives. They saw attractive full-time and part-time opportunities to teach new subjects in a new setting. It was a gratifying experience to read about their own, separate visions of a Highland university.

The Lesson of Keele

One of the earliest correspondents was Dr Clark Kerr, one-time President of the University of California and the bane of President Nixon. He was and is the doyen of American university presidents, radical thinker and immensely proud of his Scottish roots which he then revisited every year. He was strongly in support of the new university and reminded the planning group of the fate of a similar enterprise, Keele University. This, the only new university of the 40s and 50s, was also to be a higher education institution built on the then North Staffordshire College of Technology. Behind it and its vision was the towering figure of Lord Lindsay, lately Master of Balliol College, Oxford, but earlier Professor of Moral Philosophy at Glasgow University. He was the strongest advocate of the older Scottish system of the four-year broadly based first degree.

Keele was therefore to be mirrored on Swarthmore College, one of the leading Liberal Arts universities in the United States, itself a child of older Scottish Universities.

All was agreed and all was launched under the patronage of the post-war Labour Government of which Alexander Lindsay was a staunch supporter. Although at the end of his career, Lindsay himself was to be the first Vice-Chancellor. Alas, within a year or so, he died in office and it would be fair to say that his vision and influence died with him. Successive vice-chancellors, almost certainly under pressure from the other universities, gradually attenuated the distinctive character of Keele. Its all-residential nature, and its first, completely general year eventually gave way to the format, degrees and attitudes of an orthodox English university. The only university out of step was thus brought into line and served as a warning to others with fanciful ideas.

It was Dr Kerr's fervent wish that UHI would see this trap coming and avoid it.

A World of Distance Learning

Within a year after its launch the UHI Project also began to attract the interest of wider audiences. The small planning group had been aware from the beginning of similar efforts in similar surroundings and these were contacted. Others made themselves known.

Outside the UK there proved to be a number of other contenders for new universities, in British Columbia, Northern Ontario, one or two centres in the Australian Outback, Northern Norway and Central Sweden, all seriously studying the possibilities of distant or distance education. The phrase "distance education" entered the vocabulary but even such a simple concept immediately took on several different meanings.

Learning at a distance meant no more than studying in a location miles away from a college or university which supplied the student with conventional texts, assessments and other adjuncts to their studies. But distance learning took on another meaning, namely on-line or more generally off-line studies where the information was available from a range of electronic sources, including interrogation of data bases and what we now refer to as "surfing the net".

In the event, on-line and off-line studies would become the preoccupation of all students, most of them studying in the now unconventional libraries of conventional universities.

In short, there would turn out to be a complete spectrum of learning environments from didactic, face-to-face classrooms, to the Open University, a normal university but without faces, and to the personal computer or work station which could be anywhere, in a city university or up a distant glen. Given this profusion of variations which would characterise all universities, it was not surprising that the general public had little appreciation of the nature and potentialities of the new university of the Highlands and Islands, least of all its particular use of distance education.

In truth, it was not entirely clear to the founders. On-line learning, computer-speak for electronically relayed conventional teaching, was still in its infancy. The on-line label was meant to be a comfort factor in the break-up of traditional methods. It would soon become evident that the real strength of the ICT revolution lay in asynchronous procedures, meaning to learn when you like as well as where you like. Students would then at last be free from the constraints of the classroom and the teacher and able to devote their time to learning skills by applying knowledge.

The Perspective of Remote Areas

At the time, the full implications of this revolution in learning were perhaps considered too big a departure from the norms to be suitable for introduction to the general public. Within the Highlands and Islands, however, a number of professionals were growing increasingly enthusiastic about the possibility of using the new technologies to help remote areas share the full benefits of modern training and learning. With the support of Highland Regional Council, HIE and British Telecom a two day conference was held in September 1992 in Wick, on the theme of "education and training in remote areas". The conference covered the full spectrum of schools, community, further and higher education and the delegates included many future contributors to the UHI project. While confirming the view that the technology itself would be a positive factor for remote areas, the conference conclusions emphasised human factors over technology, indicating the need for distance learning provision to be backed up by a comprehensive network of guidance and support for learners and by professional development for staff.

The New Learning Paradigm

Meanwhile, the higher education sector was also coming to terms with the implications of ICT. In the early 1990s a group of academics from the Scottish Universities was set up to consider these matters, under the active chairmanship of Professor Alistair MacFarlane, then Principal and Vice-Chancellor of Heriot-Watt University. This small committee brought forth a clearly defined New Learning Paradigm. The transition to this paradigm from the timeless chalk-and-talk procedures is shown in Figure 5. At the heart of the new paradigm is the intensively supported learning environment – ISLE – described in greater detail in Figure 6. This uses the full power of ICT to effect better transfer of knowledge as information, to allow students to learn what they need to know in their time and in their space and to free up valuable time for tutorials, case studies and projects ie from on-line rigidities to off-line freedom in which to develop their personal skills.

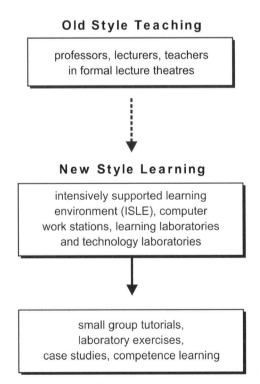

The New Learning Paradigm

Figure 5 – The New Learning Paradigm.

Traditional	Future	Anticipated Benefits
Static	Dynamic	Cheap methods of producing, transmitting and restoring acceptable quality video and animation will have greatly improved the presentation of a wide range of material.
Impassive	Supportive	Well-designed computer-based learning support systems will have been made highly supportive in dealing with a learner's difficulties. This will provide great scope for remedial teaching.
Single Medium	Multimedia	The imaginative and skilful use of a wide range of media will provide scope for attractive learning e.g. audio, video and animation.
Synchronous	Asynchronous	The space and time constraints of traditional presentation methods using lecture and laboratories will have been removed by a shift to self-paced learning using a variety of support mechanisms.
Passive	Active	Learning will be seen as an active process in which concepts are acquired, incorporated into appropriate schemas, and tested in action.
Unidirectional	Interactive	Interactivity offers scope for benefits in clarification, elaboration and consolidation, and is the key to the production of highly supportive learning environments.
Location	Network	Learning can be supported on a network basis across space, rather than in only one location.
Audience	Person	The possibility of developing learning support systems which tailor their response to an individual's needs and performance.
Real	Virtual	The use of virtual objects simulated by computer, and which are interactively accessible, offers considerable scope for linking theory and experiment in teaching and technology.

Figure 6 – The development of the New Learning Paradigm.

Although the new learning paradigm was directed at the Scottish universities (and Scottish higher education in general), it was not warmly welcomed and certainly not embraced. Indeed, there is little evidence that the opportunities it offered were welcome in any quarter. It is not difficult to see why. As summarised in Figure 5, it is a considerable challenge to existing practices and existing practitioners. Those universities with the deepest attachment to traditional methods, subjects and assessments would find it hard to set them aside and to invest in such radical alternatives. Since UHI carried so little of the formal baggage of higher education it seemed a great opportunity for it to strike out in this direction.

A Study for UHI

Apart from the studies engendered by the MacFarlane working party, UHI undertook some research of its own. It commissioned a study by a London-based educational technology consultant, Richard Hooper – later a prominent figure in the regulation of UK broadcasting. Although its primary aim was to set out the markers for UHI's first information technology strategy, in practice some of the most valuable insights in the Hooper report dealt with the effectiveness of old and new methods of teaching and learning, rather than with technology as such.

Richard Hooper defined the characteristics of what is termed in Figure 7 the virtuous cycle of learning. This sets out the five stages of a repeating cycle of learning which, big or small, few or many, make up the normal undergraduate

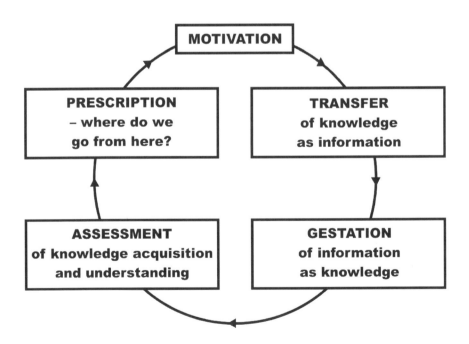

Figure 7 – The Virtuous Cycle of Learning.

	Live Teacher	Laboratory Exercise	Student/peer group	Print	Audio	Video	Computer off-line	Video Conference, etc
Motivation	✔	✘	✔	✔	✔	✔	✔	✘
Transmission	✘	✔	✔	✔	✔	✔	✔	✘
Understanding	✔	✔	✔	✘	✘	✘	✔	✔
Assessment	✔	✔	✔	✔	✘	✘	✔	✘
Prescription	✔	✘	✔	✘	✘	✘	✘	✔

Figure 8 – The effectiveness of different learning technologies.

progression from beginner to graduate. Depending on the subjects involved and on the organisation of particular universities, there may be ten, twenty or even fifty such cycles, most of them sequential but some in parallel. For all students the safe passage through one cycle is the incentive to tackle the next. Equally, failure to succeed in a cycle can and invariably does lead to demotivation and a block to subsequent progress. The failed cycle is generally the result of just one failed stage or step in that cycle. It is therefore important to get each step right. To ensure that outcome, it is then necessary to define how each of these steps can be surmounted.

Figure 8 shows a matrix of the five steps and a representative selection of pedagogic procedures to satisfy them. The row of possible ways is not exhaustive but enough to include the main methods. Most of the correlations between learning steps and learning methods are positive and on a simple pass-fail criterion, are shown as ticks. Negative correlations are shown with a cross.

The negative correlation which sticks out a mile in Hooper's matrix is that between information transfer and the face-to-face teacher. As such, it strikes at the heart of the main process of existing education, namely the lecture, the passive classroom experience of relaying information that is employed in most universities, most schools and by most teachers.

This should not have been a surprise. Any number of books have been written criticising the didactic nature of the traditional chalk-and-talk lecture. More sophisticated studies by the Open University of the in-class experience, the retention of material and its surprisingly rapid attenuation demonstrate that the qualities of the lecture experience are few. There is generally no exchange or personal interaction between staff and students or between students and students. The chances of exercising critical and rhetorical skills are small. And, of course, most teaching staff are not well endowed with gifts of spell-binding articulation, clear writing and even good humour. Lecturers are appointed for what they know not for what they can deliver.

This fundamental short-coming of the classroom experience is of course the main cause of inattention, boredom and failure of many students. It is the main cause of the failure of the virtuous cycle. The teacher must motivate by catching and keeping the interest of the class. In many subjects the face-to-face classroom experience is the only vehicle of motivation. Where the class is also burdened by information transfer, this does not easily occur.

The use of the teacher to convey information has a long history. It is that of the mediaeval scriptorium in which monks made copies of existing books by writing down material dictated by the brother at the lectern. The lecture was born and as a practice it has so far survived the invention of the printing press, the cheap book, the copying machine, PC and the Internet. But perhaps not for much longer. The reason for its survival until the end of the twentieth century was simply that there was no alternative. Now there are many and it seemed fitting that another reason why UHI would want to make the most of electronic methods of information transfer was that this was precisely the moment to do so.

Not only is information now readily available on-line and off-line, but it is available in many formats, some of them highly attractive. On-line and off-line, the material can be interactive, self-paced, self-assessed and available at any hour of the day or night. As we now know, in learning from the Internet, most students find the experience itself rewarding and the material motivating.

Even in the early 1990s these somewhat startling developments left open the ugly question of what then was the future not only for the lecture but for the lecturer and professor. There is no suggestion that machines are somehow superior to humans. The central purpose of any education is to develop the personal qualities of the student which is only possible by interaction with other students and with gifted members of staff such as professors. But it becomes essential that those professors be appointed and revered as much for their personalities as for the knowledge they have acquired. They are no longer to be seen as encyclopaedias on legs but rather as tutors, mentors and guides. Indeed one reason (startling to some) for grafting the new university onto a network of further education colleges was that these colleges already had a good reputation for nurturing their students rather than just letting them sink or swim.

The Nature of Knowledge

If the transfer of knowledge as information is best carried out by electronic means, then the time and effort of teaching staff so retrieved could be used to great advantage in equipping students with a range of skills, some intellectual, some practical, some both. Apart from their intrinsic worth these skills would render the graduate more employable and perhaps more confident in themselves. Skills add to the persona in a way that knowledge by itself does not. In any event there was also new thinking about knowledge itself.

Most traditional universities place overwhelming emphasis on what John Henry Newman, in his book *The Idea of a University*, called literal or gentlemanly knowledge. This was knowledge for its own sake and, as such, a cornerstone of almost all university courses (but not FE courses) whatever the nature of the subject, be it philosophical or practical. This kind of knowledge has several other names, systematic, codified, explicit or scientific knowledge. It is the stuff of books, journals, databases, film and other recorded material.

It differs markedly from tacit knowledge which is the internalised knowledge of experience, judgement, imagination and invention which cannot easily or faithfully be written down. This is the knowledge we call intelligence. It is highly valued in a way that codified knowledge now is not.

Up till the present time educational institutions have spent most of their time and energy harvesting, categorising, teaching and examining codified knowledge. It has been the life-blood of academics. Not surprisingly, it is the basis of cloning other academics. In its disdain for utility it has made the word academic synonymous with useless. The coming together of FE and HE was therefore seen to have positive benefits. The combining of academic studies with vocational studies might be most useful for the majority of undergraduates not set on academic careers in academic subjects. Again, UHI was seen to have a new and different future as a university, perhaps more akin to the liberal studies universities of the United States than to the standard British university with its concentration on single subject degrees and codified knowledge.

Yet one more upheaval in the field of the pedagogy of higher education overtook the early years of UHI. In 1994 six well-known educators published a book, *The New Production of Knowledge*, which set out even more clearly the argument that the world of knowledge was changing fast, from a preoccupation with codified knowledge that they called Mode 1 to a wider consideration of more useful knowledge, more contextualised and more skills based that they called Mode 2. This book, the most important for many decades, was itself not easy to read. It attracted attention of those already interested in these issues but not that of the wider constituency of teachers, professors, lecturers and administrators.

The book's message was nevertheless clear. The old authoritarian world of Mode 1 scholarship was inexorably giving way to the new more relaxed world of Mode 2, which would utilise information technology to the full and put personal skills back on the map. Graham Hills saw that UHI had the potential to be the first unashamedly Mode 2 university, less top-down and more bottom-up. But would UHI be a vehicle robust enough to deliver such a radically changed approach to higher education? And were there other reforms it should embrace on the way?

CHAPTER 11

A Reforming University?

By the early 1990s there were many signs that all was not well within the UK higher education sector. Everywhere there was pressure on the system to grow and to grow quickly, reinforced by a supposition – unproven – that national prosperity was directly related to the relative volume of educational performance. As the cheapest and least contentious way, it was decided that the new growth would therefore take place on the old wood so that what became known as mass higher education was simply a linear expansion of the existing arrangements, the courses, the researches and their range of subjects. That the existing arrangements were of an older (Mode 1) ethos, in which scholarship was all, was either welcomed or ignored. So more became more of the same.

The Foundation Degree

In Britain this had two consequences, seen as calamitous by a number of observers. First, it put pressure on new cohorts of students to pretend to be the scholars they never wanted to be. Second, it would dilute the intellectual resource base essential for the postgraduate and professional studies of those intending to be leaders. Most of the new students were not prepared for the arduous path of professional training for, say, science and engineering. Both in absolute and relative terms the numbers of students, gifted or otherwise, presenting themselves for these disciplines declined. Later in the decade this was recognised by the Dearing Committee of Enquiry into Higher Education which argued – unsuccessfully – the benefits of broader, foundation degrees for many if not all undergraduates.

The idea of a foundation degree is not just the dream of liberally minded European academics who themselves have experienced or witnessed the advantages of a broad first degree. As noted elsewhere, most first degrees in the United States are of this kind. It is regarded by many as a more than sufficient basis of citizenship, as well as a launching pad for those wishing to go further. This gifted and self-selected minority then does go on to study medicine, engineering, law and a range of other professional subjects (including research). The quality of education and training then made possible by the smaller numbers has given the United States an enviable reputation in every aspect of research and scholarship, but the strength of these graduate courses is also a powerful justification of the broad intellectual foundations of the first degree.

Notwithstanding the force of these arguments (now underpinned intellectually by the Mode 1/Mode 2 debate) British universities continued to set their face against radical reform of the undergraduate degree. Instead, intense competition between them for student numbers and financial resources gradually focused their interests onto conforming issues, bolstered by league tables and quality assurance audits.

However UHI, by adopting the strategy of independence from the conformity of existing universities, might be ideally placed to lead the UK on a reforming path – and a path which, most appropriately, looped back to the solid Scottish academic tradition of a broad first degree.

Support from Europe

During the 1990s, complementary proposals for the broadening of otherwise narrow undergraduate experiences came from another quarter. The idea that students would benefit from experience of other universities in other countries had long been a higher education tradition, but was now rarely observed. As a way of cementing the ties between their peoples and at the same time broadening the Community's higher education foundations, the Member States of the EEC adopted a scheme to encourage directly the interchange of students between different universities in different countries in Europe. The ERASMUS initiative, aptly named after Europe's most distinguished 'wandering scholar', involved subsidising the mutual exchange of students between fraternal universities.

The ERASMUS scheme was entirely voluntary and, as ever, some universities were more enthusiastic than others. However, those that got off to a flying start were quickly followed by the others. Some prior requirements of language ability were generally met without difficulty and intercalation of students into courses matching their home curricula, whilst not easy or efficient, nevertheless took place to the satisfaction of most. Of course, the greatest benefit was not from the academic material but from the social experience of new cultures and new friends. It was a great success, but it relied for its continuation on the universities themselves picking up the bill at the end of the three-year experimental period. Sad to say, it virtually died the death well before UHI was in a position to take advantage of it. It seemed that without additional financial support nothing was now possible. At the time, the resurrection of the ERASMUS concept in the Bologna Declaration could not have been foreseen.

Assessment and Accountability

In theory, the supporters of UHI had the advantage of being able to design from the beginning a new university with essential reforms already incorporated in it. But it is not that easy to off-load the baggage of the past.

Further and higher education takes place within an agreed framework of examinations and assessments. Professional authorities guard the nature, the quality, the quantity and the relevance of qualifications defining graduateness and every other level of attainment. It is one thing to set out a new and radical path to graduation; it is another to tinker with the detailed specifications of each nodal point. Every reform is therefore soon confronted with the advice of Machiavelli that change is impossible because of the weight of attachment to the present.

This innate conservatism has always been a problem within the UK education system. Three decades of attempts to broaden the English A-level examinations have so far failed. The attachment of Britain to the Single Honours Degree qualification has never been stronger and although its uniqueness qualifies it to be called an international anachronism, it remains the desirable goal of the whole of the British university sector.

But these were not the only obstacless to radical reform. Control through examination and assessment, largely self-regulated, was supplemented increasingly in the 1980s and 1990s by the growing demands of successive governments for "accountability" within the higher education system. First there was the matter of financial accountability. In the 1980s, following the near bankruptcy of Cardiff University, an edict was issued making all vice-chancellors the chief accounting officers of their institutions. Most vice-chancellors, untrained and unfitted for this new responsibility, had therefore to learn quickly to decipher balance sheets if their institutions were to survive. As a result, the mood inside the universities became more serious and introspective. The lay chairmen of their courts, councils or other governing bodies became more powerful. Statutory bodies, such as the Public Accounts Committee and the Higher Education Funding Councils, enjoyed the right to enquire into and determine the financial business of otherwise independent organisations. The Funding Councils – HEFC and its Scottish equivalent (SHEFC) – extended their authority into every aspect of university life, setting forth the criteria of what was required for the money to flow.

It was an unhappy time, made more so by the advent of other accountability criteria. Universities were to be judged on their research performance, on their teaching performance, on their recruitment successes and on their ability to convert academic know-what into commercially useful know-how. Anything that could be measured would be measured.

One outcome of direct concern to UHI was that the process of acceptance into the university "club" was likely to become ever longer and more complex, with the prospect of a lengthy and demanding apprenticeship to follow. Another was that the instinctive desire of the founders to use the new university to develop a bold and innovative approach to higher education would be increasingly at odds with the need to satisfy a proscriptive and centralised accountability system.

The way in which UHI was to assess its own students was a case in point. The centralised system tended towards a futile pursuit of objectivity, requiring a series of hurdles, supposedly of exact heights, over which graduating students would need to jump. The much more relaxed use of continuous assessment, the step-by-step process of self-improvement operated for the benefit of students, meets many obstacles in British academic life. Thus in the virtuous cycle of learning, illustrated in Figure 7, the fourth stage, that of assessment, needs to be seen always as primarily in the interests of the student. Absolute standards in most assessments are not possible and not desirable. It is essential to trust the teacher and the professor to know the nature and extent of their students' attainments. If this is best done by oral assessment then so be it. The other argument, that the death-or-glory, final written examination is a preparation for life, is nonsense and one of the best examples of an absurdity which being repeated so often becomes believable. Attitudes of mind that look for absolute standards will find comfort in Mode 1 teaching as opposed to Mode 2 learning.

If it was truly to embrace Mode 2 learning, UHI should therefore also eschew the older habits of knowledge-based, closed-book written examinations in favour of skills-based, open-book assessments. But how much reform could any small, brand new institution hope to implement – especially an institution still lacking all forms of official endorsement from those responsible for running the nation's higher education system?

The Challenge for UHI

In summary, UHI was to be born into a largely hostile climate of scarce resources and conservative beliefs in traditional procedures, where reforming instincts would find little sympathy from the established institutions and conformity would be applauded. However, the path of conformity held little appeal for a new university seeking to make its mark in the world. As we have seen, Robbins universities, such as Stirling, and polytechnic universities, such as Abertay, came into being at the end of a long queue of other pretenders. As such they would have to struggle against heavy odds to establish themselves in a highly competitive market place.

With essentially no resources, the task of UHI might have seemed a mission impossible. Indeed, most other Scottish universities wrote it off for that reason. But all such pessimistic considerations were based on the supposition that UHI would be forced into the traditional mould, there being (to its critics) no alternative. However, the progenitors of UHI held to the firm belief, born of experience, that in times of great change coming late can be a considerable advantage. The Asian Tigers were, by far, the best example of poor, small countries leap-frogging over their sluggish elders to become economic successes. Perhaps UHI could make a comparable leap and take the fortunes of its region forward with it?

PART IV

Assembling the Framework

CHAPTER 12

New Tasks and New Structures

The preceding sections of this book have sought to place the origins and initial concept of the UHI Project within the geography, history and society of its region and in the context of contemporary educational policy. To summarise, the idea was to create a new kind of university which would both reflect and take advantage of the special circumstances of the Highlands and Islands.

It was to be a one-off institution, because the Highlands and Islands is a distinctive and unique area, in both geography and culture. It would be a federation of equal partners, spread across communities from Shetland to Argyll. It would use the latest technology, for which the infrastructure was already available in the region, to overcome the barriers of distance and to make a reality of the new learning paradigm. It would bring together the regimes of higher education and further education, separate in the rest of the British Isles, in order to optimise use of existing capital resources and to provide its students with a single ladder of opportunity. It would aim to resurrect the tradition of the broad Scottish first degree, based on a common core of skills-based competencies. By its own merits and through the inherent attractions of its region, it would aim to draw in students – and staff – from well beyond the boundaries of the Highlands and Islands, including overseas students who would both enliven the social mix and contribute vitally to income. It would play an important role, directly and indirectly, in revitalising the economy and cultural tradition of its region. It was to be small in size, but would strive to be first in its own league rather than an also-ran among the one hundred or so near-identical UK universities.

At the time these aims were formulated they were not seen, either by UHI's proposers or by those working in similar fields elsewhere, as pretentious or unrealistic. However, it was by common consent a very ambitious project and one for which the necessary resources had hardly been assessed, let alone secured. There were undoubtedly many who expected it to fail, or to succeed only in part, and yet to many more UHI represented a vision and a hope which would consummate the renaissance of the region.

Guiding Structures

Now a start had to be made on forging the practical partnerships which would, over time, convert the concept into an operational institution. Thus the Highlands and Islands University Advisory Group met again on 18 September 1992, some three months after it had endorsed and launched the Hills Report on UHI. With hindsight it is possible to see that the key elements in turning the UHI concept into an operational reality were either put in place or identified for future implementation during those early months.

Three major tasks had to be tackled in parallel. The first was to maintain and drive forward the UHI concept at political and community level, until the formal governing structure for a university could be established. This was a continuation of the work of the Advisory Group which, for this purpose, agreed to reconstitute itself as the University of the Highlands and Islands Steering Group. Membership would be drawn, as before, from HIE and the local authorities, still under the Chairmanship of Councillor Val MacIver, but it was proposed that the colleges would no longer be directly represented at this level.

However, the second task placed the colleges right in the front line. As Graham Hills had recommended, the Steering Group agreed to set up an Academic Advisory Committee (AAC) involving all the participating colleges. The main aim of the AAC was to design the UHI curriculum and chart the course for its development, from the base of current further and higher education and research activities across the region. Graham Hills was invited to remain as Academic Adviser to the UHI Steering Group and additionally to chair the AAC and to represent it at Steering Group meetings. He in turn suggested that representatives of existing higher education institutions and of the Scottish Council for Vocational Education (SCOTVEC) should be invited to participate in the work of the AAC.

The third task, underpinning the other two, was to manage and develop the non-academic aspects of the project, to deal with financial planning and control and to provide secretariat support to the Steering Group and the Academic Advisory Committee. For this purpose a UHI Project Team was established jointly by HIE and the Highland Regional Council.

The task of leading the UHI Project Team was given to Robin Lingard, Director of Training and Social Development at HIE, who had already built up a strong working relationship with Graham Hills during the feasibility study phase. Although he had no direct experience of administering higher education, Robin Lingard had been a senior civil servant in Whitehall before moving to the Highlands a few years earlier as a full-time Board Member of HIDB. With HIDB he had taken a leading role in negotiating the joint venture with BT to instal the region's ISDN network. His remit at HIE already included training and learning policy and the encouragement of social and community development, so the UHI brief was a logical addition.

Robin Lingard was supported within HIE by Allan Bransbury, who had developed a special interest in the development of distance learning and had established close links with a number of the colleges both in that context and through responsibility for PICKUP, the regional access programme. Both men were able to commit only a proportion of their time to UHI, however.

Although the lead role fell to HIE, the Project Team was heavily dependent on the support of the Highland Regional Council. Their participation was led by Harold Farquhar, Director of Law and Administration, who had ably guided the earlier work of the Steering and Advisory Groups. As with HIE, the Council's efforts to push forward UHI could only be accommodated in the margins of busy people's time.

The Scottish Office Stays Cool

At the time of the Hills Report there had been hints that the Scottish Office might be willing to provide funding to supplement the UHI Project Team with consultants and additional full-time staff – including perhaps a secondment from the Scottish Office itself. However, a fly cast in that direction was not taken. More depressingly, the formal response was decidedly frosty, stressing the rigorous and lengthy academic requirements for achieving university status and referring pointedly to plans by existing institutions to expand their operations in the Highlands and Islands.

The conclusion of the Scottish Office reply was that, against this background, "it would not be appropriate for the Department to make funds or staff available to assist in the setting up of machinery to establish a Highlands University".

This was to mark the start of many years of uneasy dialogue between UHI's supporters and the guardians of the resources and approvals needed to bring the project to fruition. The UHI Steering Group, however, were not daunted.

Both HIE and the Council committed themselves to funding and staffing the initial implementation of the Hills Report – and simply informed the Scottish Office that they were doing so. UHI's first formal budget was remarkably modest – £100,000 for the financial year 1992/93, supplied in equal parts by HIE and the Council and placed under the control of the UHI Project Team. Yet from such small beginnings a major enterprise can flower.

Building the Academic Team

Graham Hills remained central to the thinking and planning of UHI, interpreting to the Highlands the views and requirements of the academic world, with all its virtues and limitations, while using his influence and access to spread the word outside the Highlands that UHI was a serious educational project which deserved attention and support. In addition, the close rapport he had built up with the colleges across the region gave him a pivotal role in bringing them from theoretical approval of UHI to direct participation in creating a new institution.

But if the college Principals were to work together, they first had to meet. Although some had worked together on the original University Advisory Group and others were close neighbours, there had never yet been a gathering of all the institutions consulted in the preparation of the Hills Report.

To rectify this and set the UHI Project off on a sociable course, HIE agreed to host a dinner in Inverness, on the evening of 7 October 1992, for the leaders of all the potential partner institutions. The whispered comments of "Who's that?" as each new figure joined the guests for pre-dinner drinks confirmed that the event had achieved its main purpose – and by the end of the evening useful foundations had been laid for the formal work of the new Academic Advisory Committee.

This first core of academic partners comprised:

> Inverness College of Further and Higher Education;
> Lews Castle College, Stornoway, Western Isles;
> Moray College of Further Education, Elgin;
> Northern College, Aberdeen;
> Sabhal Mòr Ostaig, Isle of Skye;
> Shetland College of Further Education, Lerwick;
> Thurso College, Caithness.

Completing the geographical coverage was the Education Department of Orkney Islands Council, which at that time provided further education via a unit in Kirkwall Grammar School. By the time the AAC met for the first time, some three weeks after the dinner, the group had grown to nine partners with the addition of a second college from Shetland, the newly established North Atlantic Fisheries College.

With the exception of Argyll, the grouping covered all the local authority areas within HIE's territory, together with Moray, for which HIE shared responsibility with its fellow economic development agency, Scottish Enterprise. The odd one out, on a number of definitions, was Northern College.

A Teacher Training College, with its main base in Aberdeen and a second campus in Dundee, Northern College was hard to fit into even the most liberal geographical interpretation of the Highlands and Islands and its longer term future (whether it wished it or not) was thought by many to depend on some form of partnership with an existing Scottish university. On the other hand, it was the natural destination for many student teachers from the Highlands and the island groups, it was responsible for many of the continuing development programmes available to teaching professionals in the region and its integration into UHI would have provided a valuable base load for a new university. In reality, Northern College would be sitting round the UHI Project table because its Principal, David Adams, asked to be there. Although it was felt he might prove to be more an observer than an active participant, the project was not at a stage where it could afford to discourage positive interest from any quarter. And if existing universities were to be invited to join the AAC, why not an existing higher education institution of a different kind?

The Academic Advisory Committee

The first formal meeting of the AAC took place in Inverness on 26 October 1992. It was amicable, though with some signals of the tensions ahead. The challenge of drawing together from the colleges' embryonic business plans and divergent ambitions a coherent development plan for a university and its curriculum would always loom over these meetings. The minutes also show that, even at this early stage, the partners were already beginning to focus on key issues for UHI's success – the use of video-conferencing to reduce the burden of travelling to meetings, the need to build up a research culture, the case for new buildings appropriate to a university, the possibility of setting up a company to manage the project – and the prime importance of holding to an organisational model for the new university which emphasised the network rather than the hub.

Just as important as the formal business transacted was the decision to use the AAC meetings as a deliberate means of mutual briefing, by holding each of the monthly sessions at a different venue across the network of partners. Thus the November 1992 meeting was held in Stornoway, with a visit to Lews Castle College. Meetings at Thurso College, at Sabhal Mòr Ostaig in Skye and at Moray College in Elgin followed in the first quarter of 1993.

The technology then available for linking other sites to the meetings by videophone turned out to be far from satisfactory, though it was used for the first time to enable the Orkney and Shetland members of the AAC to take some part in the Stornoway meeting. However, the benefits of visiting each other's college and seeing at first hand the links between the college and its surrounding community were generally felt to outweigh the cost and inconvenience of travel. This rolling programme of meetings also brought home to all the partners both the geographical size of the region they were seeking to serve and the significant scenic, cultural, and economic diversity within its bounds – two vital factors to build into the development plan.

During this period the case for further extension of the range of UHI partners became accepted. The need for a research base for the new university turned attention to two institutions with a strong reputation in marine science.

At Ardtoe, in the far west of the Highland mainland, the Sea Fish Industry Association (SFIA) had set up a research unit specialising in the development of new species for fish-farming. Ardtoe had become a leading centre for the commercial breeding of halibut, seen as a promising successor to salmon for the region's aquaculture industry. Further south, near Oban in Argyll, the Scottish Association for Marine Science (SAMS) had established at Dunstaffnage a major laboratory and research centre, backed by a number of Scottish universities. Dunstaffnage was also funded at the UK level through the Natural Environment Research Council (NERC) and its reputation and range of science were unique for an institution based in the Highlands and Islands.

Contacts with both Ardtoe and Dunstaffnage met with a warm response, though for both organisations their status within wider structures external to the region raised questions about how far they could be integrated into an eventual UHI. However, they were very willing to be drawn into the planning activities of the AAC, which welcomed the new dimension of scientific research which they brought to the partnership.

Perth in the Highlands

Unexpectedly, the other new AAC member came from outside the traditional boundaries of the Highlands and Islands. Perth College had been watching with growing interest the progress of the UHI Project and its Principal, Mike Webster, invited Graham Hills to visit Perth in January 1993. He found there a large college with a broad FE curriculum, a commitment to open and distance learning and ambitious plans for developing its higher education base. As to geography, it was pointed out that Perth College was responsible for a broad swathe of the Southern Highlands which was indistinguishable in cultural and economic terms from the adjacent area beyond the Pass of Drumochter. Arguably, it was these factors rather than the administrative boundaries of HIE which should define UHI's future sphere of influence.

The argument was persuasive, the active enthusiasm of the Principal and his Chairman even more so. From February 1993 Perth College became an active and welcome member of the AAC – and one whose influence on the development of UHI would prove to be significant and continuing.

CHAPTER 13

Expert Advice

The sponsors of the UHI Project had been more than ready to accept Graham Hills' judgement on the feasibility of the concept, but it was always envisaged that further work would be needed to answer those two perennial questions posed by funding bodies – "Precisely how?" and "Precisely how much?". Between late 1992 and mid-1993 those questions were examined by a group of experts whose influence on the eventual design of UHI was seminal.

The Pieda Report

In the autumn of 1992 bids were sought from a number of leading consultancies for the preparation of a prospectus and business plan for the UHI Project. The choice fell on the Edinburgh-based consultants Pieda, whose team was led by Professor Donald Mackay. He brought to the task not only professional analytical skills but also excellent contacts with the Scottish Office and the Scottish higher education establishment. In addition, his commitment to the work was given an added warmth by his own Highland background. Pieda's style was to work very closely with the Project Office and relationships were forged with the company during this initial assignment which survived through many of the twists and turns of the years ahead. Indeed Richard Collins of Pieda became in effect a full member of the UHI Project team. From an early stage, Pieda's frank advice was that the project was not yet at the point where a formal business plan could be drawn up – and certainly not yet ready for a prospectus. What they therefore sought to do was to show how the raw material for UHI – the colleges, their courses, staff and buildings – might be shaped to deliver the region's aspirations and to meet the requirements and funding patterns of the higher education system.

The policy context, as they pointed out, was not immediately encouraging. Following the creation of the new group of Scottish universities in 1992, a three year period of "consolidation" (effectively a standstill) in higher education student numbers had been introduced by the Funding Council, with no prospect of significant growth until after 1995/96. Capital funding had also been squeezed and the priority was for repairs and maintenance, with an annual allocation of less than £10 million for new buildings anywhere in the Scottish HE sector. The coolness towards UHI from parts of the Scottish Office was more understandable in this light.

In addition, although analysis showed that many of the colleges in the UHI partnership had made useful progress in building up their higher education numbers, few of their courses extended to degree level and most went only to Higher National Diploma (HND) level, usually a two year course. There was clearly a long way to go before the partnership could meet all the criteria which were then being used to judge whether an institution should be recommended for university title:

- At least 300 higher education students (full-time equivalent – FTE) in at least five broad curricular areas.
- Total enrolment of at least 4,000 FTE students on higher education courses.
- At least 3,000 of those students to be on degree level courses.
- Power to award taught course and research degrees.

On the other hand, Pieda pointed out that there were significant advantages for the UHI Project in building on the foundation of institutions currently in the Further Education sector. FE was funded directly from the Scottish Office, with no Funding Council, and the policy of "consolidation" was not being applied to higher education courses established in FE colleges. Although there was clearly no blank cheque on offer (and the hostility of the universities towards what they saw as a policy loop-hole was bound to grow fiercer), there was an ideal window of opportunity in the coming years for the FE colleges in the Highlands and Islands to use the mainstream funding system to increase greatly their contribution to the HE numbers of the future UHI. Projections made available by the colleges led Pieda to conclude that the first two of the criteria for university title (the curricular spread and the total number on HE courses) could probably be met by the UHI partnership by 2001 without great difficulty. The real challenge was to build up the numbers on degree courses and the staff with capability to teach them – and it was on this front that Pieda recommended the window of funding opportunity should be exploited to the full.

Crunching the numbers on the supply side of the UHI equation and relating them to possible funding was therefore a key task for Pieda. Just as important – perhaps more so – was the attention they paid to the demand side. Who were UHI's future students to be? Where would they come from? What would attract them to study at this remote and unusual university, when there were so many others to choose from?

Pieda were soon able to show that, in spite of having a significantly higher proportion of its school leavers going on to further and higher education than the Scottish average, the Highlands and Islands region could not in itself be expected to provide the numbers of degree students needed for achievement of university title. The tradition of leaving the area for higher education had to be recognised as more than just a consequence of the lack of a regional university. It was understandable that, entering adulthood, young people should want to get away to the brighter lights and greater anonymity of the university cities. The reasonable assumption was therefore that most of those who could go away to university would continue to do so, whether or not UHI offered them a local alternative.

That said, the increasing cost of living away from home as a student, coupled with the greater ease UHI might offer in the transition from FE to HE courses, could be expected to create a certain level of new domestic demand for degree courses run at the colleges. Just as significant was the potential of attracting to UHI adult students from the region who – almost uniquely within Scotland – had hitherto found only limited opportunities to pursue HE courses close enough to home and work to make them compatible with the obligations of everyday living. The pressures towards greater and more regular professional updating might alone be expected to provide a significant level of demand from an economy characterised by service and administrative employment.

However, even allowing for a further increase in the school leaver participation rate and for acceleration of the trend towards adult learning at HE level, Pieda concluded that it would be difficult for UHI ever to recruit more than 50% to 65% of its required student population from within its own region. That implied (as Graham Hills had suggested) that at least a third of the students would have to be attracted from outside the Highlands and Islands. Was that feasible? The consultants confirmed the broad target markets. One comprised young people, attracted to courses closely linked to the region's environment, history or culture, for whom UHI would be the obvious destination. For other young people, the appeal would be not so much the course (which might be available in ten or twenty other universities) but the mountains, sailing waters or diving locations within easy reach of their college. Last but not least, people of all ages, from any part of the globe, drawn to short courses or summer schools on topics of devouring interest to them – a market already tapped by Sabhal Mòr Ostaig.

In order to test some of these concepts, Pieda carried out a small survey of young people at schools in a number of regions of England who had already made their university choice. The survey sought to establish whether some of them might have considered seeking a place at a university in the Highlands and Islands and, if so, what factors might have influenced their choice. Although the scale of the survey was limited, it did suggest that –

(1) The course subject was likely to be the main determinant of choice.
(2) A significant number of the young people would have considered a course in their chosen subject had it been available at UHI.
(3) There were positive reactions to the concept of studying in Scotland, and particularly in the Highlands and Islands.
(4) However, for most young people the strong preference would be to study in one of the region's larger centres (Inverness being the favourite) rather than in a smaller or more remote location.

When Pieda delivered their final report in June 1993 it therefore contained three main groups of findings. The first concerned the feasibility of the UHI Project meeting the criteria for university title and the tactics and funding strategies for getting there. Here the main conclusion was that the target was achievable, but that it represented a tough challenge for the partners and that its attainment would probably take longer than had been suggested in the Hills report. The speed of progress would depend in part on the continued availability to the FE colleges of a sufficient level of mainstream recurrent funding for HE over the years ahead. However, it was also noted that funding for the new buildings needed by the central core and the local campuses of a new university was most unlikely to be found from this source and that other routes would have to be explored.

The second group of findings concerned the market for UHI, endorsing the original concept of seeking at least a third of students from outside the region, supporting it with the findings of the schools survey and pointing out that it was this incoming element (both students and a proportion of the additional staff needed to teach them) which could be expected to contribute most in terms of UHI's added value to the region's economy.

On these two heads, Pieda felt able to lend their endorsement to the sponsors' decision to press forward with the UHI Project and to the willingness of the colleges to associate themselves formally with the UHI partnership.

The third group of findings by Pieda struck a more cautionary note, however. While they recognised that in the circumstances of the Highlands and Islands the only realistic way to create a university was by bringing together the capabilities of all the existing institutions in the region, they felt that achievement of this kind of collaboration, among so many partners, would not be easy. They therefore recommended that high priority should be given to practical demonstrations of collaborative working, as a way of building up the critical mass of a federal institution well in advance of having to seek university title. They suggested that the colleges should be encouraged to formalise their collaborative relationship by establishing a Highlands and Islands College Network, as the vehicle for their joint participation in the UHI Project.

In this context, Pieda also provided a useful guide to what might be the roles of the core of the eventual university, supplementing and holding together the activities of the individual colleges. Essential core functions, they suggested, were:

1) Core management.
2) Core capital and recurrent funding.
3) External academic linkages.
4) Commercial development.

Another group of functions might be seen as "footloose", able to undertaken by the core or sub-contracted to one of the partner institutions:

- External marketing.
- Degree admissions.
- Staff training.
- Quality assurance.

This would leave as the main networked activities, involving all the partner institutions:

- Course co-ordination.
- Course design.
- Course delivery.

The Hooper Report

As mentioned earlier in the context of the New Learning Paradigm (Chapter 10), in November 1992 the London-based learning technology consultant Richard Hooper was invited to draw up an initial technology plan for UHI. As with Pieda, the insights he provided went wider than the original brief might have implied. Although he did provide advice on the technological approach which should be followed, he made it clear that it was not realistic to supply detailed specifications for systems which were bound to be technically obsolete by the time the UHI partnership was in a position to purchase them. Instead, he began to develop a series of practical guidelines on the use UHI could make of technology in implementing its vision for learning.

In an initial report he identified how UHI might apply technology in five functions of the university, its staff and its students:

- Teaching and learning.
- Non-academic pursuits (e.g. social contact across the student body).
- Domestic arrangements (e.g. smart cards).
- Administration and governance.
- PR and marketing.

Hooper's ideas on the use of technology in teaching and learning have been outlined already, including his model of the "virtuous cycle" of learning and of the optimum method of mixing ICT-based and human tuition within open and distance learning systems. These principles still reverberate. However, when looking at the wider range of functions to which ICT might be relevant he developed another principle which has illuminated (and should still illuminate) UHI's path – that although the UHI vision is not driven by technology, its imaginative and pervasive use of technology should be one of the key factors differentiating it from its competitors.

Richard Hooper's final report, delivered in March 1993, was essentially up-beat, his main conclusion being:

> The UHI vision of open-learning, distance-learning and student-centred learning, combined with institution-based learning in a geographical area of widely dispersed and thinly dispersed population, can be brought into being through the adept use of a range of technologies.

His main recommendation was for a three-pronged approach to implementing the technology plan

(1) Creation of an electronic campus, using local and wide area networks to link all staff and students, whether full or part-time, to each other and to central mail and bulletin board systems.

(2) Significant use of audio and video-conferencing systems, exploiting the ISDN network, both for teaching and learning and for governance and administration.

(3) Imaginative use of public broadcasting to provide a "university newspaper of the air" and to provide the university's shop window.

All this was to be underpinned by a number of general principles:

- That only tried and tested technology should be purchased.
- That UHI should lay down clear standards for the whole network so as to maximise connectivity and minimise costs.
- That expenditure on hardware should be matched by expenditure on software, user training and support and routine maintenance.
- That courses should not be developed in-house but should be bought in.
- That the live teacher should be used for the support of learning (understanding/tutoring) rather than for the transmission of information – a task best assigned to technology.

Hooper's provisional estimate of the capital cost of implementing this strategy was some £8 million at 1993 prices, though with the proviso that the accuracy of this estimate would depend very much on further changes in equipment costs and capability – especially as he had recommended that every student and teacher should be provided by the university with a personal computer with e-mail access to each other and to central bulletin boards.

Finally, he echoed Pieda's insistence on the need for early demonstrations of collaborative working between the colleges. In particular, he recommended that the principles of the technology plan should be put into practice as soon as possible in one degree level course, involving a group of colleges and with an appropriate commitment to the staff retraining which the new approach would require.

CHAPTER 14

External Relations

Conversations at High Table

The contacts with other universities, which had formed a leitmotiv throughout the exploratory work by Highland Regional Council and Graham Hills, were not broken off when the decision was taken to go ahead with the UHI Project. Whatever they may have felt individually about the chances of this planned new institution living beyond infancy, the vice chancellors of a small group of existing universities proved willing to meet behind closed doors to discuss UHI's future with its sponsors and give them the benefit of their advice.

As early as August 1992 Graham Hills had approached four of the vice chancellors (of Aberdeen, Heriot-Watt, Napier and the Open University) about possible membership of the Academic Advisory Committee, receiving a generally warm response. However, this step was never formalised. Instead, three or four informal working dinners were held in the course of 1992 and 1993 at which an expanding group of senior academics reviewed aspects of the UHI Project's progress against the background of the trends they perceived in UK higher education. At one time or another the group comprised:

> Professor John Daniel of the OU;
> Professor John Forty of Stirling;
> Professor Maxwell Irvine of Aberdeen;
> Dr David Kennedy of Robert Gordon's;
> Professor Alistair MacFarlane of Heriot-Watt;
> Professor Bill Turmeau of Napier.

These were unminuted sessions, not all devoted to higher thought, but for UHI's sponsors they played an important role both in helping to map the assistance potentially available from other universities – this would be an essential element in the Project's later progress – and in creating a slim bridge-head within the normally defensive world of the academic establishment. The insight they provided into higher education policy was also valuable, though it tended to confirm the coolness with which many of the concepts behind UHI were still viewed at official level – and perhaps by some of the senior academics themselves.

Other contacts with senior UK academics proved equally fruitful in this period. The plans for UHI had been well covered in the press and had found echoes in parts of the higher education sector where new ideas were being tested and new links to the community were being forged. Prominent among these was Northern Ireland, where the multi-campus University of Ulster was exploring the use of video-conferencing and related technologies both to link its sites and to reach out into the wider community. Following an approach from Professor Fabian Monds, then Pro-Vice Chancellor and Dean of Informatics, Graham Hills visited the University of Ulster in November 1993 and identified a wide range of common interests which were taken forward in an informal collaborative programme over the following two years.

Perhaps more surprisingly, there was also interest in and support for UHI from what might be seen as the most traditional end of the higher education sector. The federal and collegiate model proposed for UHI had always carried with it more than an echo of Oxbridge. In 1993 the Vice Chancellor of Cambridge University, Professor Sir David Williams, was a lawyer who had taken a special interest in the constitutional structure of universities and had advised on the constitutional problems encountered within the University of Wales. A meeting with him was arranged in Cambridge one hot day in July 1993. The Vice Chancellor proved to be not only professionally well briefed on the plans for UHI but also personally warm towards a concept which pushed at the conventional bounds of higher education. His advice on federal constitutions was simple and direct – time spent in getting the right arrangement for the institution was never time wasted. It might take fifty drafts to find the formula which suited all the partners, but that was all the more reason for tabling a first draft as soon as possible. He agreed readily to come to the Highlands at some point to meet the College Principals and talk through the constitutional issues with them. In retrospect, the fact that this generous offer could never be taken up can be seen as one of UHI's wasted strategic opportunities.

Also at Cambridge the plans for UHI had caught the attention of Dr Tess Adkins, Senior Tutor at King's College. A Scot by birth and education, with a holiday home in Iona, she was immediately able to understand the relevance of UHI to both the culture and the needs of the Highlands and Islands. This background, together with her own commitment to the cause of widening student access, made her another of UHI's most loyal and helpful external supporters in the years ahead.

Politics and Beyond

Scottish Office Ministers remained reluctant to give UHI and its sponsors any comfort in public and in their informal contacts with leading figures from the Highlands and Islands they were at best ambivalent. The reasons for this were fairly obvious. As a Conservative administration they were instinctively hostile to what seemed likely to be a heavy drain on public funds. As representatives of a party with no MPs in the region, they did not face any constituency pressure to encourage UHI's sponsors to think their efforts might eventually succeed. As guardians of higher education policy, they did not have to look far among their official advisers for someone to tell them that Scotland was still coping with a cohort of new universities, that the Funding Council had introduced a policy of "consolidation" in HE numbers and that therefore there was no need now (or probably ever) for yet another university project – especially as the Highlands and Islands already supplied so many students to existing Scottish universities.

However, the north of Scotland had a long tradition of refusing to accept that the man in Edinburgh knows best. One or two senior officials within the Scottish Office Education Department (particularly those concerned with further education) and in the Scottish Higher Education Funding Council (SHEFC) were known to be sympathetic to the UHI concept and to the educational, economic and social objectives it sought to achieve. Opportunities were found to visit them and brief them regularly on progress, but without ever asking for material help.

In parallel, the Opposition MPs who represented the Highlands and Islands were provided with regular updates on the Project, on its overall aims and on the role which could be played in it by the colleges in their constituencies. This "charm offensive" culminated in a dinner at the House of Commons in December 1993, hosted by the Liberal Democrat Member for Caithness and Sutherland, Robert Maclennan MP. While a number of the politicians present may have had reservations about the exact shape of the Project, it soon became clear that UHI was a cause they could all take to their hearts. The steady trickle of questions to Ministers which followed over the next year or two may have had its down-side for UHI's sponsors (since it is always easier to say 'no' than 'yes' to an Opposition Member), but it all helped to create the public impression that something widely sought by the people of the north was in danger of being stifled by the Edinburgh establishment.

The UHI story was even spread to the mainland of Europe, though the political benefits of doing so were recognised to be at best indirect. Intelligence from Brussels had identified one or two officials in the European Commission who were thinking about the "European University of the Future" and others who were specifically tasked with projects in the field of distance learning. In the course of a series of visits in Brussels in May 1993, these officials were found to be a well-informed and generally supportive audience – but one which could provide little direct assistance. Perhaps the most significant outcome was the realisation that there might be ways of reconciling the Commission to the concept of UHI as a generator of economic benefits at the regional level, since a recent European Court judgement had ruled that higher education should be ranked with "training" rather than "education" for Treaty purposes. This change in perspective could make UHI eligible in due course, when new buildings and other facilities were needed, for support through the EU Structural Funds, under the Highlands and Islands Objective One Programme.

Telling the Public

One of the advantages of siting the UHI Project under the umbrella of Highlands and Islands Enterprise was that it had a very professional press unit with a tradition of high quality output and a wide range of contacts. It would have been all too easy for the good news of UHI to be lost in the background noise of local journalism and parochial in-fighting. Instead, with the assistance of HIE's Press Office, steps were taken to create for UHI a high and distinctive profile within the region, across Scotland and beyond.

The first step was to create a logo. Cynics might see this as the usual triumph of form over substance. In reality, it proved to be a highly effective and durable means of giving an understandable public image to an idea about whose details even strong supporters were sometimes vague. The logo emerged from discussions within the UHI Project Team, seeking to combine the "UHI" initials with some graphical concept of the area. The best idea involved using the "U" as device like a shield, superimposing the "H" and "I" on its upper half and aligning three squares on the left and upper edges to represent the Western Isles, Orkney and Shetland in relation to the Scottish mainland. The colours – gold and a rather imperial purple – were chosen both for contrast and to suggest this was no frivolous matter. The whole device was also designed to show up as clearly in black and white.

With a modest amount of external help from a graphic designer, the in-house team produced a final version of the logo which was launched in February 1993 and began to appear on letter headings, business cards, compliment slips and fax paper. It became one of the most familiar and immediately recognisable images in the region. However, it also attracted critics. Among them were certain Scottish Office officials, who suggested that the use of the initials "UHI" in this manner was pre-empting a decision on university status reserved to the Privy Council – and with the sub-text that such a decision would be over their dead bodies. They were politely but firmly referred to the form of words inseparable from the logo ("University of the Highlands and Islands Project") and to the strap-line which usually accompanied it ("Working towards a University of the Highlands and Islands") and were told that the public was well capable of working out that this meant it was not yet a university. No more was heard of that complaint for many years.

The decision was also taken to issue a regular newsletter to chart the progress of the UHI Project. "UHI News" was to be aimed at a wide range of readers – local and national politicians, current staff in the colleges, future recruits from the academic world, potential students and their families – and was designed to catch the eye of the press so that they could spread the UHI story further. From the start, the plan was to aim for quality and a professional "feel" consistent with the project's aims. A modest first issue of four pages in black and white was published in February 1993, with the aim of it becoming a quarterly publication. Thanks again to the efforts of Allan Bransbury there were indeed four issues during 1993 and, although thereafter its frequency of appearance varied, "UHI News" (now in full colour) remains the prime public communications channel for the project up to the time of writing.

By the latter half of 1993 it was clear that the level of press interest in UHI had grown to the point where a formal press visit should be organised. The idea was to bring together in the minds of journalists two powerful themes – that the university of the future is being developed today, and that it is yet another manifestation of the renaissance of the Highlands and Islands region.

With HIE's Press Office in the lead, the event was set up in November 1993, the invitation list being designed to raise awareness mainly outside Scotland. The result was positive coverage in a number of UK and Scottish broadsheet newspapers, as well as in the educational press.

Amongst other benefits, the press response was followed by a marked increase in the number of academic staff in well-established UK universities writing in to ask when there might be an opportunity to join the teaching staff of UHI. For them, as for many of the general public, the wider telling of the UHI story had clearly struck a responsive chord.

CHAPTER 15

Changing Relationships

While the campaign pressed ahead, on the whole successfully, to convince the outside world that the UHI Project was a serious initiative of more than local significance, within the camp the business of adjustment to working in partnership also became serious. That brought the need to review and reshape some relationships – never a painless experience.

The Principals Stake their Claim

The Academic Advisory Committee (AAC) continued to meet monthly at different locations, making slow but useful progress towards defining an initial curriculum for UHI. It was clear that this would have to built on the developing degree courses of the individual colleges until new joint courses could be established.

One problem they faced was that it now seemed it would be neither easy nor cheap to convert existing course material or develop new material to suit the electronic media which it was hoped would be such a distinctive element in UHI's approach to higher education. However, others continued to encourage them down that course. In early 1993 they received a personal presentation on "the new learning paradigm" by Professor Alistair MacFarlane of Heriot-Watt, who had chaired the ground-breaking study of the application of ICT in higher education referred to earlier (see Chapter 10). He reinforced the message that by embracing ICT and applying it to degree level learning in an imaginative and highly professional manner, UHI could indeed place itself in the vanguard of Scottish learning. If sponsors could be found to pay the price, it would certainly be a price worth paying.

The AAC had also begun to face up to the challenge of broadening the capability of the partnership in research – the last and toughest of the criteria for university title. The work of Sabhal Mòr Ostaig in establishing a Research Centre for Gaelic Affairs (Leirsinn) was seen to provide a potential model for the group of colleges to follow, while the status and experience of Dunstaffnage Marine Laboratory acted as a reminder of the academic standard to be attained and of the benefits of linking research to the future of the region's key industries.

Through all this, Graham Hills had been guiding and leading the AAC from the chair, stimulating debates, opening up issues, pressing for action. That was what the UHI Steering Group had asked him to do, as their Academic Adviser, and he brought his usual commitment to the task. But beyond the first few meetings it became apparent that his agenda and that of the college principals could not be assumed to be identical.

There was no real support for (and a degree of hostility against) his proposal to invite a small number of vice chancellors from the more friendly universities to attend meetings of the AAC. They were suspected by some of wanting to use such access as a way of gathering intelligence, possibly in due course for a take-over bid. To others they may simply have seemed irrelevant to the FE-based approach the UHI Project had embraced. Although Dr Margery Burdon of SCOTVEC was a welcome participant at many meetings of the AAC, it remained in essence an inward-looking group.

There was also a conspicuous lack of warmth from the principals to match Graham Hills' continuing enthusiasm for reintroducing through UHI the old Scottish general first degree, adapted to take account of the US liberal arts model. Most of them felt that UHI was to be radical enough in its structure and its approach to learning, without taking the additional risk of trying to woo students (let alone their parents) to choose a novel type of degree course which seemed only distantly related to the world of work.

More significant than these differences of emphasis seems to have been a consciousness among the principals of the larger colleges that having won independence from local authority control they should be capable of guiding UHI's academic fortunes themselves, without being led by someone put in place by the project's local authority and enterprise agency sponsors. Whatever the motive, by May 1993 they had decided to act.

At the AAC meeting that month, held on neutral ground in the quiet seaside town of Nairn, Robert Chalmers, the Principal of Moray College, announced on behalf of the colleges that they now wished to replace the AAC with an Academic Board for the UHI Project. As its name implied, this new body was intended to be a closer analogue of the mechanism by which a university manages its academic programmes – and, like the Academic Council in a university, it was intended to be independent from non-academic influences. The logical conclusion was that it should be chaired by one of the principals, rather than by the sponsors' Academic Adviser.

Graham Hills stood down with good grace, though the move, with overtones of a constitutional coup, had come as a shock. Robert Chalmers was voted into the chair of the new Academic Board by his fellow principals – and life went on. At its first meeting, on 22 June 1993, the Board agreed to co-opt Graham Hills as a member. His involvement with UHI's academic development was in fact uninterrupted. The Project Team continued to attend the Board's meetings and to provide a *de facto* Secretariat. The same subject matter which had occupied the AAC dominated the work of the Academic Board. Little seemed to have changed – or had it?

A Change too Early?

The proposal that the colleges should take the lead in the academic development of the UHI Project was hard to fault. After all, they were the established deliverers of post-school learning within the region, the Project had been designed around their infrastructure and without them there would be no local outlet for UHI courses. Sooner or later, the colleges would have had to take the steering wheel of the AAC. But two aspects of the college's action concerned Graham Hills and the Project's funders.

The first was the timing. It was less than a year since the Hills Report had been delivered. The process of team-building within a group of very varied establishments, in both size and capability, was still at a very early stage. Constitutional arrangements for the future were still in a phase of tentative discussion. The possibility that one or two of the larger colleges would use their weight to dominate proceedings or to manoeuvre the UHI academic agenda to suit their own preferences had been latent in the AAC. In the new Academic Board, without independent chairmanship, the risk of forcing a consensus on academic progress through power politics seemed far higher.

The second area of concern, largely unspoken, was about the academic credibility of the principals and their colleges at this early stage in the creation of a higher education institution. One of the reasons why Graham Hills had been chosen to advise HIE and the Highland Council on the university concept was that, as the culmination of a career in higher education, he had actually run a university. The vice chancellors he had wanted to introduce into some form of membership of the Academic Advisory Council would have brought the same kind of first-hand experience of the upper echelons of the university world.

By contrast, only a minority of the college principals had taught in the university sector, very few had experience at senior level in higher education and only a limited number of their staff had second degrees or were qualified to teach to degree level. From this perspective, the sponsors' concern about the wisdom of the principals in "dropping the pilot" at this stage in their work can be seen as more than just academic snobbery.

The alternative view, which the principals themselves might have articulated, was that the UHI Project was a deliberate attempt to throw off the shackles of conventional academic thought and practice and that the learner-centred approach of further education, which was at the heart of their colleges' current curriculum, was far closer in spirit to the new learning paradigm than the stuffiness of university tradition. In that sense, it was essential to break away from the guiding hand of vice chancellors, however friendly their intentions, and to have the freedom to learn a new approach – including the freedom to learn from mistakes.

It is hard to say now how different might have been the pace or quality of academic progress made by the UHI Project in a further year of work by the Academic Advisory Council under the formal tutelage of Graham Hills and some other senior academics. Perhaps the frustrated ambitions of some of the principals would have soured the atmosphere of meetings and undermined collaboration.

An alternative response to the principals' coup might have been for the UHI Steering Group to strengthen its own independent role in overseeing all aspects of the Project by inviting some of the well-disposed vice chancellors to join its deliberations alongside Graham Hills. This might have been seen to water down his influence as Academic Adviser, yet it could have provided a vital counter-balance to the views now coming directly from the Academic Board, whose Chairman had been invited to join the Steering Group. There were certainly to be occasions in the years ahead when a broader range of academic experience might have helped the Steering Group and its successors to navigate the shoal waters of higher education policy more confidently.

With hindsight, the real significance of the step the principals took in Nairn in the early summer 1993 was probably constitutional rather than academic – and if so, its echoes can still be heard within UHI today. For one of the earliest decisions of the Academic Board was to adopt the title of the "The Highlands and Islands College Network" (HICN) for their future collaborative work. This deliberately picked up one of the recommendations of the Pieda report – but it did not translate the concept into the structural and organisational reforms Pieda had envisaged.

Although it was presented as a further move towards academic convergence, the HICN label carried with it the implication that UHI might be developing into a troika rather than a single powerful engine. As long as the sponsors, the colleges and the yet to be established core of the university continued to pull in the same direction, fast progress was possible, but if one of the trio sought to take a divergent course, the lateral forces would begin to slow the whole team. A constitution which bound them all together in the common cause was the desirable alternative – but so far apparently only desirable in principle as far as the colleges were concerned.

The Sponsors also Act

By the autumn of 1993, Highlands and Islands Enterprise and the local authorities in the region had also recognised the need to redefine their relationship with the UHI Project. If it succeeded, it would need the appropriate supporting structure for a complex and expensive operation. If it failed to achieve take-off speed, the sponsors would want to be able to show that at least they had done all that was expected of them by the community.

Up to that point, the investment in UHI had remained modest. The budget for the Project in 1993/94 was slightly increased – £130,000 in total, with £60,000 each contributed by HIE and the Highland Regional Council and £5,000 each by the Orkney Islands and Shetland Islands Councils. However, if university status was to be achieved early in the next decade, revenue spending would have to accelerate. A budget of over £400,000 was being planned for 1994/95, to which a further £100,000 or more would have to be added if the UHI Project paid for its own central staffing team. While the sponsors had no intention of losing control – especially as their investment level rose – they could see that a separate management structure might now be needed through which to exercise that control.

The possibility of using a purpose-built company to manage the creation of UHI had first been discussed in the context of adopting the Hills Report. With the assistance of the HRC's legal services, the legal documents (Memorandum and Articles of Association) were prepared to define the roles and responsibilities of a "company limited by guarantee". Such companies, with an independent corporate existence but with members rather than shareholders, had already become well established in the UK as a means of giving formal shape to public or voluntary sector initiatives. The lawyers confirmed that there appeared to be no obstacle to using such a company as the vehicle for setting up a new higher education institution, though the governance arrangements might have to change if and when the target of university status was in sight. They also confirmed that there was no legal objection to using the title "UHI Ltd" for the company, since it did not imply that the company had university status. As there was no company currently using the name, it was open for the sponsors to adopt it for their company – and so they did.

In parallel, the core staffing of the UHI Project was secured as a result of organisational changes within HIE. From the start of November 1993 Robin Lingard became the full-time Director of the UHI Project, still as a member of HIE's senior management team but now relieved of other responsibilities. He was also to become the Manager of UHI Ltd, though HRC officials continued to undertake the *de facto* oversight of the company's legal existence.

This form of internal secondment was also used by HIE to staff the new UHI Project Office. Allan Bransbury agreed to continue his involvement with UHI and transferred to the Project Office as Assistant Director, with particular responsibility for finance, fund-raising and ICT issues. Suzanne Sloan was recruited as Project Officer, taking on the marketing and PR responsibilities, including the development of UHI News. Soon afterwards, Linda Annal joined them as Team Secretary. It was not immediately clear how far a team of four would be able to take the Project without reinforcement, but for the present HIE had significantly increased its visible commitment to UHI by providing the staffing for the Project Office and agreeing to accommodate it in HIE's Inverness headquarters.

PART V

Regional Universities

CHAPTER **16**

Regional Universities in Britain

During the mid-1990s the sponsors and founders of the UHI project were asked to give a number of talks and lectures about the concept and its progress towards fruition. They did so against the background first of Scotland, its Highlands and Islands region and the region's needs, and secondly, of the upheavals attending higher education in general. They found that an increasing range of projected developments across the UK had picked up the message and were seeking to tackle similar educational and economic issues by means of establishing new centres of higher education. But in Britain, the two largest stumbling blocks to the foundation of new universities have been and remain finance and support – especially moral support – from existing universities.

Funding Problems

As long as higher education is wholly or predominantly funded by central government – as is the norm throughout Western Europe – then, given the retreat from socialism and public enterprise, there is no longer any prospect for significant financial assistance from government. Indeed from the mid-1980s onwards, the overwhelming dependence of British universities on inadequate government support would imbue them with a zero-sum mentality which, in turn, would lead to intense competition between them.

A further complication is that unit costs of higher education, only remotely related to student fees, are artificially low. In Britain, it is a requirement that only overseas (or more properly, non-EU students) pay economic fees on which it would be possible to operate effectively and, at the same time, to mortgage-finance capital investment. This could well be regarded as light at the end of the tunnel. Thus given the world-wide boom in education at all levels and given that education in the English language, in pleasant surroundings and involving superior educational material, will always command a premium, there is every prospect for at least a minority of British universities to be funded at least partly on this basis.

Certainly, one of the founding principles of the UHI Project was that the new institution should be capable of attracting students from all over the world. In addition to its scenery and its environment, the Highlands and Islands region enjoys a cultural tradition now largely absent from urban Europe. There seemed ample scope to develop this "Highland Experience" into the Unique Selling Point (USP) of the new university.

In addition to drumming up more paying customers there is always scope for a different kind of university to pay its way by embracing new more efficient methodologies and by offering new opportunities. But distinctiveness carries the risk that, to the conventionally minded, being different means being inferior. It takes brave people to take risks – and brave people seldom flourish in academia.

Competition in Higher Education

These considerations of orthodoxy and of the penalties for being otherwise apply with particular force to universities. Far from being the collegiate fraternity they once largely were, by the mid 1990s they appeared to have become obsessed with a competitive mentality in which anyone's gain was someone else's loss. Competitiveness had come to infect every aspect of academic life, of student performance and of staff promotion.

The collegiate spirit of generosity had all but vanished. Far from welcoming newcomers into the fold, the established universities generally sought to rubbish their pretensions. Over the last two hundred years or so Glasgow University had never concealed its disdain for its sister institution, the highly respected Royal College of Technology, now Strathclyde University. Now Glasgow, Strathclyde and the rest were not slow to look down imperiously on the even newer Glasgow Caledonian University when it got into difficulties.

To its great credit the Open University, which remains open in spirit as well as in its procedures, was one which stayed resolutely aloof from this back-biting. But the generally competitive atmosphere was bound to make the birth of any new university that much more difficult. Because governments look to older universities for guidance, the prejudice against newcomers is spread more widely. The dice are loaded against the small, the new and the different.

Yet it is too often forgotten that all British universities were once small by today's standards. In their heyday, everyone in them knew or recognised everyone else. Smallness allows that still to happen in many Scottish rural communities but not in many universities. Sadly, growth is a one-way journey. It is as easy to grow as it is difficult to shrink. "As ye grow so shall ye weep" is a gentle paraphrase of an earlier truth about sowing and reaping. But both tell the same story, that smallness, newness and the steady state have much to offer that new universities are in the best position to supply. There should therefore be no need to apologise for being a small and a new university.

The New Regional Universities Group

Much of the thinking and experience evoked by the creation of the UHI Project was therefore of interest to backers of developments in other parts of the UK. Some of the teams promoting new regional universities, in Cornwall, Cumbria, Gloucester, Swindon and other localities, contacted the group in Inverness to exchange views and visits. In other locations, existing universities had become interested in linking with their local colleges. Others wished simply to network their curricula more widely perhaps to enhance their reputations or, more likely, to increase their income. Elsewhere (for instance, around Glasgow) groups of FE colleges were spontaneously joining together to create larger and more efficient networks of curricular and other shared activities.

A number of these strands were brought together in 1995/96 in two meetings of the New Regional Universities group organised by the Royal Society of Arts and chaired by Sir Christopher Ball, then also masterminding the Campaign for Learning. Most of those present – including the UHI Project Office – represented university projects in their early stages. There was no shortage of enthusiasm, of supporters and even premises. What was invariably missing was money and the prospect of recognition by Government. It was this latter obstacle which would make it difficult, if not impossible, for a *bona fides* new British university to emerge. The exception appeared to be Lincoln.

The Lincoln Approach

A group of local champions had already determined that Lincoln, as a fine cathedral city, deserved a university presence and would be a natural regional centre of higher education if the means could be found to create it. Some other existing universities had their eye on Lincoln as a place for possible satellite campuses.

However, it was left to another, the most local and already newly arrived University of Humberside (at Grimsby) to create a second campus for itself in the city of Lincoln, to rename both campuses as those of the University of Lincoln and finally to reverse itself into a green-field site in the City with a water-front setting on the River Humber and The Wash. A company was launched, £20 million was raised and a splendid new campus begun. As a *fait accompli*, it received its Royal Charter in 1996. The speed with which it created itself, without regard to government, appeared to show what boldness and determination could still achieve even in Britain.

In one sense, therefore, the Lincoln experience gave encouragement both to the UHI Project and to other participants in Sir Christopher Ball's group. A new university had been established in a community that had fought for it and, in the process, had overcome the twin obstacles of obtaining funding and securing the active support of an existing institution. On the other hand, the route chosen by Lincoln was one which UHI had already rejected – essentially the "colonising model" offered by Stirling University in 1990 as a possible longer term development of its academic association with Inverness College. If the Highlands and Islands really wanted to establish a different kind of university, UHI would have to continue down the harder road of the evolutionary model.

The Cornwall Model

Cornwall shared with the Highlands and Islands a rural economy, a peripheral location, a comparable level of population – and the absence of any university within its borders. It was no surprise to discover that here too there were plans to use the development of a new university as a means of economic regeneration. Contact was made informally, first in Cornwall and then on a reciprocal visit to Inverness, between the UHI Project Team and the Principal of Cornwall College, one of Cornwall's four FE colleges. Their discussions found much common ground.

Within Cornwall there proved to be two different game plans for establishing a regional university. One was remarkably close to the UHI model, based round the evolutionary development of the existing FE infrastructure and linked to imaginative use of distance learning and local centres to meet the needs of learners across the county. Cornwall College hoped to be a major player in that approach, which would also have embraced the two independent and specialist higher education institutions present in Cornwall – the Camborne School of Mines and the Falmouth College of Art – to create an indigenous University of Cornwall.

The other option, emerging from the higher education sector, was for the two universities over the border in Devon – Plymouth and Exeter – to extend their neighbourly interest across the Tamar, using their ability to access higher education funding to establish a jointly-sponsored campus somewhere in Cornwall – again a version of the colonising model rejected by UHI. Sir Geoffrey Holland, Vice Chancellor of Exeter University, had a long-standing personal commitment to Cornwall and felt that this approach was the more likely to achieve the necessary government backing and hence the economic boost Cornwall so badly needed. As an ex-Permanent Secretary in Whitehall he was well placed to judge – as well as to influence the outcome.

However, neither approach was making great headway at the time discussions were held with UHI. For Cornwall had never enjoyed the benefits of a strong, multi-purpose economic development agency, comparable to HIDB, which might have supplied launch funding and staff, taken the policy lead and either reconciled all the parties to a united strategy or made a firm selection of the option most likely to succeed. The County Council did what it could, but was historically under-funded.

At that point, therefore, Cornwall had more to learn from UHI than *vice versa*. When the paths of these two projects crossed again it was at a time when both were contending for Millenium Commission funding, the higher education party having won the argument within Cornwall on the basis of promoting a single campus in the far west of the county. By a twist of irony, although Cornwall's Millennium bid failed, plans for the Combined Universities in Cornwall project caught the imagination of Ministers and a revamped scheme, with a main campus now at Falmouth, received official blessing and extensive government and EU funding support in May 2001.

The Dumfries Alternative

Like Inverness, the pleasant, bustling market town of Dumfries, in the rural south west of Scotland, had been an early contestant for the site of the new Scottish university in 1964. Like Inverness, it was bitterly disappointed at coming second or third to Stirling. It would have stayed that way but for a shift of direction in UK health policy. With the move towards undertaking more mental health care within the community, a parkland area of exceptional beauty, with many fine buildings, fell vacant as the result of the closure of the Mental Hospital element of the Crichton Royal Hospital. The decision on its future engaged both the interest and the sentiment of the Dumfries community.

As noted earlier, the original plan of the Crichton's founder had been to establish a university on the site. Now the local authority, looking for ways to exploit its new-found real estate, came to see that it might yet become a ready-made campus. With UHI already under way, Graham Hills was invited by a local group to give his view on the possible academic future of the Crichton. He recommended that Glasgow University and Paisley University, both of which had links to Southern Scotland, should together create a university presence of the kind dreamed of by Elizabeth Crichton nearly two hundred years earlier. The collection of elegant buildings in a park-like setting would make a worthy campus.

The model adopted was essentially that of a satellite relationship whereby Paisley 'adopted' the local FE college and Glasgow set about restoring its earlier traditional support of Liberal Studies. It was fortunate that a group of senior professors in Glasgow University clearly understood and supported the vision of Britain's first Liberal Arts College, American style. It was particularly fortunate that Glasgow University's Vice-Chancellor, Sir Graeme Davies, supported the initiative from the outset.

At this point in the narrative, it is necessary only to record that the plans for the Crichton were indeed implemented and that the regeneration of the site has already brought greater confidence and prosperity to Dumfries. Again, the Dumfries model is significantly different from that chosen by UHI, concentrating on a single site rather than multiple campuses and turning deliberately to existing universities to supply the site with capital funding, staff and students.

In a sense, it was a property-led solution with little attempt – at least initally – to address the tertiary education needs of Dumfries and Galloway as a whole. However, the two projects had in common the vital need to win over of the hearts and minds of large numbers of local residents and to mobilise local and national politicians to their cause. Their longer term future would depend equally on the ability to keep the confidence and support of that wider partnership.

Conclusion

These contemporary attempts to found regional universities within the UK suggested two lessons for UHI. The first is that different communities off the existing university map can indeed turn an unbridled optimism towards higher education, for the benefits it can offer and the sense of place and achievement, into successful plans for new institutions. The second is that, while all professions guard their privileged positions with a zeal worthy of any mediæval guild, no body has been more successful at that than the universities. There would be no welcome mat at their door, except on their terms.

CHAPTER 17

Regional Universities on the World Stage

In 1995 an ideal opportunity arose for the UHI Project to learn from regional university developments in the rest of the world. This stemmed from a Swedish initiative to create a new university – the Mid Sweden University – in the sparsely populated central region of Sweden centred on the town of Östersund. Sweden is a conservative country with a small number of distinguished ancient universities. The experience of the Mid-Sweden initiative was made a central feature of an international development seminar on the challenge of creating new universities, organised by Professor Urban Dahllöf and Dr. Staffan Selander in Östersund in March 1995, under the title "Expanding Colleges and New Universities".

Comparisons were invited with Scotland (featuring the UHI Project), with Australia and with Scandinavia as a whole. The seminar was generally supportive of the economic and social value of new regional universities in the development of communities distant from the larger cities. Even so the novelty inherent in the UHI Project was seen as a challenge to some in the university establishment in Sweden.

Lessons from Sweden

This reaction could be understood more readily from the presentation during the seminar of a detailed study of a small new university college at Växjö, set up in 1967 as a satellite of the established University of Lund. The parent university appointed four professors to reside at Växjö and, in general terms, to oversee and promote the new university college. That indeed was the theory. In practice things worked out differently. Because of the better facilities at the parent university, the presence there of other senior staff and the better promotion prospects from being close to the centre, the new professors tended to spend more and more time at the hub rather than at the rim.

As noted earlier, this is the fate of all satellite systems. As the Second Law of Thermodynamics inexorably reminds us, when two systems are joined, the big always absorbs the small. In homelier terms, mother universities always devour their offspring. Those persuaded to work at the satellite suffer from a sense of exile. Satellites are always the colonies to which the less promising are banished. These remarks may sound exaggerated but no centre-satellite border is ever stable.

The best a satellite can do is to strive for independence. That is what all university colleges, such as those of London University in the early 1900s, aimed to achieve and eventually succeeded in so doing. Again, as in the case of Lincoln, there were echoes from Växjö of earlier options for the UHI Project. Satellite status (whether of Stirling, Aberdeen or some other respected Scottish institution) would have given instant respectability and instant access to the parent university's reputation, facilities, staff, curricula and other benefits. But the experiences in Sweden suggested that UHI had been wise to go down another road.

There was one final message from Sweden and it had to do with the question of what really has to be done to found a university. Is the key factor to demonstrate academic excellence, to enjoy large numbers of applicants or to have splendid buildings? The answer from the Swedish side was simple. It is a political matter. Obtain political support and the rest will follow. UHI would ignore this lesson in realpolitik at its peril.

Lessons from British Columbia

A similar set of lessons for the UHI Project could be found in another case study, related at the Östersund meeting by Michael Hill from British Columbia in Canada.

In every way similar to the sentiments and ambitions of those of the Highlands and Islands of Scotland, the northern provinces of British Columbia nurtured the wish to found a university at Prince George, the local capital some 400 miles north of Vancouver. Throughout the 1980s, a group of local business and professional people combined to create a University of Northern British Columbia, building on earlier efforts of the local community College of New Caledonia.

Just as in the Highlands of Scotland, the area served by the college occupied over 60% of the land mass of the region and served a population of some

300,000. There was support throughout the northern province for the proposal that another layer of education, to university status, be added to the present arrangements. As with the Highlands and Islands of Scotland, there was easy access by road and by plane but it was time consuming and expensive. However, there was also a perpetual feeling in the Northern Region that all the big decisions relating to their local educational needs had been taken elsewhere – ie in Vancouver.

It so happens that the conurbation of Vancouver is the home of one of Canada's most prestigious universities – the University of British Columbia (UBC) at Victoria. The evidence is that from the beginning it felt it knew best about most things and that, as was the case with Aberdeen in the early years of the UHI Project, a tiny new provincial university simply was not necessary. Anything that the locals could do UBC could do better.

There ensued ten years of gradual build-up of UNBCP, the project to create a new university of North British Columbia. Almost every person of note and every single business in and around the potential campus at Prince George gave it their backing. On the other hand, political support was offered and later withdrawn. The other community colleges in other regions reacted uneasily to the prospect of one of their number stepping out of line. But the main determinant would be the say-so of the central government of the entire province – in Victoria and clearly advised by members of UBC. At the last hurdle, with victory in sight, the project failed.

It was reported that the faculties of the thirteen other community colleges in British Columbia and the Faculty Association of the existing community college of New Caledonia together opposed the founding of the new university. At the same time, a resolution questioning the educational and financial soundness (that magic word) was approved by the delegates attending a convention of the College-Institute Educators' Association held in Camuson College in Victoria. A proposal in support of the new university by Professor Dahllöf himself (who had taken a personal interest in its progress) was dismissed as lacking the controls required to ensure that the students would receive a quality education, as relying excessively on distance education and as requiring excessive amounts of money to cover capital and operating expenses. It was also stated that establishing a separate university in Prince George would erode the college-to-university programme offered at the existing College of New Caledonia and thereby damage the comprehensiveness of that College.

Within a few months all the preparatory work and the formal arrangements to oversee its delivery were set aside. The project was disbanded and the northern province of British Columbia left, as was Inverness in 1965, with a feeling of loss and of unnecessary hurt. They could reflect on the advice of the first chairman of the promoters, the Mayor of Prince George, and clearly a man of experience. His attitude to the provincial government was "Let's go ahead and build (the university) and get permission from Victoria later".

That too had been the view of the original proponents of UHI – and the evidence from British Columbia suggested that the route of hardy independence still had much to commend it.

PART VI

Gathering Momentum

CHAPTER 18

Shifting the Odds

In early 1994 a pessimist (and there were many) would have had little difficulty in rubbishing the prospect that the UHI Project would ever become an educational institution in its own right, let alone a university. The concept might be intriguing, the enthusiasm in the region understandable. But where was the substance to come from?

Highlands and Islands Enterprise could afford to lend project staff and could shave some development money off its own budget to supplement the Council's, yet there was no commitment to finding within HIE's regional development kitty the millions needed for full-scale implementation. In its early days the Highland Board, HIE's predecessor, had been responsible for some large and very visible financial fiascos. Might backing a regional university based on untried technology and clever pedagogic theories lead HIE down the same road to public criticism and official censure? Nor was there much encouragement outside the Highlands. Some back doors were still open in Edinburgh, but the front door – leading to Funding Councils and their mainstream resources for higher education – was still padlocked. The quickest way to get Scottish Office thumbs turned down for ever would have been to ask Ministers to declare how much they were willing to make available to a new university.

Meanwhile, the North's colleges and research centres, on which UHI would have to depend for its initial staff, students and facilities, were still primarily concerned with their own day-to-day affairs, on which the UHI Project barely impinged. And (this the most hurtful question, because it raised doubts even among UHI's supporters) how on earth did anyone expect to create a higher education establishment, with all the excellence that implies, on the foundation of a group of local FE colleges?

Faced with the same evidence, the optimists (a small group, but not confined to the UHI Project Office) were often tempted to come to the same conclusion. But there was enough evidence, in their eyes, that this was indeed an idea whose time had come and that by forging ahead on that premise they would win through somehow. Over the next two years, they shifted the odds to an extent that even pessimists could not ignore.

The Millennium Commission

One new factor, whose potential significance to UHI was barely understood at first, was the establishment of the Millennium Commission as one of five "good causes" designated to receive and distribute the proceeds of the National Lottery. In February 1994 the Scottish Office gave a briefing for public agencies on plans to set up a Millennium Fund, controlled by the Commission, which was to be available from early in 1995 to support projects suitable for marking the nation's entry to the third millennium. The first indications were that only a dozen projects might be funded across the UK and that bids would have to be submitted before the end of 1994, though the detailed criteria might not be available until the summer. There would be no separate allocation for Scotland.

Within HIE there was an immediate realisation that the UHI Project might be a credible candidate for funding. On the file note of the Scottish Office briefing the words – "Highland University best idea" – appear in the handwriting of the HIE Chief Executive, Iain Robertson. But the reported timescale for bidding looked all wrong to the Project Office. There was no hope of pulling together before the end of 1994 a credible business plan for a university, covering all the elements of capital and revenue funding. Too much was still in the melting-pot.

However, as further details of the objectives and criteria of the Millennium Fund became clear, the fit with UHI began to look too close to ignore. The Fund was to be used "to encourage projects throughout the nation which enjoy public support and which will be lasting monuments to the achievements and aspirations of the United Kingdom." A successful project should:

- Make a substantial contribution to the life of the community it is designed to serve.
- Look back over the current millennium or forward into the new one.
- Be seen by future generations as marking a significant moment in national or local history.

- Be of high architectural design and environmental quality.
- Include partnership contributions to demonstrate the real support of the local community.

With well over £1 billion to spend by the end of the year 2000, the Millennium Commission explained that it would hope to fund not only around a dozen very large national projects but also a far larger number of smaller capital projects of local significance, with contributions in the range from £100,000 to £15 million. This improved the chances of finding some element of the future UHI which could qualify for support.

In addition, the bidding process, as finally established, proved realistic and user-friendly, with at least two rounds of bidding during 1995 and 1996. The first step was to fill in a simple Proposal Form to test eligibility. Once that hurdle was crossed, all that was required of the bidder was to complete a three page Application Form and to submit an accompanying explanatory document of no more than 20 pages. Obviously far more paper work would have to be completed subsequently by projects which found initial favour, but the process had clearly been designed to encourage the widest possible range of interesting bids from across the community.

However, two aspects of the Commission's guidance to applicants reinforced the scepticism of the UHI Project Office. The first was the relentless emphasis on capital funding. It could be argued that UHI's deliberate reliance on the existing infrastructure of local colleges and research institutions had put new capital spending way down the list of requirements for setting up the new university, yet for Millennium funding it would have to appear right up front. The real need, in the absence of Scottish Office endorsement, appeared to be for a guaranteed source of revenue funding for UHI – and this the Millennium Commission could not offer. The second issue was the ruling out of funding to projects which would "normally be supportable from public funds". Might this be used to reject what would appear in essence to be an educational project, even if the government had declined to provide it with state support?

In addition, even for the initial stages of bidding it would be necessary to indicate, at least in principle, what money other partners would be willing to contribute to the project. The Millennium Fund would not want its own contribution to exceed 50%. HIE and the other current backers of the UHI Project, who had been providing support measured in thousands of pounds, would have to be approached for commitments of hundreds of thousands, even millions.

A Bid from Skye

For the 1995 bidding round the Millennium Commission announced that Proposal Forms would have to be submitted by 31 March and Application Forms, with their back-up documents, by 30 April. While the UHI Project Office pondered whether or not a credible bid could be constructed in this timescale, other Highland interests decided to act.

Although Sabhal Mòr Ostaig, the Gaelic College in Skye, had been one of the earliest partners in the UHI Project, it had continued to develop in parallel its own plans for furthering the interests of the Gaelic language through post-school education. Although attractive new buildings had been built on its original farmstead site, including residential accommodation, the ambitions of the college and its governing body were out-growing these facilities too. With the initiative and commercial drive which had characterised its history, Sabhal Mòr Ostaig decided to make a bid in its own right for a share of the Millennium Fund.

The project which was worked up during the first half of 1994 was given the title "Bail' Ur Ostaig", meaning "New Town" or "New Special Place", and it carried the descriptive tag – "A Place for Cultural Renewal". The idea was to acquire a site not far from the existing college and to establish there a new centre for Gaelic language and culture, with a global outreach. By August 1994, when a major planning meeting was held in Skye, the concept was taking ambitious shape, with a price tag of perhaps £20 to £30 million. However, this seemed not to discourage its potential backers, who by now included HIE and the Highland Regional Council, whose Millennium Fund Committee were supporting Bail' Ur Ostaig as the region's main bid to the Fund.

But what did this imply for Sabhal Mòr Ostaig's role within the UHI Project? And had UHI's major sponsors effectively ditched it in favour of bank-rolling a new vision in Skye? The official line was that Bail' Ur Ostaig would have to "relate to the UHI Project", just as the Gaelic College had from the start. To some in Inverness the whole scheme had the flavour of a reverse take-over bid by the "Gaelic Mafia". On the other hand, surely it was better for the Highland community to put its weight behind an imaginative Millennium Fund bid from Skye than to risk having no bid at all? Throughout the rest of 1994 the detailed planning of the Bail' Ur Ostaig project continued, gathering further momentum and support.

Two Bids – or More?

Even if the favoured Highland bid to the Millennium Fund was now emerging
from Skye, that was seen elsewhere in the Highlands and Islands as no barrier to
the proposal of other projects in the "local" category. For example, local
initiatives were under active discussion in Stornoway, Kirkwall and Cromarty.
Some or all of these might be linked to the wider UHI concept. Informal
contacts suggested that while the Millennium Commission might have
reservations about a single, monolithic bid for a new university, they might be
willing to entertain a number of smaller bids from other centres within the UHI
partnership, without detriment to the Bail'Ur Ostaig proposals. Perhaps the
cause of UHI could be best served by encouraging such diversity?

In the end, the thinking of key stake-holders swung back towards using the
Millennium Fund to support a deliberately strategic approach to the further
development of the university project. Late in 1994 the Board of HIE (now led
by Fraser Morrison, a prominent local business man) decided that they would
be willing to sponsor a single, central bid to the Millennium Fund by the UHI
Project. This left a perilously short time in which to construct a bid for the 1995
round, but with such backing it was clearly a challenge worth taking up.

To explain this change of approach it is necessary to sketch in something of
what the university project had done during that year to win such a
commitment from HIE and to deserve such a valuable opportunity to bid for
high profile national support.

Estimating the Benefits

It was easy to forget, in the complex cross-currents of relationships between the
various partners in the project, that UHI was conceived primarily as a means to
the end of regional economic development. That was and remained the main
justification for the successive roles of HIDB and HIE in helping to promote a
new university. However, there was as yet little clarity about the potential
benefits UHI might bring to the region in addition to its educational and social
aims. In the first quarter of 1994 HIE therefore commissioned an in-house
study to estimate the benefits which might flow to the Highland and Islands
economy from the successful establishment of UHI on the dispersed, collegiate
model then being pursued.

Leading the study was Dr Ken MacTaggart, HIE's Head of Economics. His
conclusions surprised even the optimists. Taking as a base the studies of
economic benefit undertaken in recent years for Strathclyde and Liverpool

Universities, together with calculations made to support the case for the new University of Lincoln, Ken MacTaggart concluded that, in each of its first five years as a university, UHI could be expected to inject some £72 million (at 1994 prices) into the economy of its region, bringing benefits to all the communities in which it operated. There were several components within this total.

The first was the additional spending effect of a greatly increased population of higher education students. The criteria for university status implied raising the total number of students on higher education courses within the UHI partner institutions from the 1994 level of 1,100 to around 4,000. This in turn should represent an increase of some £20 million in annual spending. Even more significant would be the consequential expansion of business within the colleges themselves, including increased purchases of goods and services and higher levels of academic and supporting staffing, amounting to an additional spending effect of around £45 million a year. The balance of around £7 million was attributed to the effects of capital spending, on both buildings and ICT equipment, based on the investment levels then thought necessary for making UHI a reality.

However, this estimate was acknowledged to be only a partial measure of regional economic benefit. It took no account of the commercial benefits UHI might be expected to bring to the companies currently operating in the region, through undertaking applied research and providing a local source of highly qualified staff. It ignored the potential higher success rate of a region with a strong higher education base in securing inward investment. It did not allow for the faster formation of new local companies which a university can stimulate. In all these respects, which were of particular significance to HIE, UHI could be expected to yield benefits additional to the quantifiable injection of spending power.

In short, to a peripheral region still seeking a broader industrial portfolio, a means of raising average incomes and a gateway to what we now refer to as the knowledge economy, Ken MacTaggart's conclusions suggested that the new university offered something close to a policy panacea. In scale and impact, it might best be seen as a new industry in its own right. The findings of the study were therefore of the greatest significance to HIE.

The Local Dimension

Just as important was the message to each part of the Highlands and Islands that because UHI was being built on the foundation of their local college or research institution, they could also expect to share its future economic benefits. HIE differed crucially from its predecessor body in being constructed as a network, delivering local services through local outlets.

These Local Enterprise Companies (LECs) were business-led and nominally independent, although they depended in practice on HIE's funding and administrative support. Their main strength was in the development of a local perspective on economic and social development, enabling HIE's programmes to be tailored to the differing priorities of Lochaber, Shetland or Skye. Arrangements were therefore made for the Project Office to hold a series of local briefings across the region, both for LECs and for the local authorities, on the significance to them of the plans for UHI.

Some of the LECs were already well inclined towards supporting research or specialised courses at their local UHI partner institution and for them the new message was both understandable and welcome. Others needed more persuading of the link between the academic and business worlds, which they inclined to see as separate and largely incompatible, but they too took seriously the prospect of a further boost to local spending.

Similarly, a number of the local authorities were already active partners within the UHI Project, while others had seen it as at best peripheral to their interests. There was a particular political dimension to some local authority attitudes, reflecting a residual resentment at the Government-imposed loss of control of their local college.

However, in Council Chambers throughout the region the Project Office representatives found a courteous reception and even where the initial reaction to the UHI cause was luke-warm there was an invitation to keep in contact for further briefings. Over time, all the local authorities in the wide area covered by the UHI Project would become actively involved in it.

Research and Technology Transfer

During 1994 the opportunity also arose to examine in more detail some of the possible longer term economic benefits which the HIE in-house study had indicated UHI might bring to the region. The European Commission, which had already identified the transfer of technology between the academic and industrial sectors as a major driver of the US economy, was keen to encourage the development of more effective mechanisms for the same process within Europe. At the same time, there was a political imperative to show that the European Community could help to improve the fortunes of individual regions within its Member States.

The programme which emerged from the Commission's Directorate General XIII went by the less than racy title of RITTS – Regional Innovation and Technology Transfer Strategy. It offered part funding of studies into current systems for stimulating the practical exploitation of research in various regions of Europe, leading to the development of action plans for improving regional technology transfer. Contracts would be issued after a competitive bidding process between regions. At least one of the consultants carrying out each RITTS study would have to be from another nation, in order to improve the exchange of good practice within the Community.

The opportunity of bidding for a RITTS study in the Highlands and Islands had been overlooked by the UHI Project Office and the deadline for applications was close at hand before the programme was brought to their attention by a specialist in the field. With his assistance a proposal was put together in haste, based on the premise that a peripheral rural region which had hitherto lacked any higher education institution presented an intriguingly blank sheet for the development of technology transfer systems.

Something about the bid must have caught the imagination of the European Commission. The Highlands and Islands RITTS study was one of a small number of UK winners in that round of bids, providing HIE and the UHI Project Office with the opportunity to use external expertise (from Cambridge and Norway) to help align the future research strategy of UHI with the needs of the region's business community.

The College Network

As noted earlier, the now self-governing Academic Board had adopted the title of Highlands and Islands College Network (HICN) for their collaborative activities within the UHI Project. This turned out to be no mere branding exercise. Increasingly, the colleges and research institutions were ready to share – and in some significant areas to converge – their forward planning. They now included in their number, on an informal basis, the region's nursing college (the Highlands and Western Isles College of Nursing and Midwifery) which had sites in both Inverness and Stornoway.

Demonstrating this new commitment to working together, the Academic Board produced a draft HICN Corporate Plan for the years 1993/94 and 1994/95. For the first time this brought together in one schedule all the higher education courses available across the partner institutions, together with current student numbers, and attempted a projection of course development activities through to mid-1995.

The Plan proposed that the Network should concentrate on developing and, where possible beginning to implement, six key strategic building blocks of the future university:

- A Network academic plan.
- A Network academic quality assurance policy.
- A Network staff development strategy.
- A Network research strategy.
- A learning resource support strategy.
- A financial and estates resource strategy.

In addition, the Corporate Plan document set out for the first time the HICN institutions' own concept of their mission – "to be a leading provider of further and higher education courses, recognised for the quality of its provision within the wider community". The Network would be characterised, among other things, by "its vision to develop a Collegiate network aspiring to achieve degree awarding powers and ultimately the status of a university".

Resources for the Network

In response to this closer academic collaboration, HIE made some £250,000 available to the UHI project for the financial year 1994/95. Added to the growing support from local authorities, this provided the basis for some more ambitious plans to be funded.

The first area for support was degree development. There was no provision for the cost of developing new degree courses within the mainstream budgets of FE colleges and, even though the UHI philosophy was to build from the foundation of existing HNC and HND units, progress would be slow without some external stimulus. The UHI Project Office therefore made a formal offer to the Academic Board in May 1994 to provide up to £20,000 each towards the development of the first Network degree courses. The Academic Board was invited to submit costed bids for degree courses which met identified market opportunities and could be delivered right across the Network. Early candidates were expected to include Rural Development Studies, Business Studies, Tourism and possibly Marine Science. The aim was to put together the initial components of a curriculum broad enough to attract incoming students, as well as meeting immediate local needs.

In parallel, the first tentative steps were being taken to establish the ICT infrastructure for UHI. Following the establishment of an ICT Task Force in which every partner was represented, the Project Office supplied to each institution the hardware and software then required for an in-house electronic mail system. This was soon upgraded to take advantage of the emerging Internet, standardising on the First Class software also used by the Open University.

A number of major ICT equipment and network suppliers were keeping in close touch with these developments, not least British Telecom, but as yet no-one seemed sure enough of the commercial case to commit significant resources to the use of UHI as a test-bed for their latest technology.

A Thinking Network

The growing circle of friends and supporters acquired by the UHI Project included many leading figures in the world of higher education and public policy. Although the Academic Board had been unwilling to cede them a formal role within the Project, there was much they could do informally to ensure that the planning for the new university went forward in full knowledge of wider developments.

The idea of a series of lectures by some of these distinguished supporters was welcomed by Barail, the "think tank" at Sabhal Mòr Ostaig which had organised the 1992 conference on a Highland university. With modest funding from the Project Office to oil the wheels, the Barail Lecture series was launched in 1994. Held in a variety of locations and covering such topics as the future of Celtic Studies, developments in educational technology, distance learning projects in Ulster and the role of higher education in national competitiveness, the lectures attracted wide attention and good audiences. They also served, once more, to raise the profile of the UHI Project and the awareness of its potential both within the region and more widely.

CHAPTER 19

Tackling the Constitution

Constitutions and Boredom

There is no point in pretending that constitutional documents are exciting to the non-specialist, yet because they seek to describe and define relationships the business of getting them right is of fundamental importance. The level of public interest in the devolution settlement for Scotland is a recent example of constitutional matters managing to transcend boredom.

The constitutional discussions within the UHI Project, which began in earnest in 1994 and remained unresolved eight years later, are a crucial element in its history. They illustrate perfectly the danger to relationships, both within and between organisations, of treating legal definitions and clarifications as being a secondary priority, best left in the hands of a few enthusiasts or experts. While this does not make the minutiae of structures or protocols any more interesting in themselves, their implications should be given a chance to resonate. That will be the objective of recording in this narrative the main steps through which the constitutional debate within UHI made its difficult progress.

A First Attempt

As the practical initiatives towards curriculum development and IT networking indicated, even in early 1994 the UHI Project was more than just a façade of bustle and ambition. Yet it still lacked a coherent structure for governance. The Project Team and the shell company, UHI Ltd, provided adequate accountability for the levels of public funding so far committed, while the Academic Board gave a democratic basis for the joint activities of the College Network, but the linkages between the various bodies were still largely informal.

HIE took the lead in seeking to clarify these issues of governance and constitution, driven by the twin motives of wanting to increase the organisational independence of UHI and of seeking to establish a more solid structure for future financial investment. However, HIE was not alone in this desire for clarification, though other partners might have different objectives.

The local authorities were keen to maintain a major voice in the development of the project, in order to keep it true to its community roots – and also, perhaps, so as to prevent HIE from hijacking it too single-mindedly to the cause of private business. The principals who were working together in the College Network wanted to see a clearer route mapped out towards the freedom from non-academic control that was enshrined in the traditional models of university governance. The governing bodies of these partner institutions, meanwhile, were only starting to come to terms with the possibility that they might have to give up some of their independence (newly won in the case of the FE colleges) as a result of their principals' enthusiasm for a visionary joint venture which seemed to have little to do with local priorities. They too would want a voice in future decision-making structures.

Discussions and Recommendations

A first round of discussions between the main parties was held in an Inverness hotel in early June 1994. There was unanimous agreement on the need to rationalise the existing structures of the UHI Project and to determine "the organisational requirements and associated resources which need to be put in place to allow UHI to come to fruition."

On specifics, the conclusion was that UHI Ltd should become the leading organisational structure to take forward the Project. It should become an active, entrepreneurial trading company, with an increasingly high profile, dedicated to bringing UHI to fruition in the shortest appropriate timescale. In addition, the Academic Board should be retitled the Academic Council (following university practice) and its role, functions and resources strengthened, while a new body – the UHI Forum – should be created, to bring together leading players in the project with a wide range of community representatives and academic supporters, so as to create an active "supporters club" for the Project. These bodies would subsume and develop the roles of the UHI Steering Group, which should be discontinued.

Assisted by Willie Roe, the consultant who had facilitated the June seminar, the partner bodies undertook further work on these interim conclusions during the summer and a second round of discussions was scheduled for early

September 1994. A substantial paper was provided by Willie Roe, drawing together the results of the additional work since June, with the objective of guiding the meeting towards specific decisions.

In summary, it was proposed to proceed with the tripartite structure agreed in June. The company, UHI Ltd, would lead the Project; the Academic Council would continue to be responsible for all academic matters; and the UHI Forum would provide the vital link to the wider community. The Forum, which was now seen to have an additional role in fund-raising, would have a very wide membership (effectively a mailing list) but its core activities would be conducted by an Executive Committee comprising the Chairs of the management boards of the colleges (thus recognising their locus in the Project), community representatives and "senior academic supporters". The Chair of the Forum would be, *ex officio*, a Director of UHI Ltd.

But in order to make such a structure work, it would need to be properly equipped. "It is clear" pronounced Willie Roe's paper, "that the successful advancement of the UHI Project requires that the capacity of the overall team is expanded and that a number of appointments are made to fulfil key functions." In particular, it was proposed that for the next phase of its development UHI Ltd should be led by two powerful figures:

- An independent, part-time Chairman, able to devote up to three days a week to the Project on a paid basis. The ideal candidate would be able to command respect on the basis of past academic, business or public appointments, so as to be able to represent UHI Ltd and the Project at the highest levels, within the UK and internationally.
- A full-time Chief Executive, who would be responsible to the Chairman and Directors of UHI Ltd for leading the creation and implementation of a business plan to establish the University of the Highlands and Islands.

Crucially, these were posts designed for the continuation of a development process, not for a fully-fledged academic institution. Their term was to run "until the University is ready to make appointments of a full-time nature to lead its academic and business interests". It was also recommended that UHI Ltd should recruit a small support team to work with and for the Chief Executive and to serve the UHI Forum. This would take over the role of the UHI Project Office, though its composition might be quite different. In parallel, the Chairman of the Academic Council (a two year appointment, rotating round the membership) should be freed up for perhaps one day a week from the work of his or her own institution, in order to work on behalf of the wider network, and should be supported by the establishment of a small Academic Council Secretariat with "pay and rations" links to UHI Ltd.

The Status Quo as an Option

It was no great secret that these recommendations suited HIE very well. The proposals drawn together by the consultant seemed to offer the welcome prospect of a well resourced and business-like (perhaps business-led) company, driving forward the UHI agenda towards the early achievement of university status, but also supported by the wider community through the mechanism of the UHI Forum. Although the colleges would retain their seats on the Board of the company – and indeed would represent a majority block among the Directors – their main attention should be directed in future to the work of the Academic Council. Their time in charge could come later, when UHI moved from being a multi-partner project to becoming an integrated higher education institution.

However, although the outline proposals which emerged in June had attracted general support, those with different priorities from HIE found the working out of the scheme in detail far less to their liking. The colleges were happy to see their plans for the Academic Council backed and offered new resources, but the more senior principals were bound to question whether the powerful new Chairman and Chief Executive of UHI Ltd were intended to be their servants – or their masters. Might it not be better to retain the rather less aggressive leadership of the UHI Steering Group for a while longer?

From a different viewpoint, the local authorities were coming to a similar conclusion. The terms in which the proposed new Chairman of UHI Ltd was described seemed to rule out consideration of any of the current leadership of the Steering Group. To some they read as a deliberate and wounding attempt to push Councillor Val MacIver out of the chair of UHI Ltd, by those who had already plotted to close down the Steering Group which she had chaired from the Project's earliest days. Given her personal popularity and widely recognised commitment to UHI, the reaction was wholly understandable – though the vigour of it was unexpected in some quarters.

The upshot was that all the recommendations on non-academic governance were "left on the table", with agreement that both the Steering Group and UHI Ltd should continue in existence for the immediate future, serviced as before by the Project Office. It was to be a further two years before those nettles would be grasped again.

Signing Up the Colleges

However, there was an urgent need for progress on academic governance and it was to this that HIE and the Project Office now turned their attention. It was all very well to suggest that the retitled Academic Council should receive additional support and to plan to provide more resources to the members of the Highlands and Islands College Network, but what constitutional base did those bodies rest on? Membership of the College Network brought with it in turn a seat on the Steering Group and on the Board of UHI Ltd, but was there even any form of written statement of commitment to the establishment of UHI as a condition of that membership? There were too many loose ends for comfort.

Some ambitious solutions were considered behind the scenes. The Scottish Office, as paymaster of the FE sector, was increasingly keen on structural changes which might improve the efficiency and reduce the cost of delivering further education across Scotland. The Education Department had recently encouraged closer collaboration between a group of community colleges in Glasgow, even to the extent of part funding a joint secretariat. If the FE colleges in the Highlands and Islands had been willing to enter into a formal alliance, as a first step on the road to a collegiate university, there might have been money on the table for them too. But this implied a willingness by the colleges to work through the logical steps to which such an alliance would lead, by reducing duplication of services and seeking financial savings in such areas as administration. Local boards of management, whose independence would also be threatened, would certainly see more pain than gain down that road. Principals might fear it as the prelude to being down-graded to facilities managers. There would need to be a far more substantial incentive – or threat – before such an option could command support.

Just as unpopular with the academic partners would be the reversion – still favoured by some within HIE – to a plan first advocated by Sir Bob Cowan. He had recommended finding a high-flying academic, keen to make a real mark in the world of higher education, who would be appointed as the "vice chancellor in waiting" of UHI and would be given the role of leading the colleges into full collaboration by persuasion and force of personality. But at a time when even the appointment of a full-time Chief Executive to UHI Ltd had been stalled, this option was clearly not a runner, even if a suitable candidate could be identified.

The option chosen was something far more mundane – and yet it marked an important step towards the implementation of plans for UHI. A Minute of Agreement for the "Highlands and Islands Academic Network" (a new title) was drafted, briefly discussed, then sent to all the academic partners to sign.

It would become the formal route to a place on the Board of UHI Ltd and on the Academic Council. It set out operating guidelines for the rotating chairmanship of the Academic Council and for the conduct of its business. It required signatories to work together on the joint development of a curriculum and of specific courses. It committed them to make active use of ICT in administration, development and teaching. It established the principle that degree courses developed through the Network would be delivered across the region, by direct or distance learning, and that the movement of students between institutions would be facilitated. It even required each partner to make an annual contribution of at least £5,000 to collaborative projects in cash – or, if the Academic Council agreed, in kind. This financial provision, surprisingly, proved to be less of a bone of contention than the final section of the Agreement, on external partnerships. Here the partners were asked to attempt to turn their existing bilateral external relationships into multilateral links with the Network and to agree to submit any future bilateral links to the approval of the Academic Council.

Whether such an agreement carried any real legal force was never tested. In any case, it was to remain in force only until December 1996 and there was provision for it to be amended before then by decision of the Academic Council. Its purpose was less to establish a contract than to focus the thinking of governing bodies on the nature and seriousness of the task in which they were jointly engaged. In this it seems to have succeeded. Most of the institutions signed up without problems. Only one – Northern College – took the opportunity to make the break from association with UHI, though the Nursing College also felt unable to sign up, since the independent existence of all the Scottish colleges of nursing was then in question. (Soon the Nursing College was to be absorbed by Stirling University, which in the process acquired an Inverness Campus after all).

The need for further rounds of discussion on the Minute of Agreement with Inverness College and Moray College proved later to be significant, but at the time their reluctance was not seen by HIE to stand in the way of concluding that the academic partners were now adequately tied to the future of UHI and that a solid basis for further investment had been secured.

CHAPTER 20

The Millennium Bid

When Scotland's Millennium Commissioner, the Earl of Dalkeith, gave a briefing for potential Highland bidders at Culloden House Hotel near Inverness, he made it clear that the Commission were concerned to discourage applicants from committing themselves to heavy expenditure on professional services even before their basic eligibility for a grant had been established. He emphasised that initial bids did not have to contain full business plans or detailed architectural drawings.

The UHI Project Office took this advice to heart, not least because there was so little time for them to prepare a bid for the 1995 round of applications. Setting out the UHI concept was no great problem. Nor should it be difficult to explain how closely the concept was linked to the future well-being of the communities of the Highlands and Islands – and hence how the UHI Project could be seen as a suitable vehicle for marking the start of the new millennium. But the Commission's money was designed for capital projects. There was at that point no estates strategy for UHI as a whole and only a few of the individual institutions had up-to-date development plans for their own campuses.

In their 1993 work towards a UHI business plan, the consultants from Pieda had made a very broad estimate of the capital investment needed to realise the UHI concept on the ground. For the group of partners then involved (rather smaller than in 1995) they suggested that some £21 million would be required for the replacement or refurbishment of existing buildings, with a further £34 million to meet the needs of the new cohorts of higher education students – perhaps £55 million in all. Pieda were therefore asked to revisit their estimates in the light of developments in the past two years.

Not surprisingly, the figure they now proposed for campus developments was significantly higher, at just under £85 million. This included £28 million for the replacement or upgrading of existing buildings, £30 million for new academic and communal accommodation, £22 million for residences and sports facilities and £5 million for land and infrastructure. In addition there would be the cost of building up the data communications networks, equipping the campuses with computers and establishing libraries of a standard suitable for higher education.

This last requirement had been the subject of a recent study by a team of specialist consultants, led by John Fielden of the Commonwealth Higher Education Management Service (CHEMS). In spite of instinctive hopes among the Project Office and its advisers that UHI would be able to use electronic access to the knowledge base as a means of avoiding heavy investment in library buildings and stock, the study concluded that the poor state of the existing FE college libraries, the uncertainties about technology and the essentially inflexible requirements of those responsible for granting university status would combine to make major new investment unavoidable right across the network of colleges. The library experts from CHEMS recommended earmarking as much money for libraries as for the development of UHI's IT infrastructure – perhaps £8 million.

The total bill for capital investment in UHI therefore came to some £100 million. Even at a 50% share – probably more than could be offered in practice – the bid to the Millennium Commission would amount to £50 million, bringing it into the category of large strategic projects. Would this appeal to an organisation with a UK-wide remit and an obligation to avoid giving grants to projects which the state should be funding? There was only one way to find out – by submitting a bid which included the minimum of detailed information and hoping that the concept would attract enough attention to qualify for further investigation.

The First Bid

Graham Hills was asked to write the 20 page document designed to catch the imagination of the appraisal staff within the Millennium Commission. His draft, with input from the Project Office, was formally approved both by the UHI Steering Group and by Highlands and Islands Enterprise, the latter acting as the lead partner for the bid. It was submitted just before the deadline of 30 April, accompanied by a map and a series of explanatory appendices about the project.

Nowhere in the pack was there a single drawing or costing of a specific building on a specific campus. Those would have to come later, if the chance to do so could be won by this first throw. And if the first throw failed, there was no fall-back plan for finding £50 million from another source.

The document was as bold as the gamble it represented. It launched straight into the substance and made no concession to false modesty.

> This bid … is for capital funding which will make possible the establishment of a new federal, collegiate university of the Highlands and Islands of Scotland. It will be a university with campuses throughout the region, linked by one of the most modern communications networks in Britain. The principal purpose of the new foundation is to underpin the sustainability of this part of Britain by regenerating its economy and thereby enabling its people, its culture and its environment to flourish… In a sentence, [its vision] is that of a new kind of university, the best of its kind, showing the way out of the past and into the future, both for the region and for Scotland – perhaps as did the monks of St Columba in the first millennium.

Although much of the rest of the document was taken up with matters of governance and investment, at its core was a description of how it was hoped life would be led in the new university. This was an elaboration of Graham Hills' initial vision, now encompassing the first results of practical collaboration between the partners. It covered the approach to learning, the curriculum, the role of research, the staffing requirement and the student experience. The buildings were also described, but only in a generic way in order to illustrate what they would be used for, and with the disclaimer that:

> We are not able to put forward at this stage drawings, site details and costings for a specific development at a specific location. We expect these to come forward steadily…..once it is clear that there is a real prospect of substantial capital developments being funded. What we would therefore propose is that the Millennium Commission should agree in principle to fund 50% of the capital cost of making UHI a reality, within an envelope of £50 million to be committed over the six years 1995-2000. The partners in the project would then commission a full estates strategy, leading to a schedule of expected investments, for discussion and agreement with Commission staff.

The bid then ended on a suitably confident note:

> We believe no single project has received such widespread support in the Highlands and Islands and that none could equip the region so well for the contribution it can make to the nation in the next millennium.

Cool Reactions

There was immediate confirmation that the Millennium Commission would be no push-over. The Project Office had had to submit a Proposal Form in advance of the bid and the Commission's reaction to it crossed in the post with the submission of the Application Form and the bid document. This followed one of a number of standard formulae used by the Commission, confirming that the project had been accepted as eligible but that when it came to considering the full application the Commission would "wish to be assured of the project's long term viability and the availability of running costs support."

The opportunity was provided to deal with the point by submitting a supplementary note to the bid. A letter was therefore sent in reply by the Project Office, drawing attention to the sections of the bid document which explained how it was assumed that UHI might fit into the mainstream of the higher education funding system. However, the lack of any official commitment to such funding for a new university remained an obvious point of vulnerability.

Further disappointment was to come. In mid-June 1995 the Millennium Commission published its first "long list" of projects which it would be taking forward to the next and more detailed round of investigation. UHI was not on the list. Nor was Bail' Ur Ostaig, the planned development on the Isle of Skye. At first it seemed that the game was up, yet the letter of explanation sent to the Project Office confirmed a level of continuing interest. Informal contact with the case officer suggested that there was nothing to stop a revised bid going forward for the next year's bidding round. In essence, what had been supplied so far was too generalised to warrant detailed appraisal. It was hard for the authors to disagree.

Filling in the Details

Having come so far with the Millennium Commission – and with no alternative white knight in prospect – the UHI Steering Group and HIE took little persuading to agree that a revised bid should be prepared by the end of 1995. This time as much as possible would be done to fill in the details.

A fresh contract was prepared for Pieda. They would have to develop their outline capital costings into at least the first draft of a UHI Estates Strategy. In parallel, they were asked to construct a persuasive case to show how UHI might expect to attract sufficient mainstream revenue funding to answer concerns about viability. With the Scottish Office no nearer to giving the UHI Project a green light, this second task required particular ingenuity. The construction of an estates strategy was more straight-forward, though it called for patient working alongside the colleges to draw out their ideas for the development of buildings and campuses and to derive costings from them.

But dry figures of capital cost would not be enough to fix the UHI Project in the imagination of the Millennium Commission as a venture worthy of their nation-wide mission. Architectural concepts would have to be shown – yet the Project Office was in no financial or constitutional position to appoint an architect to design a new university. The compromise solution was wholly consistent with the collegiate vision of UHI. Each partner would use a local architect to prepare initial designs and drawings in sufficient detail to underpin Pieda's costing exercise. Once they were ready, a small expert group of volunteers assembled by the Project Office would review the plans and make the minimum necessary suggestions for improvement or greater consistency. It was made clear to the architects that they could be offered no more than an honorarium for their professional work at this stage – though of course they would be in pole position for substantive contracts if the overall bid proved successful.

With at most five months in hand before a revised bid would have to be submitted, the Project Office prepared for a very busy summer and autumn. If relations within the UHI partnership had been going well, the task would have seemed less daunting. However, on that front there were now some troubling skirmishes behind the scenes.

CHAPTER 21

Tension Between Colleagues

The Academic Council, in line with its revised constitution, had elected a new Chairman to serve during 1995. Mick Roebuck was the Principal of Lews Castle College in the Western Isles, not one of the largest FE Colleges in the Highlands and Islands Network but an institution deeply rooted in its community and an early supporter of the UHI concept. He was highly committed to partnership and collaboration between institutions across the region, both as the foundation stone of the new university and as a practical counter-weight to the influence of the Scottish Office. In his new role he saw signs of tension which alarmed him.

On the surface there was calm and good order. Joint development work on six UHI degree courses was under way or planned – Rural Development Studies, Environment and Heritage, Business Administration, Arts and Social Sciences, Marine Science and Tourism. Video-conferencing was beginning to allow staff from different institutions to work together without incurring the cost and time of travel. The Academic Council continued to meet regularly, with a substantial agenda. By the end of the year a revised UHI Corporate Plan would be completed, covering the period 1995-1997

Yet in reality this was still a fragile partnership and the underlying attitudes sometimes spoke more of competition than of co-operation. At root, there was still a great uncertainty. Would UHI ever win through to funding and acceptance, or would the whole project hit the buffers? If the vision crumbled in the face of financial and political realities, where would that leave institutions which had committed their future to a partnership without substance? Was it not more prudent to talk the language of partnership while quietly maximising individual benefits? It might be all very well for the principals to make grand joint declarations, but staff implementing the projects often felt they had their own futures to protect.

Mick Roebuck did what he could, leading by example and working behind the scenes with his fellow principals to influence their thinking, but there were limits to what he could achieve in the single day each week officially devoted to UHI affairs. At the same time, he had to direct the fortunes of his own college. During the year his sense of frustration grew. Much of it he shared with the Project Office, which was still acting as the secretariat to the Academic Council. That the agreed plan for an independent Secretariat had never come to fruition was another small indicator of UHI's problems.

Seeking Signatures

Meanwhile the Project Office had been wrestling with a related problem on the constitutional front. As noted earlier, all the institutions in the College Network had been asked to sign a Minute of Agreement to govern their collaboration on UHI matters. Most had done so without query, since the text had already been reviewed in the Academic Council. However, for two colleges – Inverness and Moray – what lay behind the wording proved to raise serious difficulties.

Both were significant institutions, locally and in the context of UHI. They were large FE colleges with a growing level of higher education activity. Inverness College was the largest partner in UHI and the one with the best developed links with an existing university, through its academic association with Stirling. It was also situated in the capital of the Highlands, where it was still seen by some as the potential kernel of an independent university. Moray College was smaller but no less ambitious. Geographically it was linked as closely to Aberdeen as to the Highlands and it had continued to develop its association with Aberdeen's Robert Gordon University.

In such matters, personalities can be as important as institutions. The Principal at Inverness, Jim Hedley, was nearing retirement but he continued to be a dominant figure among his staff and with his Board. He was justly proud of his college's status as an academic partner of Stirling University and of the Professorship granted to him personally. While he was content for the college to play its part in the development of the UHI Project, he often gave the impression that it was a secondary priority when compared with the delivery of Stirling's degrees to Highland students at Inverness. Stirling's decision to celebrate the first graduations through Inverness College at a formal degree ceremony in the town's Eden Court Theatre underlined the contrast for Inverness between what already existed and what might – or might not – still come to pass.

Dr Robert Chalmers, the Principal at Moray College, had already exercised effective leadership within the UHI Project as the first Chairman of the independent Academic Board. Having held that post for the better part of two years and given way to Mick Roebuck, he continued as Vice Chairman until June 1995. However, he now seemed to have redirected his priorities and his energies to his college and its immediate interests.

Copies of the Minute of Agreement were trickling back to the Project Office from the other UHI institutions, with signatures in place, while the first bid to the Millenium Commission was being prepared. The objective was to be able to say in the bid that all the current partners had signed up. Queries to Inverness and Moray at first suggested that any delay was just a matter of getting the item onto a crowded Board agenda. Then came the news that their Boards had declined to sign the document as presented. The Project Office offered briefings and explanations. A presentation was duly given to the Inverness College Board, in a fairly frosty atmosphere, but it became clear that progress would only be made in private discussions with the Principals and their Chairmen.

In both cases the root of the problem turned out to be the freedom of an incorporated college to enter into and maintain bilateral academic relationships outside the UHI partnership. The document contained two clauses which their Boards were reported to be reluctant to accept. The first required all partners to review their current bilateral academic agreements "in order to determine whether they can become multilateral links with the Network as a whole". The second required all future bilateral academic agreements to be approved by the Academic Council. The intention had never been to terminate existing agreements, such as the academic association between Inverness and Stirling, and the wording recognised that no current university partner could be forced to extend its collaboration to the whole UHI grouping against its will. However, it was felt consistent with the other partnership obligations in the document that from now on any bilateral academic deals should be subject to the agreement of the other UHI institutions.

Encouraged perhaps by their university partners, Inverness and Moray objected to both clauses. The first was said to be inappropriate and unenforceable. The second was said to undermine the prerogative of their Boards of Management to be free agents in determining the future of their institutions, because it would give an external (and strictly unconstitutional) body the right of approval over their association with another academic institution. This latter point went to the heart of the argument about the proposed federal nature of UHI, though it was not presented in those terms. The Project Office was pressed to drop both clauses, but since they had already been accepted by the majority of institutions this was resisted.

By this time the initial bid to the Millennium Fund had been submitted. It included the text of the Minute of Agreement as an appendix, described as a document which the participating colleges "had recently formulated.....to govern their current co-operative activities". It had not been necessary to specify how many had signed it. However, once it became clear that the Millennium Commission were willing to look at a revised bid from the UHI Project, the terms of discussion with Inverness and Moray shifted. Only those institutions which signed the Minute of Agreement would be able to put forward their capital development plans as part of the detailed funding bid.

In the case of Inverness, the potential cost of their plans was over £13 million, at a time when their overall financial position was thought to be comparatively weak. When it was made clear once more that their current agreement with Stirling was in no danger, they began to soften their objections to the two clauses. It looked for a while as if a deal was also on the cards with Moray, at the cost of replacing "approval" with "endorsement" as the Academic Council's role in relation to new bilateral agreements. But then rumours began to spread that the Board of Moray College had decided to withdraw from the UHI Project. As if to confirm the rumour, Moray College staff began to pull out of UHI planning meetings.

It proved impossible to ascertain the formal position. There were doubts about what – if anything – the Board had decided. No notice of withdrawal was ever received from Moray. However, even when Inverness College eventually signed their copy of the Minute of Agreement there was no corresponding move from the other dissenter. Therefore the revised bid to the Millennium Commission would not include any capital expenditure or conceptual drawings from Moray College, though the omission was understandably not referred to and Elgin remained on the map of UHI sites.

A Stand-Off with Skye

Both the UHI Project and Bail' Ur Ostaig had been placed on the Millennium Commission's List B, comprising bids which were judged insufficiently detailed for full appraisal but whose sponsors were invited to make a further and fuller proposal to the next round of appraisals in 1996. There was clearly some concern at the thought that two major Highland projects might go into the next round without indicating what relationship there was between them and why they were persisting as separate bids.

Although Sabhal Mòr Ostaig had readily signed the Minute of Agreement and remained a firm backer of the UHI Project in all public pronouncements, there were occasional rumblings of disquiet from the Gaelic community that UHI's late Millennium Fund bid in the previous round might have worsened the odds against Bail' Ur Ostaig. There were even hints of an anti-Gaelic bias within the Project Office. However, elsewhere among the UHI partners there were matching worries that Bail' Ur Ostaig might represent the launching pad for establishing an independent higher education project in Skye, replacing the current commitment to the UHI Project. Some formula was needed which would clarify the position, for both external and internal audiences.

This proved far easier than dealing with Inverness and Moray. The Project Office was able to confirm that a significant part of the capital funding within the revised bid would be for the upgrading of IT and learning resource facilities. This would apply to all UHI partner institutions, whether or not there were plans for other capital investment on the site, and so both Sabhal Mòr Ostaig and (if funded) Bail' Ur Ostaig could expect to benefit from success for the UHI Project. In turn, Sabhal Mòr Ostaig agreed that, if their project gained its funding, they would make available to the UHI partners the planned higher education offerings of Bail' Ur Ostaig, to be taught through the medium of Gaelic – though it was also emphasised that their project was about far more than higher education. A form of words to convey this reciprocal arrangement was agreed and would be used in both revised bids to explain the relationship between them.

The outcome seemed sensible, even if it resembled a stand-off. At this stage neither side was keen to explore whether the two projects might improve the chances of securing a major Millennium project for the Highlands by merging their bids.

CHAPTER 22

Plates in the Air

At this crucial stage in the development of the UHI Project its backers had to work on the assumption that the necessary funding package would materialise. With Pieda's help, they felt it should be possible to prepare a convincing and thoroughly revised bid to the Millennium Commission, but at the same time the reality had to be filled in behind the words.

The first step was to strengthen the Project Team, which urgently needed a kernel of technical expertise. The recruitment of Patrick Dark as ICT Co-ordination Manager marked a real milestone in the Project's progress, its significance belied by his quiet personality. His post-graduate experience (at Cambridge and Robert Gordon's) gave him the necessary professional credibility to co-ordinate ICT developments at the partner institutions and to provide overall strategic direction of UHI's future networks. The fact that he was recruited by UHI Ltd – and thus became the company's first employee – also signalled the growing maturity of the Project. In parallel, Margo Taylor was seconded to the Project Team from HIE, to strengthen the finance and administration function and improve the service to the Academic Council.

Time Out at Dunkeld

This was also the time to address unfinished business on the policy front. The Millennium Commission assessors would undoubtedly keep worrying away at UHI's weak point – how could the new university secure sufficient recurrent funding to keep it viable? Pouring money into the capital account would be pointless if the government refused to let UHI into the charmed circle of mainstream revenue funding – and so those millions would remain firmly locked away unless a more convincing story could be deployed. Some shifting of the official stance had to be attempted, though for the present it would have to be behind closed doors.

In one of those hidden and "deniable" gatherings which more usually form part of a peace process between warring nations, an informal briefing on the progress of UHI was arranged at a quiet riverside hotel in Dunkeld, conveniently situated mid way between the Highlands and those Edinburgh offices where Ministers and officials usually pondered UHI's future. Although it was felt inappropriate to invite Ministers in person, the fact that they did not veto their officials' attendance was taken as a good sign.

It helped that the invitations to the event came from someone who had only just left the leadership of a Scottish university. Professor Bill Turmeau, on his retirement from Napier University, offered his services to the UHI cause, which he had long supported. He agreed to front the discussions at Dunkeld, which drew together the key players from the UHI Project, the Scottish Higher Education Funding Council (SHEFC) and the Scottish Office Education Department, together with the principals of the other two universities most closely linked with the UHI story – Aberdeen and Stirling. It was an amicable gathering, informative rather than decisive, though for some the speed and extent of the Project's recent progress seemed to be an eye-opener. Although no minds were changed on the day – indeed, SHEFC remained basically frosty to the idea of offering any of their money to such a strange and unproven institution – the briefing seemed to achieve the purpose of convincing people who mattered that the Highlanders were still determined to pursue their dream.

There was also a hint of agreement on a way forward. It was suggested that some of the worries about UHI's ability to meet the quality standards of higher education might be stilled if other universities were to lend a helping hand. Perhaps this was intended as a back-handed way of reviving the colonising model rejected in 1992, but since both Aberdeen and Stirling were present at the discussion there was no scope for an overt take-over bid.

Subsequently the Project Office drew up a draft Declaration by University Partners, in an attempt to tie down the idea of a joint approach to bringing UHI into being, which might also have attracted some form of SHEFC financial support. The document was discussed further with a number of the university principals, but no-one was keen to be the first to sign even a bland declaration of intent and that initiative soon ran into the sand. On the other hand, after the event at Dunkeld there were few signs of opposition to UHI among the established universities – at least in public.

Curriculum and Colleges

Through small and gradual steps the staff across the College Network were also learning to collaborate more readily. Progress was most marked in preparing units for the new curriculum, where the Rural Development degree was emerging as front runner among the batch of courses under joint development, building on material already in use up to HND level.

Although the first degrees would be validated by the colleges' existing university partners, discussions were progressing well with the Open University Validation Service (OUVS) on a UHI-wide approach to validation for the longer term. But this initiative brought the spotlight back to another weak point in the Millennium bid. How was a university curriculum going to be delivered at the college level?

By November 1995 the Project Office was in a position to attempt an answer, following a series of informal Roadshows to discuss the UHI concept with staff in the partner institutions. A paper for leading figures in the Academic Council suggested that the UHI curriculum should be planned in two complementary blocks:

- A common core curriculum. This would be a group of subjects, of broad economic and community relevance across the region, available at every college.
- Local and regional specialisms. These would be subjects which reflected particular academic strengths or specific aspects of local or regional heritage, culture or industry. They might be the specialist preserve of a single college, or an area of joint expertise among a small group of colleges. Ideally they should be linked to a collocated research capability. Crucially, they would give UHI its distinctive edge in the market for students and resources.

The paper proposed that each individual college should put forward plans to deliver this curriculum, in three modes of operation:

1) Core Delivery. By a certain point in UHI's development, every college should have the in-house capability to deliver all subjects in the agreed core curriculum up to degree level.

2) Exporting. Each college should be able to offer at least one of the local and regional specialisms up to degree level, both to its own resident/local students and, through distance and open learning, to any other college which had identified local demand for it.

3) Importing. Each college should make arrangements to act as a delivery point for the exported teaching of other elements in the specialist curriculum, from other UHI colleges to any local students seeking access to it. Wherever possible, this should be backed up by some form of local tutorial support, perhaps at community level.

In this way, it should be possible to achieve the dual objective, central to the UHI concept from the start, of making the whole curriculum accessible to the whole of the region while providing centres of expertise capable of attracting in students from elsewhere.

As the paper recognised, there was a significant gap between this ideal model and the reality of what the UHI partners could actually deliver. The development or franchising of enough degree courses to provide reasonable coverage of a varied curriculum would take a good deal of time, money and staff effort. However, that was no new problem for UHI. The tougher issues would be about relationships, with local communities and within the College Network.

Taking the community level first, the concept proposed by the Project Office assumed a responsibility on each college to act as the access point for UHI courses to any students within its catchment area. This fitted well with the mission of the existing FE colleges, but other partners had a different focus. Two of them – Ardtoe and Dunstaffnage – were research institutes with no local infrastructure for delivering tertiary education. (In the years ahead this problem was to be solved by the development of new colleges in Lochaber and Argyll under the UHI banner.) Another partner – Sabhal Mòr Ostaig – had a constitutional commitment to deliver courses through the medium of Gaelic and it was far from clear whether its Board would permit the college to take on the additional task of providing access to English-medium tertiary education for the people of Skye and Lochalsh.

At the College Network level, the Project Office assumed implicitly that although students would have a local and corporate link to an individual college they would "belong" to UHI, so that the exporting or importing courses across the network would be centrally administered and – from the perspective of the college – neutral in financial terms. This was of course based on the federal, collegiate model which the partners had all accepted in principle as the way forward. Yet until some form of collegiate constitution was in place it would be difficult in practice for colleges to see students as other than an income-generating resource for their own institution. The longer this tension continued, the slower would be the development of networked courses and the delivery of an integrated curriculum.

Not surprisingly, the Project Office's proposals were greeted with polite interest and accepted as the basis for filling out the relevant parts of the revised Millennium bid – thus achieving the immediate objective. But real progress on tackling the fundamental constitutional issue was again deferred.

New Political Leadership

By this point a Government reshuffle had brought new political leadership to the Scottish Office, with Michael Forsyth replacing Ian Lang as Secretary of State. Lang had never been more than cool towards UHI, so a change might be positive for the Project. Yet Forsyth's record did not inspire hope. His reputation as a hard-liner, on the Thatcherite right of the Conservative Party, suggested he would be readier to cut the throat of a new institution than to offer it a transfusion of public money.

In practice, Michael Forsyth confounded many of his initial critics across Scotland by showing an open-minded approach and a populist touch, though he never lost his "dry" credentials. The backers of the UHI Project were still in no position to approach him directly, but there were opportunities for informal contact – and these were used, though sparingly. It seemed that the UHI Project was no worse off for the change of Secretary of State. Whether its prospects had improved, it was too early to say.

The Revised Bid

As the culmination of this busy period, in which the champions of the UHI Project felt they were running from plate to plate in order to keep everything spinning, a revised bid to the Millennium Commission was submitted in November 1995.

This was a great contrast with the initial proposal. The main submission, complete with financial tables and drawings, was supported by ten detailed appendices covering key issues from ICT strategy to building design principles. One appendix, put together with the enthusiastic assistance of a small local consultancy, was bulging with letters of support for the UHI project from community and business sources, from key agencies and from a surprisingly wide range of existing universities.

Above all, the November 1995 bid for the first time gave the Millennium Commission an idea of what kind of long term legacy their money might buy. There were illustrations of new buildings planned for Ardtoe, Dunstaffnage, Inverness, Kirkwall, Lerwick, Perth, Scalloway, Stornoway and Thurso. These were to be the new campuses of UHI, making its presence across the region a visible reality. With the illustrations came the ability to attach sums of money more clearly to specific construction plans. The campus developments were estimated to cost £55 million in total, with a further £21 million required to supply the ICT and library infrastructure and to cover project management costs, making a total of £76.7 million. It was proposed that the Millennium Fund should meet 50% of these costs, with the balance coming chiefly from the UHI Project partners (public agencies and academic partners) and from the EU Objective One programme.

As before – but now with the added conviction of independent assessment – the bid assumed that the revenue costs of the new institution could and would be met through mainstream Scottish Office funding for further and higher education and through full cost recovery where appropriate. Although the policy of "consolidation" (ie standstill provision) of higher education student numbers was still in force across the UK, it was pointed out that the policy did not affect a number of UHI's target markets, particularly part-time HE courses, post-graduate courses and full-cost courses offered to mature students and businesses. Looking further ahead, the bid (somewhat prophetically) concluded that:

> whether in fact the "consolidation" policy affects the pace at which UHI numbers can be built up will depend at one level on the develop-ment of general Government policy towards HE growth . . . and, at another level, on whether the regional economic advantages of imple-menting the UHI Project are seen to justify the marginal increase in total Scottish HE numbers which would be implied . . .

However, although much of the new material in the bid was about college buildings and student numbers, the emphasis remained firmly on the UHI Project's economic and community benefits. Now that the professionals had done an excellent job in filling in the essential details, the central message that UHI was truly "a project of the Millennium" could be delivered even more confidently.

PART VII
Breakthrough

CHAPTER 23

The Turning of the Tide

By the beginning of 1996 the existing backers of the UHI Project had played almost every card in their hand. They had already achieved a great deal. A loose association of public agencies and academic bodies, rallying round an economic and educational idea, had grown into a strongly motivated partnership capable of delivering joint courses and making a credible bid for large scale funding. Yet UHI was officially unrecognised and unblessed. In response to press enquiries, a Scottish Office spokesperson would still go no further than hinting that Scotland was already well provided with universities and that they saw no case for adding to their number.

A Gesture of Confidence

At this critical point the Academic Council had another change of leadership. Mick Roebuck left the region to become the Principal of Kilmarnock College and was succeeded as UHI Academic Council Chairman by Ray Murray, the Principal of Thurso College, one of the smaller FE colleges in the partnership. Both the college and its principal had a reputation for innovation and independence. The new Chairman made clear to his Academic Council colleagues, as well as to the Steering Group and the Project Office, that he was ready to redouble the efforts to make UHI succeed.

It was accepted by the partners that a further restructuring of the Project would be essential if they secured the backing for implementing their plans. They now had to decide how to achieve it. In mid January a joint meeting was held of the Academic Council, the UHI Steering Group and the Board of UHI Ltd – in large measure an overlapping cast. Conscious of the need to demonstrate their confidence in success, they agreed to re-affirm their joint support to the UHI Project, to commit to giving the highest priority – in effort and resources – to collaborative delivery of the curriculum and to review the management structures for the project. Work started immediately to implement this renewed commitment. The Academic Council's Curriculum Group scheduled a major meeting for early February and Ray Murray began a series of informal brainstorming sessions with Val MacIver, Graham Hills and the Project Office to draw up the options for a new management structure.

The Scottish Grand Committee

In parallel, the UHI Steering Group agreed to make the most of a fresh and unexpected opportunity to use what political influence it could command. In pre-devolution Scotland the nearest thing to a Scottish Parliament was a hybrid body called the Scottish Grand Committee. This brought together all the MPs from Scottish constituencies and gave them the opportunity to quiz Ministers on matters of specific interest to Scotland. It took no decisions and commanded no great respect as a means of achieving political ends, but it did provide an additional platform from which the opposition parties could lob verbal hand grenades at the government of the day.

The new Secretary of State for Scotland, Michael Forsyth, had recently taken the political establishment by surprise (something he clearly relished) by declaring that the next meeting of the Scottish Grand Committee would be held in Inverness. The date of the meeting, 5 February 1996, fitted perfectly with the need for the UHI Project to convey to the Millennium Commission the breadth of support it commanded among the region's political representatives.

A few MPs were briefed about the recent progress of the project, in case they should find an opportunity to ask the Secretary of State about his Department's attitude to the university which the region so desired. There was no great expectation of an encouraging answer, but it was hoped that a wholly negative response would be more difficult to make in the capital of the Highlands.

What actually happened was astonishing. As they filed into the meeting room, Michael Forsyth said casually to Jim Wallace, the Liberal Democrat MP for Orkney and Shetland – "Jim, ask me a question about UHI." These things happen in politics, across the party lines. When an opportunity arose, Jim Wallace therefore said, in the course of a general commentary on Scottish Office policy towards the region: "I also hope that the Secretary of State will show more enthusiasm than we have seen so far for the concept of a Highlands and Islands University."

The Secretary of State's response is worth giving in full, as set down in the Official Record:

> The Honourable Member for Orkney and Shetland asked me specifically about the idea of a university for the Highlands and Islands. My briefing tells me that it would be too difficult. Having recently visited the Gaelic College in Skye, I believe that there is a tremendous opportunity to use the new technology to create a new style of university. This is the 250th anniversary of a dread scene in the Highlands. What better year to use new technology to make a new beginning? I am happy to pursue these ideas, as the Hon. Gentleman suggests.

For those who were present, the surprise shown by MPs at this response was far less interesting than the visible consternation of the Scottish Office officials who had come up to Inverness to "mind" the Secretary of State. Clearly they had had no warning of what he intended to say. Indeed, he had taken the very unusual step of revealing the negative tone of their briefing on this topic. It is not unknown for governments to make U-turns in policy, but they are usually heralded by hints and well-placed leaks in advance of any announcement. This shift of direction, from opposition to positive support, came out of the blue. It seemed to be the result of a personal – and political – decision that a change of attitude to the UHI Project was needed and that there could be no better place and time to declare it.

Rationale for a U-Turn

Once again, as all the lessons from abroad had suggested it would, the future of a regional university was being determined by political will rather than by academic judgement. But what was the political angle in this case? Both on the spot and in subsequent conversation the MPs and the commentators found it hard to work out why Michael Forsyth had decided to back UHI, by deeds and resources as well as words – and to do so openly against the advice of his officials. It seemed an improbable way of shifting Highlands and Islands votes – notoriously ungrateful for favours – towards the Conservative Party. It would not play particularly well in the rest of Scotland. It would irritate much of the higher education establishment. It would require real money to be spent. So why now embrace this orphan child, so warmly and so publicly?

Before long the speculation faded away, as the practical implications of the decision came to dominate attention. For his part, Michael Forsyth did not elaborate the reasons for his decision while in office. Informal contact with his officials confirmed that they remained as puzzled as anyone else. But the authors of this book felt it was an event so central to the UHI story that they should ask Lord Forsyth of Drumlean, as he now is, if he was willing to explain what had led him to shift Scottish Office policy so radically six years earlier.

The answer was both unexpected and simple. He had seen UHI's significance in national rather than regional terms.

Two factors, brought to his attention in his official visits around the country, had led him to conclude that the new university deserved support. The first factor was the need to broaden Scotland's industrial base, which he thought was too dependent on inward investment at the less skilful end of electronics, vulnerable to competition from lower cost countries. For longer term prosperity, Scotland had to become a design centre rather than an assembly line. The second factor was the deeply conservative outlook which seemed to dominate Scotland's existing universities. Their ability to play a dynamic and transforming role in modern society seemed to have been abandoned in favour of financial security and academic exclusiveness.

From this perspective, what he saw by contrast in the plans for UHI (and had clearly recognised in microcosm in his visit to Sabhal Mòr Ostaig) was a new approach to the use of technology in learning, with no tradition or established structure to hold it back. If it worked, it might shock the existing universities out of their complacency. Better still, it might be the basis for a new Scottish industry, exporting to the rest of the world a technology of learning with the hardware and software to go with it. There was no guarantee that it would work, but unless it was given a chance to prove itself, UHI would remain a might-have-been for Scotland. He had decided it should have that chance – and in the pre-devolution Scottish Office it needed little more than his personal conviction and the backing of his immediate Ministerial colleagues for a Secretary of State to be able to announce such a decision almost as soon as it had been made, leaving officials to cope with the consequences.

The Consequences

At the press conference following the meeting of the Scottish Grand Committee, the journalists pressed Michael Forsyth on what his pledge of support for UHI meant in practice. How would he and his officials "pursue these ideas"? His response was brief and to the point – they should, with the Project's backers, "find a way of doing it which is cost-effective, and do it." Behind the scenes urgent talks were being arranged between the Project Office and the key Scottish Office officials on what this meant and what practical assistance might be offered to UHI's development. It was clear that the assistance would be initially through the loosening of policy strings, rather than purse strings, though there was the prospect of some financial support too.

The critical policy factor was "consolidation" – the bar on growth of higher education numbers, which stood in the way of UHI developing towards the degree student population necessary for university status. If this barrier could be lifted, exceptionally for UHI, it would answer many of the concerns about revenue funding and longer term viability which were known to be troubling the Millennium Commission. Beyond that, the need was mainly for assistance in linking the UHI partners to the mainstream academic IT networks and for selective support with innovative projects in applying that technology to both teaching and administration. In reflection of their Secretary of State's enthusiasm, officials were careful not to cross anything off the UHI shopping list in this initial meeting, though there would obviously be some months of negotiation ahead.

CHAPTER 24

Managing for Real

As noted earlier, the need to revisit the management arrangements for the UHI Project had been recognised by the leading partners even before the change of heart at the Scottish Office. Now the requirement to put matters on a more appropriate basis for the longer term had become urgent.

Ray Murray pointed out to his colleagues on the Academic Council the potential confusions which remained at the heart of the project. The membership and functions of different bodies overlapped – this was particularly true of the Steering Group, the Academic Council and the Board of UHI Ltd. The company, UHI Ltd, had no separate management from the Project Office, yet it was taking on employees in its own right. Meanwhile, the core staff of the Project Office remained on secondment from HIE and Robin Lingard, the Project Director, was also a member of the HIE senior management group. Ray Murray concluded: "A simpler model would be for all staff to be employed by UHI Ltd, with a Chief Executive responsible for implementing the strategy agreed by the Board of Directors."

To all of which, the Project Office gave a hearty amen. The previous attempt to streamline management of the UHI Project on those lines in 1994 (discussed earlier in Chapter 19) had foundered on the different but converging reservations of the local authorities and the colleges. What made it likely that a fresh approach would succeed? Four factors seemed to have improved the chances:

- The need to demonstrate to the Millennium Commission that UHI would have the central structure and professional discipline appropriate for managing a major capital project, to be implemented at sites across the region.
- The need to speed progress centrally on course and curriculum

development, staff training, marketing and student services, in order to move credibly towards a bid for university status.

- In the wake of Michael Forsyth's public statement of support, quiet but firm encouragement from the Scottish Office for the colleges to give a more visible expression to their commitment to collaboration.
- The fact that this time the Academic Council Chairman had taken the initiative to make the proposal to his colleagues.

Possible Structures

Ray Murray was now to be found at the Project Office up to two days a week, often in company with Graham Hills. They began to draw out alternative structures for UHI, recognising that there was a need to plan not only for the rest of the development phase but also for the operation of a fully-fledged university at the end of that phase.

Ideally, the initial structure should be readily convertible into university mode when the time came. Graham Hills' advice was therefore to try to "shadow" the organisational structure of a university from the start. Traditionally, a British university would have two governing bodies with complementary roles:

- The University Court, a strategic body chaired by a senior figure from outside the university and including both academic and community representatives. The role of the Court should be to root the university in the society and economy it serves. It also acts as the guardian of financial accountability for the university.
- The University Senate, an operational body chaired by the Principal and bringing together representatives of all the staff of the university. The role of the Senate should be to govern the activities of the university as an academic institution and to set relevant policies for it.

On this model, the day-to-day management of the university is normally delegated to a University Management Group, involving the Principal and senior colleagues, and to a number of specialist committees reporting to the Senate.

How could this system be replicated in the development phase, before university status was granted? The concept of the Court was perhaps the easiest to translate, given the comparable role of the UHI Steering Group as a manifestation of the bond between the UHI Project and the communities of the Highlands and Islands. In the 1994 proposals the recommendation had been to broaden and formalise the role of the Steering Group through the creation of a

UHI Forum. This idea was resurrected, with the new title of "UHI Foundation", to be a University Court in waiting.

In one sense, the forerunner of the University Senate might be thought to be the UHI Project's Academic Council, which already brought together the senior executives of all the academic partners. However, its current role was limited to the oversight of joint courses and other academic initiatives undertaken collectively. It was not constituted to manage resources or to develop policy outside that domain and it was not conceivable that the major funders of the project would confer such a role on the Academic Council in advance of the creation of a university institution. This was where the hybrid but still necessary role of the company, UHI Ltd, came again into focus.

The proposal which emerged from these first discussions at the Project Office was for the Board of UHI Ltd to manage the development phase of the UHI Project, advised and supported on the one hand by the Foundation, representing the community, and on the other by the Academic Council, representing the colleges. Once university status was achieved, the Foundation would be transformed into the Court, taking the financial accountability role of UHI Ltd, the Academic Council would become the Senate, absorbing the operational management roles of UHI Ltd – and the company would disappear, its job done.

For the remainder of the development phase it was recommended that day-to-day management would be undertaken for UHI Ltd by:

- A full time Chief Executive, taking over the role of the Project Director but specifically charged in addition with bringing the project through to university status.
- An Executive Office, whose staff would all be employees of UHI Ltd, working under the leadership of the Chief Executive.
- A University Management Group, with delegated responsibility from the Board of UHI Ltd for the operational activities directly relevant to the academic development of the new institution. This would be made up of the principals of the partner institutions, plus the Chief Executive of UHI Ltd, and would give them a far more direct role in the management of the project than through participation in the Board of the company.

No proposals were made on this occasion about the ideal template for the future Chairman of UHI Ltd, one of the issues on which the previous discussions about management of the project had foundered.

UHI in Fashion

While these management proposals were in preparation, the chances that they would soon be needed for real became far stronger.

Michael Forsyth announced that he had decided, exceptionally, to remove the cap on the growth of higher education student numbers in the Highlands and Islands colleges. Although it was initially a commitment for one year only, this was a significant breach in the "consolidation" policy and a further earnest of the commitment of the Scottish Office to do what it could to bring the UHI concept to reality. But there was more to come from the Secretary of State.

On 26 April 1996, delivering the Williamson Memorial Lecture at (ironically) Stirling University, he articulated his own vision for UHI:

> . . . a University of the Highlands and Islands delivering courses through the 'information superhighway' to the towns, villages and homes of the area, providing new or 'second chance' opportunities for school leavers and adults to progress from basic skills to the highest standards of intellectual attainment. From this must flow economic, social and cultural benefits significant enough to kindle a new Highland Enlightenment.

Almost lost in this political endorsement of the longer term ambitions of UHI was the announcement of a further practical step to assist its current activities – Scottish Office approval of the first UHI degree course, in Rural Development Studies, subject to validation. This he described specifically as "a signal of my support for the UHI Project".

By the time that lecture was delivered, there had also been highly encouraging news on the funding front. The Millennium Commission had moved the UHI Project on to the "long list", signifying that the bid now had enough credibility against their funding criteria to justify detailed external appraisal by an appropriate expert. However, they made clear that the bid should first be further revised to reduce the call on the Millennium Fund, both in absolute terms and as a percentage of the total investment programme. They also hinted strongly that all student accommodation projects should be excluded from the revised package.

While there was still no guarantee of a grant, this response was a powerful sign that – helped no doubt by the change of attitude at the Scottish Office – people who mattered were beginning to recognise the real potential of this community-based initiative. Sadly, the Bail' Ur Ostaig project in Skye failed to make it to the long list and there was initially some local resentment at the apparent inequity of the outcome. Then came private guidance from the

Millennium Commission, both to the backers of Bail' Ur Ostaig and to the UHI Project Office, that room should also be found in a revised UHI bid for a version of the new campus for Sabhal Mòr Ostaig. Given the simultaneous need to reduce the overall level of grant sought, this would present quite a challenge to the Project Office and their technical advisers, but it was recognised that the inclusion of the Gaelic College in the UHI bid would further strengthen its community credentials – and hence its chances of success.

Listening to the Community

With so much now at stake, it was decided that the new management arrangements for UHI had to be discussed as openly and widely as possible, to ensure there was community backing for the changes. A special meeting was therefore arranged by the Steering Group, at which all the stakeholders would be offered the opportunity to review and comment on the proposals.

On 29 May 1996 over 50 people assembled in Nairn (so often the location for critical moments in the UHI story) to agree a way forward, assisted once more by Willie Roe, the facilitator who had helped to formulate the 1994 proposals. This time there was a strong local authority presence and the colleges were represented by members of their management boards as well as by the senior executives, so the balance of views was perhaps more likely to favour a community-based approach to management than the business-based approach which HIE had advocated two years earlier.

The outcome turned part of the structure developed by Ray Murray and Graham Hills on its head. The majority view was that the most important player in the next phase of development should be the UHI Foundation, an organisation with wide community representation which would take on the roles of both the Steering Group and UHI Ltd. Indeed, it was envisaged that the existing legal structure of UHI Ltd would be adapted to create the Foundation.

As the meeting note recorded:

> The UHI Foundation will be created as the lead organisation to carry through the work programme leading to the creation of the University. It will be the guardian of the University concept. It will have a high public profile.

In order to carry through this remit effectively, it was proposed that the Foundation should elect from its members a Board of 12, of whom six would be representatives of the colleges. The Board would be responsible for determining the overall implementation strategy for the University and would set targets for the Chief Executive and the Executive Office, whose operational role would be unchanged from the proposals to the meeting. Also unchanged would be the role of the Academic Council, though the concept of bringing the college principals and the Chief Executive together in a University Management group was dropped.

At the Nairn meeting the opportunity was also taken to revisit the constitutional and organisational model for the university. Again quoting from the meeting note:

> It was reaffirmed that UHI aims to be a federal, collegiate university, broadly as proposed by Sir Graham Hills, and pursued to date by the partners. It was also reaffirmed that the central principle of governance should be the maximum delegation of functions and responsibilities to the college level, consistent with maintaining the integrity of the University. Expressed another way, the minimum centralisation of functions and responsibilities required to enable the University to prosper.

Pressing On

Action to follow up the main conclusions of the consultation in Nairn was swift. The next day the Steering Group and the Board of UHI Ltd met formally, as planned.

The Steering Group approved the establishment of the UHI Foundation to take over its role and remitted to its Chairman (Val MacIver) and the Project Office to come forward with proposals for membership. The Board agreed to set in train the drafting of a legal constitution for the Foundation, to be derived from the Memorandum and Articles of UHI Ltd. It also authorised the recruitment of a Chief Executive and commissioned the preparation of a job description and an advertisement.

So could it now be assumed that everyone was happy? The new management arrangements certainly seemed to contain something for all parties. Those who wanted to see a business model adopted had secured agreement to placing day-to-day responsibility for delivering UHI on a Chief Executive, backed up by an Executive Office. Both were to be independent of HIE and would be answerable to a small Board of Directors able to set testing operational targets. Those who wanted to see the community in the driving seat had established the UHI Foundation in a lead role, guarding the university concept and electing the members of the Board. As for the colleges, they had been offered half the seats on the Board and had received confirmation that the future university would be run on the basis of minimum centralisation.

It was, in sum, a good enough deal on which to base the final bid to the Millennium Commission.

CHAPTER 25

A Final Sprint

The summer months of 1996 saw all the resources of the UHI Project at full stretch. While day-to-day work could not be abandoned, priority had to be given to two areas of action which were now time-critical. By August a final bid would have to be ready for the Millennium Commission, with all the figures and supporting detail, so that it could be considered at a meeting of the Commission scheduled for 25 September. By late September also the selection process for the new Chief Executive of UHI Ltd should be completed.

Recruitment

Assuming – as they had to – that at least the critical minimum funding package for UHI could be secured in the coming months, what kind of person would the partners need to recruit to take the project forward to university status? The note of the recent consultation in Nairn had recorded the conclusion that: "In making the appointment, the emphasis should be on finding someone with first-class project leadership and management skills and experience, rather than academic excellence."

Yet ideally the Chief Executive should also be familiar with the university world and its arcane funding mechanisms, and thus able to command respect among policy-makers whose current enthusiasm for UHI could not be guaranteed to last for ever. Some time earlier the current Project Director, Robin Lingard, had made it clear that he would not wish to lead the next development phase, which he felt required someone who had already made a name for themselves in a career in or around higher education. All the partners were agreed that they were not seeking a Vice Chancellor in waiting. The post would be offered for a fixed term to complete the development process. Nevertheless, most of the partners felt it would be important for the Chief Executive to be able to strike up a close relationship, effectively as an equal, with the leaders of Scotland's existing universities.

It was recognised that it would not be easy to find the right balance of management skills and academic experience to meet this demanding specification. Unless a generous salary could be offered, there was a risk that the best candidates would simply not apply.

And this was a potential sore point for the college principals. While their heads told them that the project now needed new leadership, with a strong figure driving forward towards the goal of university status, in their hearts some seemed to resent the implied threat to their own status. Although a Project Director seconded from HIE might have irritated them and tried to push them around for the good of the project, he could never have been a threat to their position within their own institution. But a Chief Executive fresh from a successful university career might have few scruples about moving confidently into their own management territory, as long as it could be presented as essential for UHI's success. If the Chief Executive was, from the start, offered a higher salary than they commanded, the implication might be that they were out-ranked and could indeed be ordered about, even on their own home ground.

At the root of this concern, predictably, was the unresolved constitutional relationship between the colleges and the future university. The common objective still agreed in all public statements was to create a collegiate federation, which had to imply that the colleges and the university would at some point become "one flesh". What was lost in autonomy would be gained in partnership. Yet even if this changed state was some way off, perhaps beyond the point of retirement for some current principals, it brought deep personal concerns about what leadership role would remain at the college level and in the local community served by the college.

Since others around the table at the Board of UHI Ltd were sensitive about the local precedent of offering too generous a salary for a time-limited post in Inverness, the final agreement was to offer an initial salary of between £45,000 and £55,000 – thought by some to be too low to attract a strong field of candidates. In the same spirit of economy – again probably a false one, with hindsight – it was decided not to use a "head-hunter" to spot potential candidates or to support the recruitment process.

On this basis the post of Chief Executive was simply advertised in the recruitment pages of the press, with a closing date of 26 August 1996, seeking someone who "…will be an effective project manager and will work to maximise the educational and economic impact of the University in the Highlands and Islands."

The Third Bid

The third and final bid to the Millennium Commission was completed in late August, tight against the deadline. Its main emphasis was on capital costs and how to meet them. By a good deal of juggling, room had been found for a more modest version of the new campus for Sabhal Mòr Ostaig, together with a Learning Resource Centre for Moray College – at last firmly back in the UHI partnership. The total cost, with an allowance for inflation, had now reached £86 million. However, between one bid and the next the call on the Millennium Fund had been reduced by £5 million, to just over £33 million. This represented 38.5% of the total, as against the 50% share assumed in all previous bids.

The rest would be found from a consortium of all the interests bound up in the UHI Project. HIE and its network of Local Enterprise Companies had pledged just over 10% of the total, with a further 5% from the local authorities. Private sector sources and Health Boards were written in for some 9%, while 11.5% was to be levered from the European Regional Development Fund, through the Objective One special programme available to the Highlands and Islands. The balance was to be found, in one way or another, from funding sources controlled by the government, either through capital development support available to the FE colleges in mainstream provision or through special funding offered to UHI. Although the firm promises for the latter amounted at the time to only £500,000 – a sum offered by the Secretary of State to help establish the first stage of UHI's video-conferencing network – it was a sign of the changed times that assumptions about future Scottish Office support to UHI could be made with confidence in a formal bidding document.

All this was to cover work which met the Millennium Commission's rules for eligibility. Some other items of capital work (particularly student residences) had been excluded from the calculation on eligibility grounds and would be financed in other ways. However, if these were added in to the total it was fair to say that the UHI Project was still – as in the earliest bid – a £100 million vision for the Millennium.

And the millennial vision was still as much economic and social as educational. Revised estimates of economic benefit were included in the bid, this time from an independent consultancy. These forecast that, once UHI had expanded its student and staff numbers to fill the new buildings now planned, the additional direct and indirect jobs created across the Highlands and Islands would amount to 825. Together with the temporary jobs associated with the actual building programmes, the total would be little short of 1,000. From this perspective, UHI would indeed represent a new industry for the region.

As to the social vision, it was summarised as follows:

> The social consequences of the laws of thermodynamics are mostly brutal, the big growing bigger, the margins more marginalised and the centre dominating all. Human ends will insist that small is beautiful and that the big needs to be resisted. For this to be done intelligently requires the insight and resources of intelligent people. UHI will be a mainspring of this kind of regional robustness. [This] is the heroic aspect of the University's mission and the leavening of its more mundane responsibility to keep the Highlands and Islands economy and culture well and truly afloat.

Validation

Meanwhile the grooming of the UHI Project for life as an academic institution continued, now with the encouragement of the Scottish Office. In order to build up the framework of the university's curriculum, UHI Ltd had recently appointed a Curriculum Development Officer – David Shepherd. The pace of events was now so swift that he was the company's fourth employee, two more having been recruited already to support Patrick Dark in developing ICT systems.

But for the present the main focus of academic development was on the colleges – and particularly those engaged in the submission of UHI's first degree for validation. Michael Forsyth had approved the Rural Development Studies degree from the Scottish Office perspective, but only a university could validate it for offer to students. After a thorough grilling of staff and investigation of the course material, a team from Aberdeen University gave it that endorsement just as the final bid to the Millennium Commission was being completed. Since some students had just completed the Higher National Diploma level of the course, there was now the prospect that they would become UHI's first graduates in the summer of 1997.

As yet another sign of official favour, the Scottish Office sent one of their Ministers – Lord Lindsay – to Inverness on 26 August to announce the good news at a press conference. The event was hosted by HIE and included a prominent role for HIE's Chairman, Fraser Morrison. It also provided an opportunity for Ray Murray to explain to a wider public how, within the UHI partnership, individual colleges had already found ways of making common cause for the benefit of students. The seeds of the degree had been sown some years earlier, when Lews Castle College in Stornoway worked jointly with

Sabhal Mòr Ostaig on the development of a single unit within a Higher National Certificate. That in turn grew into a full HNC, then a Diploma, with development led by the group at Lews Castle College but drawing in other partners on the way. With validation, four colleges would now be able to offer the UHI BSc in Rural Development Studies, with the prospect that others across the network would pick it up for their students in the years ahead. The fact that another team from across the colleges was on the point of submitting the second UHI degree (Environment and Heritage) for validation by Robert Gordon University added emphasis to the message from the press conference, that even without its own university title or ability to validate degrees, UHI was effectively in business already.

Second Thoughts on Structure

The agreement on future UHI management structures, reached at Nairn only a few months earlier, was already looking ragged at the edges. As noted in the previous Chapter, the wider community's enthusiasm for keeping a firm guiding hand on the future direction of the Project had won the day, with the community-based Foundation given the right to elect from its members a Board of 12 to direct the work of the Chief Executive, half of whom would represent the colleges. HIE – and in particular Fraser Morrison, from his business experience – felt this solution provided insufficient insurance for funders that the major investment they were being asked to make in UHI would be tightly controlled and that swift and efficient progress would be made towards university status. Val MacIver, as Chairman of the UHI Steering Group, was persuaded that some adjustment of the deal had to be made before the Millennium Commission reached its decision on the funding bid. In a rapid exchange of phone calls and faxes a further revised structure was drawn up, to be discussed at a special meeting of the Steering Group (still the supreme policy-making body for the Project) arranged for 28 August.

The first – and least controversial – proposal affected the Foundation. At Nairn its membership arrangements had been left vague. It was now suggested that it should be formalised into four groups of 15, representing the academic sector, the local authorities, the business community (including the HIE Network) and the wider community. This was readily accepted in principle, for the details to be filled in later.

The second proposal was more fundamental, since it changed the size and balance of the Board. As Fraser Morrison's paper put it, the issues to be tackled were operational effectiveness and breadth of representation:

I am concerned that the proposals . . . for the Foundation to nominate half the Directors may result in a weak Board or one which finds no place for some of the visionary supporters who have helped us so far. The categories of Directors proposed also seem to offer too limited a role for the "customers" of UHI, so that the whole project could appear supply-led rather than demand-led. A somewhat larger Board than the 12 members proposed at Nairn could help here. I believe it will also be necessary to adjust the proposed balance of the Board so that the Academic Council, while retaining a major role, nominates less than half the Directors.

The alternative now put forward was for a Board of 16, of whom five would be nominated by the Academic Council and five (representing the wider community) by the Foundation. The remaining six Directors, whose role would be "to represent in particular the customer and employer interests" (previously seen as the role of the UHI Foundation) were to be selected by an unusual method which might have – but apparently did not – set alarm bells ringing. They would be chosen by four individuals – the Chairman of the UHI Academic Council, the Chairman of HIE, a local authority Elected Member (in the first instance Val MacIver herself) and a representative of the Scottish Office. It was further suggested that the same group should identify one of their six nominees as the first Chairman of the new Board.

Since there was no bar on the "Group of Four" nominating one or more of its own members to the Board, this arrangement would clearly open the way for Val MacIver to be retained as the Chairman of the new policy-making body for UHI, thus assuring continuity. But it was also recognised by some as offering a convenient route for HIE, in the person of Fraser Morrison, to take effective charge of the Project once more. The fact that the Scottish Office swiftly declined to take part in the process made that outcome yet more probable.

Within the Steering Group, the main objection to this revised structure for nominating Directors might have come from the colleges. It was their power base on the Board which would be most clearly weakened. However, the third proposed change to the agreement reached at Nairn was designed to win them over. In order to balance the loss of strategic influence, they were to be given an enhanced executive role. Resurrecting the concept put forward earlier by Ray Murray and Graham Hills, it was suggested that the college principals and the Chief Executive should form a UHI Management Group, under the Board, to direct the Project at the operational level.

Thanks to some astute preparation – and aided by the imperative of keeping a united front at this critical point in the bid for funding – this package of proposals was endorsed by the Steering Group. Although there would still be the need to seek formal agreement to the deal from the wider group consulted at Nairn (and this did lead to later variation of the details), the structure for guiding and managing UHI through its next phase of development now appeared to have been fixed to the satisfaction of all interests.

Final Questions

Those at the heart of the enterprise had to keep clearly in mind, throughout all this headlong progress, the possibility that the Millennium Commission would decide to fund only part of the ambitious plans for UHI or, worse still, would finally rule the whole project ineligible because of its educational roots. It was therefore in equal measure worrying and reassuring when an invitation was issued in early September to meet the Scottish Commissioner, the Earl of Dalkeith, and the Commission's Chief Executive, Jenny Page, for an informal discussion in Edinburgh.

By now the Millennium Commission would have had all the basic data they needed for a decision. In addition to the various written submissions and financial spreadsheets, they had been receiving reports from their own independent consultant, Douglas Wynn, who had travelled across the region to make his own appraisal of how well the concept was rooted in reality. At the Edinburgh meeting the discussion therefore turned on the nature of UHI rather than on its physical or financial attributes. How could a project of this kind best be reconciled with the mission of the Millennium Commission and with the selection criteria which had been developed?

Four questions were posed to the UHI team, for further consideration and a written response in the coming days:

- As a university-based project, how is the UHI Project distinctive and perhaps unique?
- What are the wider benefits of the UHI Project?
- How are others, especially the private sector, making a commitment to the Project?
- What is the basis for confidence in UHI's long term viability as an independent university?

None of these questions was new and all had, to some extent, been answered in the successive submissions. However, this was an opportunity to address them in the context of a final decision on funding, clearly now in the balance. Two aspects of the Project Director's reply, sent on 10 September, may be worth highlighting at this point in the history of UHI.

The distinctive nature of the project was summarised as follows:

> The UHI Project is distinctive both in its institutional concept and in the nature of the region it serves. It is unique in the way the concept has emerged from and been tailored to the region. The objectives and history of the UHI Project have grown from the community, not from an existing university wishing to extend and develop its role. The applicant is not an educational institution, but a community based partnership.

The response on long term viability, while resting partly on educational demand, also emphasised the importance of strong community roots:

> We would also suggest that the community's faith in and support for UHI is as powerful an omen for success as any other. . . . The UHI Project is seen as the flagship Millennium initiative for the Highlands and Islands, with an impact and significance going beyond the bounds of the region itself.

Finally, the reply was able to offer a further and very recent endorsement from the Secretary of State for Scotland, in support of the partnership's belief in UHI's longer term viability:

> I anticipate that it may become a model for regional universities elsewhere in the world and of new ways of accessing learning and knowledge.

The Chief Executive

The selection interviews for the UHI Chief Executive had been set for the week beginning 23 September – the same week in which the Millennium Commission was to reach its decision on a grant. There was obviously a risk that the successful candidate would find within days that the project they were to lead had been denied the core funding necessary for its launch. However, it was agreed that, as long as the position was made clear to all candidates, the selection process should proceed as planned. Anyone unwilling to take that level of risk was unlikely to have the qualities required for such a demanding job.

At the short-listing stage there was some disappointment about the response to the advertisement. Few of the candidates had experience at senior level in the university system. Even fewer had a track record in managing major projects. However, with the assistance of personnel experts in the Highland Council an interview panel was established and a core of credible names agreed.

At the end of a number of probing interviews, the decision was taken to offer the post to Brian Duffield, then a titular professor at Leeds Metropolitan University and Dean of the Faculty of Cultural and Educational Studies. He had been the most senior academic on the short list. He had held posts in the FE sector in Scotland and in Edinburgh University, so he was well versed in UHI's tertiary education context. He was also familiar with and committed to the Highlands and Islands and its communities, with a holiday home on Barra in the Western Isles. He had clearly read many of the original papers setting out the aspirations of UHI and, both in his application and in his interview, he reiterated a belief in the guiding principles of a collegiate federation, of the seamless robe between FE and HE and of the "polo-mint" configuration rather than the hub-and-spokes model of satellite status at the periphery.

On this basis, the panel made its choice and the offer was accepted by Brian Duffield. UHI now had a Chief Executive. But would it have its funding?

Standing by the Fax

As the last days of September 1996 ticked by, the tension in the Project Office rose steadily. It was known that the Millennium Commission had reached a decision on UHI and on a number of other projects, but no hint was given of what the decision might be or when it would be announced.

Finally, early on 30 September the Project Director received a cryptic telephone call from the UHI case officer at the Commission, Jennifer Iles. A letter was about to be faxed through, but she could not say what would be in it. As a small group clustered by the fax machine in the corner of the office, the atmosphere was sombre. This didn't seem the way to convey good news. The letter that emerged was therefore all the more of a shock.

Subject to contract negotiations, the UHI Project was being offered a grant of up to £33,354,000 – the full sum sought in the final bid – and the formal announcement would be made later that day.

PART VIII

In Transition

CHAPTER **26**

A Project in Transition

The award of £33 million from the Millennium Commission – the largest Millennium Fund grant yet awarded in Scotland – was the single greatest event in the life of the project to found a University in and of the Highlands and Islands of Scotland. It turned the impossible dream into a funded investment programme. In the face of a sceptical audience it affirmed the substance of the arguments in favour of a new foundation of higher education, a distinctive foundation likely to bring new prestige and enhanced prosperity to this singular part of the United Kingdom.

What proved to have tipped the balance in favour of such a large grant – and in the face of intense competition for the available funds – was precisely this link between the project and its region. To the Millennium Commissioners, who would not have been able to back a traditional university project (one which would have provided predominantly young undergraduates with facilities they could have found by travelling to Aberdeen or Stirling), UHI was attractive as a way of offering access to higher education for people otherwise denied it, as a vehicle for lifelong learning and as a flagship for modern educational methodologies. It was recognised as a major community-based project which would provide these new opportunities right across the Highlands and Islands.

In terms of money, the grant and the matching funding it unlocked could be regarded as a substitute for the dowry which had previously been the government's birthday present to every completely new university. This caused a stir among the Scottish universities, their principals in particular, and the academic fraternity as a whole. There was a deal of clucking and pursing of lips of those concerned that the new arrival would be a drain on the other universities, already brain-washed into the zero-sum mentality of those perpetually on the defensive.

More significantly, in spirit the announcement of the grant marked a leap of the kind that separates the Old Testament from the New. There was a vision to be given life, there were plenty of prophets to be off-loaded to make way for newcomers and there was a prospect of heaven to quarrel about.

However, the rejoicings were in a low key. The main celebration was a dinner hosted by the Board of UHI Ltd in the Inverness Town House on 25 November 1996, but it was a modest and quiet event, more thoughtful than triumphal. For the UHI Project as a whole, it appeared, the immediate issues to be faced were not spiritual but practical.

Tying Down Relationships

The Millennium Commission's grant offer had been, like a house purchase, "subject to contract". Discussions began immediately, with a new group of officials, on what this condition implied. The first impression was of an onerous procedure, mainly concerned with defining penalties. In practice, negotiations soon settled down to a constructive level, aimed at tying down the purposes for which the money was to be paid. A further light touch was added by the realisation that the future of this major project in the Highlands and Islands was being dealt with in the Millennium Commission by staff with the apposite names of Richard Mountain and Jennifer Iles.

With Brian Duffield not expected to take up his post before the end of 1996, the contract negotiations on the UHI side were dealt with by the existing Project Office, under Robin Lingard. It soon became clear that although the primary contract – formalising the obligations between the UHI Project and the Millennium Commission- would be relatively straightforward, it would not suffice for the purposes of accountability. Most of the money would be spent at campus sites which UHI did not own and on new buildings which it would not own. As yet, the only formal expression of the relationship between the colleges and the UHI Project was the Minute of Agreement put in place a year or two earlier and due to expire in December 1996. A legal document now had to be drawn up to prevent the possibility – remote as it might seem – that a college would pull out of the UHI Project once its new building was completed.

The prospect of having to sign legal commitments was not popular with the colleges, but they could not fault its logic. If UHI had to enter into formal obligations to use its grant money properly, there had to be a back-to-back obligation on the owners of the buildings which that money would create. The sanctions sounded terrifying – full repayment of grant in certain circumstances of default – and there was much sucking of legal teeth as to the wisdom of individual colleges accepting such potential sanctions.

In the end, however, the documents were all signed and the relationship between the UHI Project and the colleges was for the first time placed on a basis of legal rights and responsibilities.

With hindsight, just as important as this formalisation of relations within the UHI Project was the way the Millennium Commission agreed to formalise its own objectives for the Project, in the terms of the principal contract. At first there was pressure to include a clause which set as the objective the achievement of university status by a given date – and which by implication might have created a default state if that target date was not met. After much persuasion, it was accepted that setting such a date was neither realistic nor necessary. Even if the tests of eligibility for university status were not passed until all the building work was completed, the fundamental community objectives of the project would still have been met. It was therefore agreed that a reference to the objective of creating a federal, collegiate university would be enough, without tying it to a specific date for the transition to full university status.

However, the contractual discussions did hint at a potential future dilemma for the Millennium Commission. Only a small part of their grant would be directed at developing the academic and technical infrastructure through which UHI would eventually establish its claim to become an institution with university status. Most of the money would be used to create new buildings appropriate for a university and this expenditure would inevitably be the focus for their monitoring. But whose responsibility was it to monitor whether the UHI Project itself was developing satisfactorily towards the quality standards required for university status?

More fundamentally, given the terms in which their grant award had been justified, what was the Millennium Commission's responsibility for ensuring that UHI really did become the distinctive and different type of university which the community in the Highlands and Islands had been led to expect?

Finding a New Home

The UHI Project also found itself having to plan a transition to new premises. Although HIE was in no hurry to eject the lodgers, there was a growing feeling among the colleges that it was time for UHI Ltd to distance itself physically, as well as organisationally, from its original sponsors.

The new Chief Executive and his Executive Office should have a home of their own. But should it also be seen as the headquarters for the eventual university? This was a complicating factor in sifting the options. The question of where to locate the headquarters of the future university had always been an awkward one. It was awkward because, although its airport, rail and road links made Inverness the obvious and most convenient place for siting any headquarters (as both HIE and the Highland Council had already demonstrated), the rest of the region resented the dominance this implied. In UHI circles that resentment was compounded by concern among the smaller and more peripheral academic partners about the ambitions of Inverness College. It was felt that one college – and that the largest in the Highlands – would somehow be favoured if the administrative centre was physically close to it.

Pleasantly small towns such as Dingwall or Strathpeffer, some 15 miles to the north, were canvassed as alternative possibilities but telecommunications links and perceptions of the ease of travel eventually narrowed the choice back to Inverness, at least for the short term. Once UHI really was a university, it could decide for itself where the headquarters should be.

Unfortunately there was at the time little office accommodation on the market in Inverness. Even scarcer was accommodation that both suited UHI's immediate needs and could cope with the prospect of rapid growth in staffing numbers as new funding accelerated the pace of development. Against a very tight deadline the Board of UHI Ltd decided as an interim measure to lease an upper floor (later a second was added to the lease) in a British Telecom building in the middle of Inverness.

Caledonia House was a featureless office block dating from the 1960s or 1970s – arguably the ugliest building in the town, though the HIE offices which were to be vacated ran it close. Here the UHI Project would be even more hidden from the public gaze than it had been as a lodger with a major regional agency. It was also an unattractive working environment for the staff, bearable on a short term basis but oppressive beyond that. It shared the narrow corridors, segregated spaces, poor lighting and inadequate ventilation which were the lot of so many of the buildings of its period. With limited refurbishment, the best would be made of a poor job. Unfortunately, what had been intended as a temporary home turned out to be UHI's base for many years to come.

Constitutional Endorsement

On the constitutional front it only remained to formalise the decisions reached during 1996 on the establishment of the UHI Foundation and the new composition of the Board of UHI Ltd. At least, that was what was hoped.

An Extraordinary General Meeting (EGM) of the membership of UHI Ltd was therefore arranged for 30 January 1997, at which the revised Memorandum and Articles of Association of the company were to be tabled for approval. By the time the meeting was held, however, two formal proposals had been received for varying the proposed membership of the Foundation. The first, from the National Union of Students, sought to increase the number of student representatives from two to three. That was accepted readily. The other proposal was more unexpected and, in part, more contentious.

Behind the scenes the Boards of Management of some of the larger colleges had been making common cause. They wanted to ensure that their views, not just the opinions of their principals, would help to guide the future development of UHI. They sought the addition of a new category of Foundation membership, to be drawn from the management boards of the incorporated or independent colleges – that is, all the UHI partners except Orkney College and Shetland College, which were still under local authority control. This would increase the total membership of the Foundation (the eventual total would be 75, rather than the 60 initially planned) and it might also swing some of the balance of power back to the academic partners, but it was hard to resist what could be – and was – presented as a further broadening of community representation in the affairs of UHI. This first part of the proposal the membership of UHI Ltd therefore accepted.

But some of the proposers then took a step too far. The Chairmen of the Boards of Moray College and Perth College argued that representatives of the college boards should also be automatically granted membership of the Board of Directors of UHI Ltd. The prospect of the big colleges seeking to dominate UHI had always been feared by the smaller partners and this looked to them, as to HIE and the local authorities, like the beginning of a take-over bid.

Put to a vote, the supplementary proposal was heavily defeated. Yet it had been another reminder of the precarious and unresolved nature of the relationship between the UHI Project and the colleges on which the future university would depend for its students, staff and courses.

With these issues resolved, the long trek towards a constitutional settlement for the UHI Project's next phase seemed to have reached its destination. In the following months the 75 places on the UHI Foundation were filled and the Foundation members in turn began the process of electing the new Directors of UHI Ltd. When the dust settled, in May 1997, it revealed the not unexpected sight of Fraser Morrison as the Chairman of the company, with Val MacIver translated to Chairman of the UHI Foundation. From that point the main burden of leading the final ascent to university status was therefore firmly on the shoulders of Brian Duffield and Fraser Morrison.

Politics in Transition

Against all the odds, a Conservative politician had given the UHI concept the endorsement and the practical support it needed, just when it mattered most. Now that the Millennium Commission's capital grant was confirmed, the Scottish Office had to clarify how they were going to massage the various funding streams in order to ensure a sufficient flow of revenue funding from which the UHI partners could develop towards university status.

The initial solutions, not surprisingly, had little to do with higher education funding. With further education still administered directly by the Education Department, it was relatively easy for officials to find ways of supplementing existing college budgets or lifting other barriers to growth. This was not the answer for all UHI partners, however. Some did not qualify for FE funding under the relevant Act and in parts of the area covered by the UHI partnership – particularly Argyll and its islands in the rural south west – there was no infrastructure in place for the delivery of tertiary education. To deal with this latter problem, officials went out of their way to encourage the development of plans for a network of local learning centres and for the creation of Argyll College as the umbrella body to administer them.

But there were limits to what even the most enthusiastic official could promise to UHI at that stage in the electoral cycle. A General Election was imminent and the polls suggested that the Conservative Party was unlikely to hold on to power much longer. Although the UHI concept had received cross-party support, an incoming Labour government committed to financial prudence would want to take very careful stock of all its predecessor's promises.

CHAPTER 27

Universities in Transition

The founders of UHI were conscious from the beginning that the project to create a new university would be taking place at a time of great change in the university sector world-wide. Governments everywhere were articulating their concerns that higher education should play a larger role in preparing their country's industries for the revolutionary changes in technology, notably those in the information and communications technologies. In essence they were seeking better trained technologists and better value for money. Two particular imperatives of the 1990s were the growth in undergraduate student numbers and the eruption of the Internet as a global telecommunications system and a universal learning tool. It was UHI's great good fortune to be born in the midst of these upheavals which presented singular opportunities for newcomers.

In Britain, there would arise a persistent, nagging fear that the country's industries, universities, colleges and schools might fail to ride the crest of this extraordinary wave. In terms of user numbers, hardware and innovation, the technology gap between the USA and Europe seemed ever widening. Inevitably governments called upon the universities to play a greater role in the education and training of the young, especially in relation to the new possibilities driven by ICT.

The Dearing-Garrick Enquiry

In Britain this quest for better performance took the form, as it often does, of a high level committee of enquiry, in this case led by a distinguished one-time civil servant, Sir Ronald Dearing. He had built a reputation as a national "trouble shooter", sorting out awkward problems for the politicians. This time he was invited by the government (then still a Conservative administration) to enquire, over the period 1996-1997, into the long-term development of higher education in Britain. In particular, how could diminishing financial support be reconciled with ever increasing student numbers? In parallel a separate study, chaired by Sir Ronald Garrick, was set up to examine the implications for Scotland of the main enquiry and to put forward its own vision of the way in which higher education might develop in Scotland. This allowed account to be taken of the different characteristics of the Scottish education system and of such factors as the higher HE participation rate among young people.

History will record that the Dearing-Garrick enquiry had the opportunity to consider and propose fundamental changes across the British higher education system, in response to the imperatives of rapidly changing social demands and changing learning procedures. New phrases were entering the vocabulary, including The Learning Society and The Knowledge Society. Neither was anywhere defined but both came within the compass of the enquiry. From the submissions to it, and from its own enquiries into similar exercises being undertaken world-wide, it became aware of what might and possibly what should be done radically to reform the present arrangements. The UHI Project, in its own written submission (made jointly with HIE), highlighted the importance and the implications of the New Learning Paradigm, of the Mode 1/Mode 2 debate, of the doors opened by the Internet, of problem-based learning initiatives and of fundamental changes in the epistemology of knowledge itself. On these and similar issues Dearing, Garrick, their colleagues and their specialist advisers had therefore much to think about.

Disappointed Hopes

With his usual efficiency, Dearing reported on time, in July 1997. The main report was a very substantial document of over 450 pages, accompanied by a summary report, the report of the Scottish Committee and eight other volumes of Appendices and Special Reports, the whole fitting into a box over 4 inches deep. There were 93 recommendations in the report of the main committee, looking at the United Kingdom as a whole, with a further 29 in the report of the Garrick committee looking at HE in Scotland Yet in spite of its apparent substance, the outcome of the enquiry has to be regarded as a disappointment.

The Dearing Report started well. It listed the characteristics which the Committee concluded UK higher education should display for the coming decades. It should:

- be increasingly responsive to the needs of students and of clients (such as employers and those who commission research);

- structure qualifications which can be either free-standing or built-up over time, and which are commonly accepted and widely recognised;
- offer opportunities for credit transfer between courses and institutions;
- adopt a national framework of awards with rigorously maintained standards;
- work in partnership with public and private sector employers;
- respond fully to the need for active policies for developing, retraining and rewarding its own staff;
- maintain its distinctiveness and vitality through linking research and scholarship to teaching;
- take full advantage of the advances in communications and information technology, which will radically alter the shape and delivery of learning throughout the world;
- be explicit about what it is providing through learning programmes, and their expected outcomes, so that students and employers have a better understanding of their purposes and benefits.

To all of this the UHI Project team – and many others looking for a boost to new thinking on higher education – could give a hearty cheer. But the Committee's ability to turn this analysis into a blueprint for change was limited by an innate conservatism and an underlying concern with funding above all other considerations.

The Dearing Committee's conservatism can be summed up by the quotation chosen, as a preface to their recommendations, to convey the essence of a university. Taken from the works of an earlier Poet Laureate John Masefield, it read as follows:

> It is a place where those who hate ignorance may strive to know, where those who perceive truth may strive to make others see; where seekers and learners alike, banded together in the search for knowledge, will honour thought in all its finer ways, will welcome thinkers in distress or in exile, will uphold ever the dignity of thought and learning and will exact standards in these things.

It is unlikely that this was chosen because it sounded like Margaret Thatcher and it would be unkind to describe it as a tepid motherhood statement. However, it is a far cry from the priorities of a country struggling to equip itself to meet the challenges of the 21st Century. Similar vague and nostalgic sentiments are also to be found in the phrasing of the general aims and purposes of higher education, as adopted by the enquiry.

They were four-fold:

1) to inspire individuals to develop their capabilities,
2) to increase knowledge and understanding for their own sake and to foster their application to society,
3) to serve the needs of an adaptable, sustainable knowledge-based economy, and
4) to play a major role in the shaping of a democratic, civilised and inclusive society.

No one could quarrel with these as words. Indeed they are timeless. But therein lies their fault, for they express none of the urgency of the times and nowhere suggest how these lofty ideals could be more effectively pursued. The phrase highlighted in point 2 says it all. "For their own sake" is a straight quote from Newman and his (Oxford) idea of a university. Its stress on academic interest over social utility would be played out in full in the years following the report of the enquiry. Academic research would continue to head the list of desirable activities. In the form of the Research Assessment Exercise it would eventually become the main determinant of the differential distribution of resources between universities

As to funding, the Committee found itself facing some large figures. It identified a very significant funding gap if quality standards were to be maintained while resuming growth in student numbers. The estimated immediate requirements were for an additional £350 million in 1998/9 and £565 million in 1999/2000, with a total additional requirement (net of savings) of £2 billion at current prices over the next 20 years. Its main solution was to share the pain more widely. Having rejected options which would yield too little money or add unacceptably to student debt levels, Dearing proposed the charging of £1000 per annum tuition fees (roughly one quarter of the annual average grant) to all full-time students, to be paid when in work through an "income contingent mechanism", preferably recovered by the Inland Revenue. At the same time Dearing recommended retaining the current system – means-tested grant plus loan – for student maintenance.

Funding concerns and a basic wariness about change combined to make most of the rest of the Dearing Committee's recommendations little more than an endorsement of the status quo. Indeed, it specifically recommended that the Government should maintain the current criteria for university status in the medium term.

The report said specifically that: "for the future there should be a period of relative stability in the number of universities, with the weight accorded to the numerical criteria reduced and greater emphasis placed on a distinctive role and characteristics in awarding this status."

The Dearing Committee was also keen to maintain and, if anything, strengthen the line between FE and HE. While recognising the growing role of the FE sector in delivering higher education, it sought to confine future growth of such activity to the sub-degree level, requiring students to move on to universities for their degrees – though, perhaps with the UHI Project in mind, it allowed a possible loop-hole for "remote or rural areas". It identified the importance of ICT to the future development of higher education, particularly in terms of lifelong learning, but proposed very undemanding targets, suggesting that all HE students should have open access to a networked desktop computer by 2000/2001 and "expecting" that by 2005/6 all students would be required to have access to their own portable computer.

In spite of the range of possibilities for change and reform, the Dearing Report therefore left the impression that British universities were deemed to be on the right rails, needing only more money to keep them happy whilst realising at the same time that extra resources were unlikely to be forthcoming.

Uncharitably it could be said that the Dearing Enquiry not only failed to go forward, it actually went backwards. Much of the Dearing report was therefore concerned with bureaucratic niceties of resourcing, accountability and quality assurance. These tedious matters would come to dominate university thinking throughout the late 90s and the early 21st century. Nowhere was the sea change from subject-centred teaching to student-centred learning given the prominence it deserved. The New Learning Paradigm might as well have not been invented.

The Scottish Variant

Mercifully, the Garrick Committee had been able to consider a wider agenda, particularly in relation to the distinctiveness of Scottish higher education. Even the quotations it deployed were more apposite.

Thus it quoted Lord Robbins, following his installation as Chancellor of Stirling University, as saying: "All my life as an academic I have been conscious of a quite special debt to Scottish intellectual influences and a quite special admiration for the Scottish university tradition, both for its achievements and for the education principles on which its rests."

Another, more hard-hitting quotation was taken from George Davie's "The Democratic Intellect". It invited:

> . . . a belief that Scotland has kept alive, not just in the universities but throughout the length and breadth of the land, a continuing sense of the value of the national idea of the democratic intellect, illustrating its social relevances by reference to Continental and to American as well as to English experience.

Here then was a small country never likely to presume that it knew best but always that it had much to learn. The Garrick Report was in tune with this sentiment. It was short. It did not quarrel with what its parent committee had said but tackled some more immediate issues. In this it was forward looking whereas the Dearing Report had stood by the *status quo*.

Garrick had invited oral evidence from HIE and the UHI Project team and it was therefore encouraging that the report took note of UHI and saw it as a pioneering experiment that might lead as well as follow. In the body of the text much was made of the New Learning Paradigm and its emphasis on tutored learning and machine readable information.

The Garrick Report also tackled the structure and length of first degree courses, in the context of further increasing access to higher education across the population. It recommended to all higher education institutions in Scotland that the 360 credit-point Bachelors Degree should become widely available and that they should, with the support of the Scottish Higher Education Funding Council, begin to develop or extend their provision in this area. This support for a more general first degree of three year's duration would be particularly welcome to those in and around the UHI Project who had from the beginning advocated this kind of degree as its staple qualification.

At the same time, the Garrick Committee recommended two further proposals:

1) that HEIs should develop more diverse programmes at the fourth year, Honours level, and
2) that colleges of further education and institutions of higher education should collaborate in enhancing and publicising access and articulation routes into degree programmes for students in FE colleges.

A "busy" diagram was used to illustrate the numerous pathways into, out of and across the network of possibilities. Its implicit flexibility was all that was needed to allow post-school education in Scotland continuously to evolve and thus to meet the future requirements of the entire system of further and higher education.

The Garrick Report also made a number of specific comments and recommendations which suggested a ready understanding of UHI's potential to span the divide between FE and HE and a recognition of the validity of its distinctive regional role.

In proposing the establishment of a Scottish funding council for further education, taking over the roles then carried out by the Scottish Office, it recommended that the FE Funding Council should fund further education and sub-degree higher education, while the HE Funding Council would fund all degree courses, including those run by FE colleges and – specifically mentioned – UHI.

In commenting on the links between higher education and the Scottish economy, it again made specific and positive reference to UHI:

> . . . we believe that higher education can also have a powerful long term regenerative impact. This is one of the arguments that has been put forward in favour of the UHI Project, although we cannot, of course, make any predictions about the success of the Project at this stage. We consider that in such cases regeneration can best and most sensibly be achieved through partnerships between the institution and local and regional interests. We have therefore noted the contribution which the region and local industry is making to the UHI Project, over and above the funds which are being made available by the Government.

However, the Garrick Committee held back from recommending that the UHI Project should actually be allowed to become a university in the near future. Perhaps it could have gone no further, given the Dearing Committee's decision to recommend "relative stability" in the number of UK universities. In any case, what it did say on the issue would have been positive enough as the foundation for a political initiative if the Government had been so inclined.

It summarised its views as follows:

> We are fully supportive of the need, for economic and equity reasons, to make higher education provision available to rural communities, from Wigtownshire to Cape Wrath to Kirkwall and beyond. Whilst we acknowledge the special circumstances in which the UHI Project has been established, we agree with the National Committee that intentions to establish further new universities should be considered against a set of agreed criteria and that greater clarity is needed about where ultimate responsibility lies for decisions about the establishment of additional universities.

Thus in both spirit and letter, Garrick's analysis of the way ahead for higher education was far more favourable to the UHI Project than Dearing had been. In spite of disappointment with aspects of the Scottish report, it could also have been interpreted as at least offering the prospect that change might be for the good. Given the right lead, it would have been possible for individual universities (and colleges) to respond positively to it and to make the most of the opportunity to reconsider their own visions and their own practices. The UHI Project, in particular, could have used it as a policy launching pad for a number of its pioneering initiatives.

Unfortunately, it soon became evident that Garrick – and Dearing – might as well not have bothered.

Politics and Priorities

By the time the two reports were completed and delivered, the General election had come and gone. A Labour Government was elected in May 1997, in a landslide victory. In spite of its overwhelming mandate, it adopted a policy of strict control over public expenditure. Its priority in higher education was to balance the books.

There was to be no further money for higher education, and since change is always expensive, it follows that there would be no changes. To make matters worse, on the day the reports were published – 23 July 1997 – the new Government out of the blue announced that it intended arbitrarily to impose a flat-rate annual tuition fee on every undergraduate and to abolish the maintenance grant completely. Although these moves were presented as a "preferred approach", subject to further consultation, there could be little doubt that the Treasury had already incorporated the changes into forward budgets.

The direct effect on UHI was minimal, because its HE student numbers were small and because its dependence on the Treasury was at that stage limited. In any case, within a few years the devolved Scottish Parliament would have abolished tuition fees for Scottish students at Scottish universities, in the first of a series of acts of defiance of Treasury dominance.

But the indirect implications for UHI were more serious. Although the Government promised to return to the other aspects of Dearing and Garrick later in the year, in a White Paper on education and training, the opportunity to take a fresh look at the role of higher education in a changing world – and to take up the new learning agenda – had by then been lost. In pre-devolution Scotland there was apparently not the political will to separate out the Garrick recommendations from the generality of Dearing.

The report of the Garrick Committee had directly or indirectly endorsed the model and most of the ideas of UHI. It was therefore recognised as a university of the future and decidedly not one of the past or seeking to pretend to be one. It would have needed no further encouragement to adopt an integrated qualifications network, to pilot the 360 credit-point Bachelor's degree and to seek the closest collaboration between FE and HE. Had the Scottish Office wished to try out Garrick's ideas in a controlled environment, it had just the vehicle at hand. Instead, other political priorities took precedence. Those priorities would now help to determine in which direction the UHI Project developed – and how fast.

CHAPTER 28

A Book in Transition

At this point in the narrative, the authors have to come forward briefly to make an explanation.

Since 1991/92 we had been at the centre of the UHI Project on a daily basis. We were present at the main events described, initiated or wrote many of the key documents and had access to a wide range of other papers. Previous chapters have been based on first-hand knowledge or on accounts given to us by others with whom we worked. We can be reasonably sure – within the usual limits of authorship – of both the factual accuracy and the overall balance of what we have written. But our account now has to take on a different nature, reflecting our own changing relationship with the project.

Changed Status

At the end of May 1997, Robin Lingard took early retirement and left HIE to set up his own consultancy company. In the process, he gave up all formal links with the UHI Project and with the structures which governed it. He felt it important that his successor had a free hand with the next phase of development. While he would have been happy to offer advice to the new management, if asked, he was content to concentrate on developing his own freelancing career.

Graham Hills, on the other hand, remained on a number of UHI committees in an advisory capacity – initially as a member of the Academic Council and the UHI Foundation, then additionally on a group set up to advise on external fund-raising and "friend raising". He later gained a different angle on the progress of UHI by joining the Board of Management of Inverness College. However, none of this offered the kind of day-to-day insight into events which had characterised his earlier involvement. He now had a peripheral rather than a strategic role.

This was a proper progression. As Brian Duffield put it during one of the early hand-over meetings – "You gave us the blueprint. Our role is to be the artisans who build from it." But, from the narrow perspective of writing a book and attempting to take the history of the UHI Project up to the present day, their change of status means that the authors have thinner material to work on beyond the middle of 1997.

Other Difficulties

If that were the only issue affecting the rest of this narrative, it would hardly be worth stopping the flow of the story to note it. It might fairly be asked why the authors did not simply seek access to the UHI or HIE archives in order to fill any gaps. The answer lies in some of the other difficulties which need to be mentioned here.

The first difficulty is that – particularly in the period 1998 to 2000 – the UHI Project appeared to become a very secretive institution. Although public information, newsletters and glossy documents were still being issued, it became very difficult to know from the outside what was really occupying the time of the management, how well the work was going or even whether the original blueprint was being followed. Those seeking – but not finding – information "from the outside" can be taken to include many in the Foundation, in the local authorities and in the wider community who had been staunch supporters from the first.

The second difficulty is that the authors could not ignore a growing impression that they, in particular, had become *non grata* with the new management, for reasons that still remain unclear. In these circumstances, even the fact that they were planning to write a book would have been badly received. To ask for access to papers would have been provocative.

The third difficulty is that – perhaps as a consequence of the first two problems – information did still reach the authors about what was going on within Caledonia House. It came informally and unattributably, mostly by word of mouth, sometimes corroborated on paper. Much of it was offered by people who wanted to unburden themselves to an ex-colleague or to someone who understood the roots and original aspirations of UHI. Both because of the nature of its source and because of later events in the story, most of this information cannot be drawn on for the purposes of history. While it is not possible to unlearn what was said or read, it can be used here only if it has been corroborated subsequently from other sources.

The question was therefore whether these difficulties, compounding the lack of first-hand material, made it preferable to terminate the narrative at this point, or whether it was possible to proceed with caution.

Going On

The decision to continue was taken in part from a natural wish to pursue the story as far as it could be tracked. It also reflected a genuine wish to celebrate the very substantial achievements, since mid 1997, of those who have faithfully sought to make UHI a reality. Both the positive and the negative sides of the later history of the UHI Project should be equally instructive to those who, across the world, may still be looking for guidance on how to go about delivering modern higher education in remote or rural areas.

What follows is therefore something of a hybrid history, necessarily incomplete but seeking to convey what happened next in the context of what went before. The hope must be that when UHI achieves university status an official history will be prepared which can tell the full story. Meanwhile, the authors will step back from the footlights and try to let the rest of the narrative tell itself.

Part IX

Clouds Across the Sun

CHAPTER 29

Artisans at Work

Yet More Resources

Blessings were still being showered on the UHI Project. The incoming Labour administration soon proved keen to show itself no less generous than its predecessor. When the new Scottish Office Minister for Education and Industry (Brian Wilson) made an official visit to Inverness in September 1997 he announced the commitment of a further £3.6 million, for such essentials as curriculum development, academic infrastructure and ICT development. Earlier investment had already allowed completion of the initial phase of UHI's video-conferencing network and the Minister used the network to give the good news to all the college sites from the Inverness office.

Part of the money was also to be used for the running of the UHI Executive Office. By now this was turning into a substantial operation. At the time the Millennium grant was made, the project was being run centrally by eight staff. When Brian Wilson visited Caledonia House less than a year later the staff had reached 20, reflecting the move to an operational phase.

The most important task of any Chief Executive is to appoint outstanding staff beneath him. During 1997 Brian Duffield began to assemble his team. Patrick Dark (Head of ICT) and David Shepherd (Curriculum Development Co-ordinator) were already on board, together with two other IT specialists. Two of the original HIE staff (Allan Bransbury and Margo Taylor) applied successfully for posts in UHI Ltd. Other posts were now advertised.

Many of the new staff members had given up equally good or better jobs in universities elsewhere to take part in the new venture, enthused by its potential to create something new and special for Scottish higher education. The first group recruited to the senior management team included Dr John French (Head of Academic Development), Eric Gibson (Head of Finance and Corporate Services), Jenny Tizard (Staff Development Co-ordinator), Dr Neil Chisholm (Research Co-ordinator) and Sharon Jones (Academic Standards Co-ordinator). Their task was to push forward the volume and quality of UHI's activities on all fronts.

Towards a Curriculum

In turn, the Executive Office team had to rely heavily on the largely voluntary efforts of busy staff in the colleges, especially for the steady development towards a university curriculum. Still co-ordinating and guiding these efforts was the Academic Council, now led (in the annual progression agreed earlier) by Mike Webster, Principal of Perth College. He had been the driving force in bringing Perth into the UHI partnership and his strong personality would be a critical factor in the project's next phase of development.

On the surface, at least, progress towards the common curriculum was encouraging. Across the colleges, eight degree courses were available by 1997, including the first two networked UHI degrees. In the pipeline were six further degree courses (Tourism, Marine Science, Environmental Science, Computer Sciences, Social Sciences and Music), together with a number of post-graduate certificate and diploma courses. An Academic Partnership Agreement was now in place with the Open University, covering both validation services for the UHI degree programme (through the OU's own Validation Service) and more general support for quality assurance and staff development programmes. The signing of this Agreement had given particular satisfaction to Dr John Cowan, the Director of the OU in Scotland, who had lent the project liberal doses of his own enthusiasm and experience since its early days.

The Academic Council also established two new working groups to give greater depth to its work and to draw in external expertise. A Working Group on Cultural and Heritage Studies was set up, under Norman Gillies of Sabhal Mòr Ostaig, to ensure that the UHI curriculum reflected the area's rich mixture of cultural and historical influences. A Working Group on Learning Environments and Technology was given the task of providing central guidance on how technology should be used to support the individual's learning, with particular attention to the needs of students outside the traditional age groups for higher education. This Working Group was chaired by Professor Alistair MacFarlane, now retired from running Heriot-Watt University and available to bring to UHI his own expertise on the application of new technology to learning. In the coming years he would be summoned to the aid of the UHI Project on a number of critical occasions.

With hindsight, this gives particular significance to what Alistair MacFarlane had to say about his own future vision for the university. In a keynote lecture to mark the launch of his Working Group he said: "The new UHI institution will not be just a collection of providers, but will offer supportive learning driven by real needs within an integrating framework of provision that links all institutions of the network. We have to make sure the technology enables this."

Building Projects

Meanwhile the real bricks and mortar business was under way, at sites across the region. The new building work would be spread out over a period of four or five years, with scheduling determined both by local conditions and by the mix of funding required at different locations.

Here again fresh expertise was taken on board to assist the Executive Office in this complex task – an architectural adviser and a project manager, the latter charged with ensuring the proper expenditure of funds released by the Millennium Commission.

At one location, in particular, there was by now some regret that the plans included in the endorsed bid had not been more radical. Inverness College had secured funding for a new Learning Centre at its main (Longman) site, which was on the industrial estate closest to the centre of the town. If UHI had settled in the ugliest modern building in central Inverness, the College certainly inhabited its main rival – an uncompromising concrete block beyond the railway bridge, with a filling station and a bus depot for neighbours. When the Millennium bid was being planned it was suggested to the college that this might be the opportunity to relocate to somewhere more redolent of both Highland life and higher education. The reply was robust. The Longman site suited current client groups and was convenient for those without cars. An extension to accommodate the new learning technology was all it would need for its new role within the university.

However, the burghers of Inverness – or at least a faction among them – felt let down by this lack of ambition. When it became clear that the regional psychiatric hospital at Craig Dunain would be closing, in response to the movement towards providing a greater volume of care in the community, pressure came on the college to re-examine its options.

Craig Dunain Hospital had – not surprisingly – many of the features which had made the Crichton Hospital in Dumfries such an attractive location for a higher education initiative. The buildings were large and well spaced, the grounds were extensive and imaginatively laid out. There would have been plenty of room not only for teaching and social facilities, but also for high quality student accommodation. It would have been a natural place to establish a small science park, with incubator units for small firms. In addition, unlike the Crichton, it was on an elevated site with extensive views over and beyond Inverness.

However, although initial drawings were done and an option appraisal confirmed the attractions of Craig Dunain, Inverness College was unable to implement the plan. It cannot be a coincidence that soon afterwards the extent of the college's financial woes began to become public knowledge.

New buildings – even those paid for by generous benefactors – bring with them running costs which benefactors rarely cover. Thus it would soon become evident that the capital investment provided for the creation of UHI's new estate carried an extra price-tag which would have to be met by an enhanced income at each college. However, one of the arguments in favour of recruiting more undergraduate students from outside the region, especially from overseas, was to provide that additional income stream – and such students were far more likely to be attracted to a Craig Dunain campus than to the Longman site. While in the short term the decision by Inverness College to stay put may have seemed prudent, its impact on longer term income generation and on the future marketing message of UHI seems not to have been given sufficient weight.

Strategic Planning

All the strands in this complicated business of working towards a new university were brought together by the Executive Office early in 1998 in a remarkable document – "The UHI Strategic Planning Framework – 1998-2001". Around 120 pages long, it endeavoured to set out how the goal of university status would be achieved in 2001, preceded by gaining full degree giving status late in 2000. In these targets and in all other important respects, the Strategic Plan held to the model of UHI first articulated by Graham Hills and subsequently endorsed by the Highlands and Islands community, by Michael Forsyth and by the Millennium Commission.

The document, whose Preface bore the signatures of Fraser Morrison and Brian Duffield, confirmed the new management's commitment to the overall strategic aim of establishing: "a new university for the region for the new millennium. This new university will be an innovatory federal and collegiate institution committed to achieving for the region . . .

- Wider access to high quality tertiary education and training.
- Increased participation in tertiary education and training.
- An indigenous research and development structure."

The Strategic Plan also reaffirmed the original objective of delivering through UHI a seamless approach to tertiary learning – an integrated curriculum "at all levels of post-school advanced education". In more detail it explained that:

> UHI will expand its portfolio of courses at further and higher educa-tion levels. The university criteria naturally concern higher education courses and, accordingly, much of UHI's corporate development will be in higher education, while the responsibility for further education expansion will lie principally with UHI partner colleges. However, it is emphasised that UHI will develop a 'seamless garment' of tertiary education and that all developments will be co-ordinated to this end.

Similarly, the Strategic Plan restated the aim of developing a "polo mint" university structure:

> UHI is committed, both conceptually and practically, to maximising the autonomy of management and administration at the local/commu-nity level, commensurate with ensuring that it fulfils its corporate responsibilities as an institution of higher education. Within such a devolved environment, the role of the UHI Executive Office is to act as a facilitating unit . . . .

This last declaration sat somewhat oddly with figures elsewhere in the document which suggested that about a third of the estimated annual recurrent and development costs for the rest of the development phase (£1.5 million out of £4.5million) would be attributable to the Executive Office. Nevertheless, no reader of the Strategic Plan could be in any doubt that in early 1998 the new team of artisans was still following the original UHI blueprint – and apparently doing so with enthusiasm.

Future Governance

In one important respect, the new management seemed to have taken strategic thinking one step further than the project's founders. Drafting a constitution for the future federal university had previously been seen as a step too far, particularly by some of the larger colleges, even though a wise external adviser had argued unsuccessfully for an early start on the process.

Under Fraser Morrison and Brian Duffield a UHI Constitutional Working Group was at last set up, chaired by Mike Webster. Its activities will feature again in the next Chapter, but a first indication of how its thinking was developing appeared in the 1998-2001 Strategic Planning Framework. This sought to place the future university in the specific legislative context of the Scottish Further and Higher Education Act of 1992.

As its date implies, the Act had been part of the background to the planning of UHI's future from the start. However, it had never featured as a problem or a hurdle in previous discussions with Scottish Office Ministers and their officials about the way ahead for UHI. Its main role was to set out the legal basis for Scottish Office support to the provision of further education and for support to higher education through the Scottish Higher Education Funding Council (SHEFC). It did, however, allow the Secretary of State for Scotland to recognise an educational body – for instance, a Further Education College which had developed an extensive higher education portfolio – as a designated Institution of Higher Education, eligible for SHEFC funding, even before it secured full university status. This provision had perhaps been the stimulus for the Garrick Committee's suggestion that the UHI Project could be funded in future by SHEFC rather than by its proposed new Further Education Funding Council.

The Constitutional Working Group had therefore looked in particular at how to reconcile two crucial governance issues: "First, UHI governance will need to reflect a federal decentralised structure of governance which embraces the various governance arrangements of the UHI partners. Secondly, UHI will need to satisfy the requirements of a Designated Institution of Higher Education. . . ."

As was explained in the Strategic Plan, the expert advice they had received made it clear that the current voluntary arrangements between the UHI Project and its constituent colleges would be inadequate either to guarantee UHI's academic and financial management responsibilities or to secure Designated Institution status. Their conclusion was bold:

> Accordingly a new single legal entity, consisting of a federal university encompassing the incorporated colleges and other UHI partners, will be required to be constituted. This entity must preserve the individual identity of the academic partner institutions.

In other words, their view at that point – early in 1998 – was that a federal constitution was not just the best way forward for UHI. It was also seen as compatible with the operational requirements of the 1992 Act. If such a structure could now be implemented it would be constitutional progress indeed.

CHAPTER 30

Amending the Targets

Although the UHI Project seemed to be so well set on the course to success by the early months of 1998, it can now be seen that the seeds of future crisis were being sown around the same period.

A Shift of Emphasis

Ironically, the generous new resources won for the venture were themselves a source of tension. Under the circumstances, it was forgivable – even laudable, from one perspective – for those now in charge to be mainly concerned with the organisation and management of these new resources. However, this shift of emphasis had two consequences (neither of them desirable and both of them avoidable) which would have a profound influence on subsequent developments.

Firstly, it gave the project a predominantly managerial ethos. This was reinforced by the composition of the Board of Directors of UHI Ltd, which would increasingly reflect a business viewpoint. Almost by definition, management is a top-down process, immediately at odds with the vagaries of bottom-up thinking which characterise academic communities. Secondly, the effort consumed by the management process would gradually drive out the time and energy required for the constant reflective processes of deciding where the UHI was going and what it needed to do in order to sustain the vision on which everything rested.

In parallel with this change of strategic focus for the Board and the management team, a number of complicating factors were developing behind the scenes. Each separately might have been managed without terminal damage. In combination they would come close to sinking the whole venture.

Scottish Office Scrutiny

In spite of Graham Hills' perennial warnings about the downside of universities' dependence on Government funding, it had never been realistic to contemplate the creation of UHI without significant support from mainstream education budgets. Indeed, had it not been for the Scottish Office intervention in 1996 it is most unlikely that the project would have won its capital funding from the Millennium Commission.

But now the Scottish Office began to tighten what had previously been a very loose rein on the direction of UHI's development. Brian Wilson's speedy and welcome endorsement of UHI on behalf of the Labour administration had carried a sting in the tail. He announced that the Scottish Office was to review the project and its progress.

This was not necessarily sinister. The declared objective of the review was to satisfy Ministers that the financial and educational assumptions underlying the project would deliver the best possible outcome for potential students, in terms of quality and educational experience. Brian Wilson himself had declared that he wanted "nothing but the best for the Highlands and Islands". Within the Executive Office there were surely hopes that the Scottish Office might also take this opportunity to pick up some of the positive hints in the Garrick Report about adopting a bespoke approach to UHI's progress towards university status.

Hitherto, those responsible for higher education in the Scottish Office had largely kept their distance. Nothing special had been asked of them, except to take notice of the change of attitude to UHI initiated by Michael Forsyth and endorsed by Brian Wilson. All the positive support had been channelled through officials responsible for further education – including the uncapping of the permitted number of HE students. But the review now offered – indeed, required – the project to be considered within the context of Scottish higher education policy.

That too might have been in UHI's favour, had there been any inclination to take the distinctive path mapped out by Garrick rather than endorse the conservative spirit of Dearing, which had clearly won the day in England. As Michael Forsyth's *coup de main* had already demonstrated, even before devolution it would have been within the political gift of Scottish Ministers to declare, paraphrasing the words of the late Donald Dewar, "Let there be a new university".

However, there was a danger that the formal process of a review might instead give a golden opportunity to those concerned about the radical aspects of the Highland vision – and indeed about Garrick's proposals – for introducing a policy of containment, ensuring that UHI was confined in future within the traditional framework of university roles and structures. In the event, it was this faction that won the day.

For their purposes, it was not even necessary to run the risk of challenging the Ministerial enthusiasm for UHI. Indeed, on 20 May 1998 Brian Wilson was able to announce to the Scottish Grand Committee (this time meeting in Westminster) that the project had passed its evaluation with flying colours.

As he said: "The UHI Project has demonstrated conclusively to me that the university [sic] is on course to become a first class institution. Academic quality and the richness of the educational experience lie at the heart of any successful university and the study has convinced me that the project and its partner colleges are as committed as I am to securing the highest academic standards and the most fulfilling educational experience for its students."

But were the academic standards – and the students – he had in mind still the ones UHI had been designed for?

Higher Education Hurdles

The demanding but relatively broad criteria for achieving university status which had applied in the early days of the UHI Project – essentially based on numbers of students across a range of full-time degree courses – had already been supplemented under the Conservative administration by a new emphasis on meeting specific academic quality standards. Existing universities would be required to jump over an increasing number of hurdles to prove that they were putting public money to good use. Aspiring universities faced a steadily lengthening process of having to show themselves worthy to enter such august company. There was the familiar sound of barriers to entry being piled higher – a move which the Dearing Report had effectively endorsed.

New Labour, once in power, showed no inclination to go soft on academic quality. Indeed, across a wide range of public sector policy it favoured an "evaluation culture", in which targets of all kinds would be established and progress towards them would be the key determinant of future favour and funding.

Specifically, this approach to higher education had three major implications for the UHI Project. The first was that a great deal of the in-house academic development effort would have to be devoted to proving that the network of colleges could meet required standards in existing higher education courses, rather than into extending the breadth and depth of the overall curriculum. Significant attention therefore had to be given both to developing and running internal procedures for quality assurance (adding greatly to the bureaucratic infrastructure) and to preparing for external audits by the Quality Assurance Agency (QAA).

The second implication was that assumptions made about the process of being designated by the Secretary of State for Scotland as a Higher Education Institution (HEI) had to be rethought. Designation had been presented in the recent UHI Strategic Plan as an imminent and largely symbolic event, but it would now be linked directly to the achievement of satisfactory academic standards, as tested by the QAA. It was almost as if the criteria previously relevant to becoming a university were now being applied to the stage of becoming a recognised HEI. The immediate practical implications affected the route through which public funding was supplied, since designation was the key which unlocked the door of the Scottish Higher Education Funding Council – the Scottish Office having decided to ditch Garrick's recommendation of using SHEFC to fund all degree courses from any level of institution. However, in presentational terms the achievement of HEI status now had to be seen as a major test of the new management's capability. The focus of effort therefore moved from the task of creating a university to the immediate challenge of passing the tests for this essentially interim status.

The third implication was that university status for UHI might now be a far more distant objective than even the pessimists had predicted. The process of external quality auditing was to extend out beyond HEI designation, with the need to demonstrate consistent academic quality to the QAA over a period of years (perhaps five, perhaps more) before any recommendation could be made that an institution deserved to be even considered for university charter. Unless some Ministerial short-cut could be engineered, the prospect of the Highlands and Islands celebrating the foundation of its University in 2001 was now gone.

Priority Markets

The Scottish Office, under its new Ministerial team, also began to exercise a significant influence on the attitude of the UHI Executive Office to its potential markets and the balance between its potential client groups.

Two of the central planks of New Labour policy were the importance of lifelong learning and the need to promote social inclusion. Higher education, it was felt, could and should contribute more to both objectives. A University for Industry was being developed, not as a formal institution but more as a brokerage mechanism for improving the accessibility and relevance of courses. If UHI wished to remain in political favour it would have to respond to the same priorities, both in its own right and as a means of delivering the objectives of the Scottish University for Industry (SUfI).

The provision of tertiary learning for people of all ages had been one of the founding principles of those planning the new university. Its mission to make courses available to students in the most remote corners of the region was intended to overcome an important aspect of social exclusion. The new Scottish Office priorities for higher education were in that sense another endorsement and encouragement of the UHI concept – and were eagerly embraced as such by the management team. So how did they contribute to driving the project off course?

The answer is twofold. Because the Ministerial perspective was domestic and local, it took the attention of UHI away from the vital need to recruit students and staff from outside the region and from beyond Scotland. What had always been intended as an "and" option (the provision of learning opportunities to local communities) was interpreted as an "or" option. Although plans for addressing this wider market had earlier been prepared internally and even approved by the Board, reference to the recruitment of students from outside the Highlands and Islands began to disappear from progress reports and policy statements. Plans for student accommodation were shelved.

This narrowing of the market perspective both circumscribed the ambitions and aspirations of those now running UHI and denied to its financial planners the "free" income which overseas students – in particular – would have brought. The exchange for some additional money from Scottish Office, SUfI or the EU was a poor one in anything other than the very short term.

In addition, the new priorities for serving student markets brought UHI into potential competition with its own constituent colleges. The further education sector had a long and honourable record of providing accessible routes into higher education for those whose location or conventional educational attainment would have left them otherwise excluded. But if these were now to be the target market for the would-be university, why should they not be recruited directly by the colleges?

The more UHI gave top priority to issues of access and social inclusion, the more it raised the question of what value all the millions of money and years of effort had really added to the infrastructure of local institutions which existed independently before 1992.

CHAPTER 31

Centralised Control

The Scottish Office review and its implications were an external complication, bringing dangers of diverting the UHI Project from the breadth of its original mission while pushing into the distant future the goal of university status. Other complications were home grown.

The Farrington Report

The UHI Constitutional Working Group worked hard in the first six months of 1998 – or more accurately a consultant laboured on its behalf. Dennis Farrington, from Stirling University, was an academic expert in the constitutional niceties of British universities. He was also familiar with the Highlands and with the concept of UHI. He had even participated in the Wick conference on Distance Learning back in 1992. Now he had been called in by the Executive Office to bring professional support to the task of designing a suitable constitution for the new university. In addition to his meetings with the Working Group he was involved in informal discussions between the UHI management team and the Scottish Office.

Farrington's report, delivered to the Board of UHI Ltd in April 1998, assumed that the project was set on a long road to university status, via the unglamorous route mapped out in the Further and Higher Education (Scotland) Act 1992. Designation as a Higher Education Institution would precede the award of degree-giving powers, leading eventually to the granting of full university status. Quality hurdles would have to be crossed at regular intervals along the way. As noted earlier, this was clearly the preferred route among Scottish Office officials and it is hardly surprising that the consultant reflected this as the main option in his report. He did, however, recognise that other options existed.

An alternative might be termed the political route. If enough people and organisations in the Highlands and Islands could persuade their local politicians to back the cause, then it was within the power of the Scottish Office to promote an Act of Parliament, carrying a message to the Privy Council that the creation of a new university be put in motion – as had happened with the establishment of Stirling.

This approach would still have required the UHI partners to demonstrate respectable standards of academic quality and it might have retained HEI designation as a step on the way, but it would have been wholly consistent with the political view of UHI as being a different kind of university with a specifically regional mission. In an early paper to the Constitutional Working Group Dennis Farrington called this populist and direct approach the Private Legislation Route and thought it an exciting possibility – but it was not what was finally recommended.

His final report focused instead on the constitutional arrangements appropriate for what was soon (if all went well) to become a designated HEI. In this he said he had been guided by the UHI Strategic Planning Framework and that his proposals were "predicated on a federal, decentralised structure of governance, building on the pre-existing strengths of the UHI partner institutions".

"A Model University Structure"

However, what the report recommended was a complete constitutional separation between the partner institutions and UHI. The partner institutions would retain their individual identities and local roles as providers of further education, while UHI would become a new corporate entity responsible for all higher education courses – including the colleges' existing provision. It would receive funding for higher education courses and on that basis would contract with the colleges to deliver them. Instead of the network of institutions becoming a federal, collegiate entity which would achieve HEI designation, UHI would now seek designation in its own right, as a body separate from all the colleges. Instead of adopting a decentralised structure, UHI was to become a highly centralised mechanism built around the Executive Office.

The contrast with all previous constitutional concepts for UHI – including those on which Farrington's proposals were said to be predicated – was stark. Yet at no point did his report (of which a final version was endorsed by the Board of UHI Ltd in June 1998) explain why the abandonment of all that had gone before was necessary. What was presented, without reference to the past, was "a model university structure".

Were there internal debates about the change? Was it pointed out that the structure now proposed was inherently unstable, giving the colleges only a secondary interest in the fortunes of the new university, while the university would be wholly dependent on the colleges to deliver its courses? If so, powerful arguments must have stilled the dissent.

Perhaps the larger colleges secretly welcomed the lifting of the threat of a federation, with its inherent loss of autonomy. Since the new model of UHI would have no role in further education (in spite of the earlier goal of weaving a "seamless robe") they would also be free from the prospect interference on their home ground.

Breaking the Community Link

But it may have been other elements in Farrington's package of recommendations which swung the various interest groups within the Board in favour of acceptance. For the "model university structure" included some other radical departures from the governance arrangements hammered out only a year or two earlier. It was argued that UHI should prepare itself for HEI designation by adopting straight away a system of governance suitable for a university. The clear but unstated complementary objectives would be on the one hand to reduce the level of community influence over UHI's affairs and on the other to increase the power and freedom of manoeuvre of its governing body.

Thus the Foundation, as the guardian of the community stake in UHI, was to be limited in future to an infrequent consultative role, under the chairmanship of a Rector who would be, in effect, the creature of the governing body. Members of the Foundation would also lose their status as the membership of the company taking the UHI concept forward. Under the new Articles of Association proposed for UHI Ltd, the Board of Directors would be replaced by a 25 strong Board of Governors, of whom 7 would be appointed by the Foundation to represent the wider community. Only later did it become clear that the Board of Governors would also be the only legal members of the company they ran – in other words, that they would be answerable only to themselves for the conduct of a major project on which the fortunes of the whole region could be said to depend.

Nor were the Foundation members the only losers in this arrangement. Within the limit of 25 Governors it was ruled that there would not be room for all the heads of the partner institutions, thus abandoning the last pretence that this could be seen as some form of federal constitution. As a sop, an additional consultative body called the UHI Forum would be established, in which all the academic partners would be represented. No-one seems to have believed that the Forum would really make any difference to the way UHI was run in future – which is perhaps why it was invented.

Pushing Through the Changes

Of course, it was one thing for new constitutional arrangements to be recommended, but they still had to be legally endorsed. This process would take place at the Annual General Meeting of UHI Ltd, set for mid-September 1998, at which the new Memorandum and Articles of Association would be offered for agreement. Given the fundamental nature of the changes, it might have been expected that key issues would have been presented to the Foundation in advance, as matters for discussion in a spirit of give and take. On the contrary, a new authoritarian note was struck both by the Executive Office and by the Board. The Board itself had already approved Dennis Farrington's report back in June, without reference to the Foundation. These matters were not up for debate. They were up for validation.

Nevertheless, it would have been quite possible for the Foundation – as the membership of the company – to refuse to accept the new constitution and to send the Board back to produce something different. After all, there would have been no legal vacuum in the interim, since the existing constitution would have remained in force. At this point, it is no exaggeration to say that the fate of the constitution was in the hands of the community which had willed UHI into being. Although the time for planning concerted action was short and the documentation complex and hard to unravel, there were those in the Foundation who saw enough of the implications to consider making a stand. A small group of earlier supporters opposed the new constitutional proposals on principles which may have seemed to many as hair-splitting details but which – as in the case of the abandonment of federation – were fundamental to the founding concepts of UHI. A much larger number opposed them as a gut reaction to what was perceived as arm-twisting, by the authoritative centre of an organisation now far removed from the decentralised, community-based model sold to the Millennium Commission.

Some within the colleges saw as the sticking point a little heralded provision in the new Articles of Association which would put the Chief Executive of UHI Ltd in the chair of the Academic Council, mimicking well before the event one of the roles of a university Vice Chancellor – and, more than incidentally, adding immediately to the centralised power of the Executive Office.

Great pressure was brought to bear on the dissenters, who included the Convener of Highland Regional Council, the 'elders' who had so far supported UHI and certain of the college principals and boards of management. In private discussions before the AGM some minor changes in the legal documentation were offered and agreed, enough to sway some waverers though without altering the overall impact of the proposals. It was made clear that at the AGM itself the motion would be for the adoption of the new Memorandum and Articles in their entirety, with no procedure for the introduction of amendments from the floor.

At no point, either in these behind-the-scenes discussions or at the AGM itself, was any adequate explanation given for the need to implement changes which took the project in such a different direction from both the original blueprint and the Strategic Plan issued by the current management only months previously. The official reasoning for recommending the new Memorandum and Articles, as given in papers prepared for the AGM, was that the existing constitution of UHI Ltd was inappropriate for a designated Higher Education Institution. So much had already been established when the Strategic Plan was published, but the implication now was that only the "model structure" endorsed by the Board would meet the requirements for designation. This was, at the mildest, misleading.

The more powerful argument, deployed in private by the Chairman and Chief Executive to sway the dissenters, was that the Scottish Office required the model proposed by the Board, as a condition of designation, and that what had gone before was no longer deemed appropriate. The complications of a federal UHI, possibly spanning the HE/FE divide and seeking an unorthodox route to university status, were unwelcome to those now holding the purse-strings. Worse still, public disagreements within the Highland community might be taken as the excuse to refuse designation, or to withdraw or scale back the commitment to UHI once the devolved Scottish administration came to power the following year.

If the region really did want its own university, this was now the only way to get it. Trust us and our expert, they said.

At an emotionally charged AGM on 21 September, the Chairman of the Board called for unity. Anything less would send the wrong signals to government. The new constitution was endorsed by a show of hands and the matter was settled. Or so it seemed.

CHAPTER 32

In the Executive Office

The debates about the nature of UHI, the constitution and the decision to opt for designated status filled out much of the thinking time of 1998. It was an example of academic politics which have preoccupied universities and colleges over many centuries. All this went on largely above the heads of many of the full-time staff of the Executive Office who, throughout this period and beyond, were busily getting on with creating the framework for the new university.

Coherence in the Curriculum

The core academic task in front of the Executive Office was two-fold. It was to create and operate the essential mechanics of integrating the separate activities of the individual colleges into a coherent programme of UHI higher education courses. It was also to identify and stimulate developments at undergraduate and postgraduate levels germane to the Highlands and Islands but not necessarily yet a college responsibility. In due course, good examples in this second category would be mountain studies and rural healthcare research.

The larger task was the assembly of an integrated higher education curriculum. At least the new constitution had clarified responsibility in that area, by bringing all HE resources under the wing of UHI Ltd and hence of the Executive Office. But there was much to be done to give a logical form to the mixture of course materials thus inherited. Some originated in earlier college initiatives to build modular degree courses on the foundations of one or two year (HNC or HND) courses. Others were the result of collaborative ventures with existing universities, mostly pre-dating UHI. There was also the growing portfolio of network degrees, originated by UHI, validated by the OU and delivered by the colleges.

The range of subjects was broad rather than focused. It included topics of a general kind to be found in most higher education institutions, such as information technology, social studies, business studies and other vocational subjects, together with the distinctive defining subjects for UHI, all at various stages of development – such as Celtic and Gaelic studies, environmental science, archaeology, rural economies, fishing and forestry.

Not surprisingly, in several of these distinctive areas of the curriculum colleges had in place key staff with postgraduate university experience, many of them of university calibre, who could act as champions.

The principal developmental activity of UHI was therefore a set of parallel processes of assembling twenty to thirty degree programmes, each the product of a small inter-college team assisted by the staff of the Executive Office and an external assessor drawn from an existing university. The outcome of each was then tested by the Quality Assurance Agency (of Scotland) and finally submitted to the Open University Validation Service for validation as a *bona fides* degree course leading to an OU degree. The OU was ever helpful. Its support and encouragement was greatly appreciated, subject only to a faint anxiety by some in UHI that relying on just one university was not necessary or desirable.

Eventually a range of some twenty five separate themes emerged, to be clustered into five generically related groups, the new embryonic faculties. These were:

- Arts, Culture and Heritage;
- Business and Leisure Studies;
- Environmental and Natural Systems Studies;
- Health and Social Studies;
- Information and Engineering Systems.

In the ensuing years of 1999 and 2000, the curricular superstructure of the future university was gradually built up, as reflected in successive issues of the UHI Prospectus. Its outputs were in the form of networked courses (some networked in practice, most still in theory), mainly leading to an unclassified first degree.

They suffered generally from two flaws. The first was that articulation from HNC and HND to BSc or BA would be anything but smooth. To many students, HNC and HND were ends in themselves and not Part 1 or Part 2 of a degree course. A more serious flaw was that several courses, whilst credible and desirable, had to be aborted for lack of student numbers, a fear from the beginning. To compound the problem, colleges had little practical incentive to set up new courses on a networked basis, where they might draw on multiple markets and share student numbers across the area.

The ICT Infrastructure

If there was one feature of UHI that was to distinguish it from other universities at that time it was its planned reliance on one of the most modern and efficient electronic networks, linking college to college and college to the centre and beyond. Overcoming distance, and therefore time, by instantaneous exchange of information in the form of text, of voice, of pictures and by videoconferencing (VC) of all three formats, was the platform on which the novelty of UHI rested. It was also intended to be the magic ingredient which gave the new university the economic edge in course delivery, allowing one set of course material and one lecturer to support simultaneously the learning of groups of students hundreds of miles apart.

Three significant development projects were undertaken by the Executive Office in this formative period, involving the network infrastructure, the applications infrastructure and the information systems. A team was established, from Executive Office and college staff, to push forward all three. Whilst there was no lack of enthusiasm and knowledge, a practical handicap was the difficulty of recruiting highly skilled technicians at salaries compatible with further education budgets.

The first and most pressing task was to establish the Wide Area Network (WAN) together with the fibre optic and microwave infrastructure that would interconnect all of the partner institutions. Beyond this, the Local Area Networks (LANs) would provide high speed links to the desktop of every student and member of staff. UHI contracted with Scottish Telecom in 1997 to build the WAN, together with the fibre-optic and microwave infrastructure that would join the institutions and provide an onward connection to SuperJanet (the UK university network) and the Internet. These physical links were 'enacted' by Cisco System's switches and routers that helped establish an integrated voice, data and video network, one of the first in the UK. The development was awarded the Networking Industries Network Project of the Year Award in 1999.

The network infrastructure paved the way for applications and services on which UHI's mission depended, using integrated video-conferencing, e-mail and telephony systems alongside "web-enabled" services. Video conferencing was seen as a particular success, building up to wide-scale uptake – though at first primarily for administrative purposes.

In the early days it was a curiosity used by a few. For these individuals it was rather like a 'spectator sport' in which they simply enjoyed a window on to a remote meeting. However, with time and with the adoption of multiple synchronous connections, genuinely 'distributed' meetings became the norm. By 1998/99 UHI had implemented an extensive network comprising 14 video-conferencing studios – the 13 academic partners plus the Executive Office. This radically altered the management, organisation and conduct of meetings and also significantly increased the opportunity for active participation across the partnership. As an alternative to a one or two-day round trip of several hundred miles it had much to offer.

Support for teaching was initially not a priority. There was a balance to be struck between early synchronous technologies and the broader bases of learning and teaching. Nevertheless, the uptake of video-conferencing in course delivery accelerated, with over 55% of its use eventually involved in teaching. The first UHI degree, Rural Development, was successfully taught between three sites using VC, the Web, e-mail and local academic support, while video-conferencing was also used to facilitate international student collaboration with Finland and Sweden. This greatly enriched the course. Video-conferencing also proved particularly useful for local outreach by the colleges to community learning centres.

There were, of course, some problems to overcome. The real challenge lay in co-ordination of use in teaching, which required the standardisation of timetabling, resource booking, and confirmation processes and systems. This was never fully resolved, mainly because of broader organisational and constitutional issues, thus reducing quality and increasing wasted effort.

The commitment of the individual partner institutions to the system was also patchy. Because it was not certain how or when UHI would materialise as an integrated institution, required levels of trust and mutual support were difficult to achieve. Colleges did not always promote user training, thus limiting understanding of the technology and affecting the quality of its use. The search for standardisation highlighted the different objectives of the partners, often driven by self-interest and a residual desire for autonomy. This was demonstrated by their enthusiasm for local teaching as opposed to shared learning. Some colleges even compounded this by using the technology to secure competitive advantage over each other.

In short, as a communications tool video-conferencing was highly successful. It had a significant impact, but it could not function effectively as a stand-alone system. As part of a broader inter-organisational environment it necessarily depended on other systems and activities. As a means of cementing individual institutions into a single entity it was limited by the way the relationships between the colleges and the Executive Office had been constructed. If these other organisational – and human – issues could have been resolved, further gains in quality and performance would have been possible.

The Virtual Library

There remained, of course, the ever more vexed matter of the transformation of information into knowledge and ultimately into useful knowledge. Up till the present time, knowledge has crystallised into the form of books, journals and other text materials. This is where libraries came in. Many seats of learning have owed their distinction to the size and character of the books and library buildings that they owned and managed. The rapid inflation of the growth of knowledge and of the texts to contain it would, in the second half of the 20th century, present insoluble problems to libraries everywhere. The cost of shelving, seating and book management everywhere outstripped the financial resources available. Even the most dedicated bookworm had to yield first to the electronically managed library and finally to the electronic library itself. But for UHI, and perhaps only for UHI, the consequence of what was a problem for others could be seen as an asset.

As earlier studies had confirmed, the existing college libraries were barely adequate to support higher education courses. Simply bringing them all up to standard was not feasible, even with the extra money provided by the Millennium Commission. However, the vision for UHI, in the New Learning Paradigm, was that it could live with the most modest of 'fixed-assets' libraries and could thus make the virtual university library a virtue out of necessity. Even the hallowed word 'library' gradually gave way to the new description of Learning Resource Centre. These would still be libraries in appearance, with extensive reading and writing places, but they would now be managed by IT professionals rather than bibliographers.

Linking all the college libraries together and linking them collectively to the UK university network might have been a small step for the bigger libraries but it was a great step for UHI. A new library management system was selected, at the leading edge of technology, and was piloted at Inverness College with the aim of rolling it out across the network of colleges by the end of 1999. However, while useful progress was made, other factors (particularly those organisational factors which affected the commitment to technology-based teaching) prevented full achievement of the vision.

Evidence of Progress

The pages of the UHI Newsletters between Summer 1998 and Summer 2000 present a picture of consistent progress and positive achievement. New courses were being validated, new faces kept appearing. In February 1999 UHI's first research students took up their posts across the network of colleges, marking a major step towards the establishment of a research culture which would be one of the important criteria for university status. The concept of associated institutions was developed, with the acceptance of the Highland Psychiatric Foundation into the UHI family. A Development Trust was established to help UHI generate income from external and private sources. At the local level, in the communities which had given such loyal support to UHI since it was little more than an idea, new buildings were being completed and proud formal opening ceremonies held. From Shetland to Argyll and from Stornoway to Elgin the progress towards a new university was becoming steadily more visible. Figure 9 shows the extent of the development of the network.

Unhappy Days

Yet in spite of all this constant activity on the surface, signs began to emerge that in some fundamental respects the project was suffering from a loss of impetus. It was as if the Executive Office, having succeeded in centralising so much power through the new constitution, lacked the skills to put it to effective use. If so, this was ironic. From the days of Sir Robert Cowan onwards there had been voices arguing for the recruitment of a powerful academic figure to drive the project forward, banging heads together as necessary in order to ensure that individual colleges did not hold back the progress of the partnership. Arguably, all the tools to carry out that job were now in the hands of the Chief Executive of UHI Ltd, from a well resourced Executive Office and control over a generous budget to the chairmanship of the Academic Council. The Board of Governors had secured significant freedom of action. Ministers still declared their complete support for UHI and its aims. It would have been reasonable to expect acceleration towards the goal of university status, in an atmosphere of exhilaration. Instead, these seem to have been unhappy days in the Executive Office. The evidence points to as many as five inter-related problems.

One was the complex mechanism set up within UHI for taking or endorsing decisions. Committees proliferated, with recommendations being referred from one level to another and conclusions emerging only after lengthy process, if at all. The root of the problem seems to have been in the procedures required for

Lews Castle College, Isle of Lewis, Outer Hebrides.

Broch of Clickimin, Lerwick. Shetland College: archeological research.

Perth College: Aircraft Engineering.

Lews Castle College: Rural Development Studies.

Moray College: Learning Resource Centre.

The cultural heritage of the Highlands and Islands:
its land and its people.

Inverness College: Forestry and Conservation.

Photo: Iain Sarjeant (www.iainsarjeant.com)

Photo: by courtesy of North Atlantic Fisheries College, UHI.

North Atlantic Fisheries College, Scalloway, Shetland.

Photo: courtesy of UHI Millennium Institute

SAMS: the Scottish Association for Marine Science, Dunstaffnage, Argyll.

The Gaelic College at Sabhal Mòr Ostaig, Slèite, Isle of Skye, Inner Hebrides.

Photo: Ian Smith, by courtesy of Sabhal Mòr Ostaig.

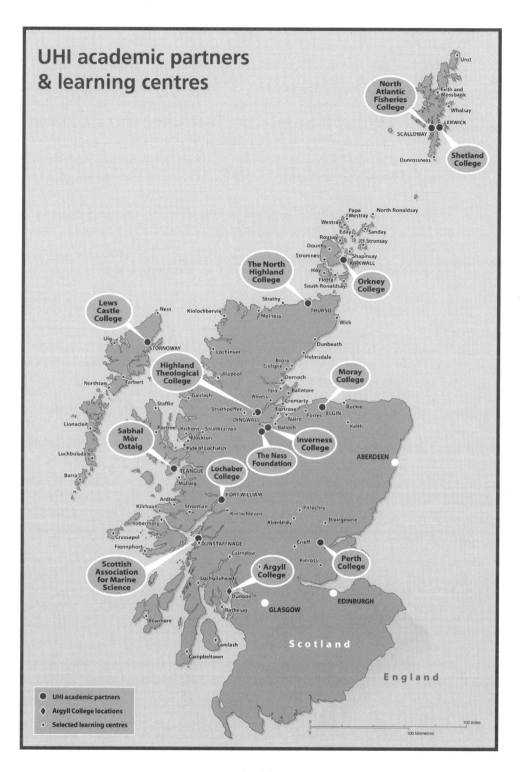

Figure 9 – Details of the UHI network.

academic quality control, but the infection spread widely. This had two visible effects. The first was that ideas brought to the Executive Office from outside sources – for courses, contacts, sources of funding and so on – tended to vanish without trace. In the absence of any apparent response, people took their ideas elsewhere or let them drop. The second, mainly internal effect was that even senior staff seemed unable to take decisions without reference to "due process", however simple the issue. The scope for individual initiative and imaginative action had been circumscribed, in a way which seemed wholly inappropriate for a development project.

The second, closely linked problem was the absence of encouragement and space for open debate and discussion about the way forward for UHI. Meetings of the Foundation received reports but were clearly not expected to probe beneath them. Within the management team discussions were confined to small, closed groups.

This was perhaps a reflection of practice in the FE sector – and also in the polytechnic sector that had been incorporated into the university family. Both were inclined to managerial thinking. Things tended to be done by decree rather than by persuasion. Yet it is a simple fact of university life that it thrives on argument and give-and-take. It is invariably the case that the right people coming into universities are those who do so to fulfil their own desires and to dream their own dreams. This is not a romantic sentiment but the recognition of why some very bright people work longer hours for smaller salaries just in order to make their own contribution to the greater scheme of things. In brief, universities are like orchestras, bottom-up organisations which thrive on freedom and chafe when managed. If UHI was to attract and retain such people, then a loose managerial rein was essential. Instead, the scope for debate and for the contributions from 'the least of their number' amongst the academics would be limited, both within the Executive Office and in the Academic Council. The healthy luxury of allowing a thousand flowers to bloom would be stifled and the road to university status made that much longer.

The third problem was the continuing tension between the ambitions and priorities of the Executive Office and those of the colleges. As noted earlier, any federation is liable to give rise to tensions between its focal point and the federal partners portrayed as the periphery. The centre has to lead but not to drive. It can create most of the options but then it has to leave it to the network to choose between them. By abandoning the federal model, the Board of UHI Ltd had apparently opted for a command economy approach, allowing the Executive Office to drive the partnership by taking control over all the resources for higher education through a separate institution. But this was not the same as giving it control over the other partners. Because the Executive Office was wholly dependent on the network of colleges to deliver the higher education courses, it must have been obvious to them that UHI now needed them far more than they needed UHI. For many of them, further education remained their mainstream business and their main management preoccupation. An increasing number were finding it impossible to balance their financial books on the FE account. In none of this could UHI, as now constituted, offer them any help at all. There grew up an atmosphere of "them and us", where "them" was always the Executive Office and sometimes also their fellow colleges, viewed as competitors rather than partners. This was the unavoidable and predictable legacy of defining the central institution as something separate from and other than the partner colleges.

The fourth problem was the neglect of those links to the wider community which had been so essential in launching the UHI concept and sustaining it through its early stages of development. With the departure of Val MacIver from local politics, the Board of Governors lost their last link with the region's local authorities. No attempt seems to have been made to recreate the link. Instead, much energy and management time went into the establishment of formal agreements with institutions in far flung places, from Cape Breton to Iceland. Papers were delivered to a conference in Morocco. A UHI delegation visited Barcelona to explore collaboration. Another delegation visited UHI from Rwanda. None of these contacts seemed to be used to open up new markets for UHI and to bring in the "free" income which overseas students could provide. In the case of Iceland, at least, the main effect seems to have been to convince another small nation to adopt the UHI concept and to implement it before the Scottish prototype was really airborne.

In the Highlands and Islands, however, UHI was becoming less and less visible. At community level the local college remained the focus, its links with the wider partnership rarely obvious. Even the UHI logo was hard to find on signs, buildings or marketing material. At Highland and regional level the Executive Office seemed unwilling to play a prominent role in policy discussions or joint ventures. For many, who had looked forward to the contribution a new university would make to the intellectual and cultural life in and beyond Inverness, this was a source of real disappointment and puzzlement.

The last of these problems – not the least of them, but perhaps the hardest for external observers to pin down – concerned relationships within and around the Executive Office itself. The house style of management clearly suited some staff well. They and their careers thrived under it and the responded with a fierce loyalty. For others, it proved hard to cope with. Some went on sick leave, quite a few simply left.

Whatever the full story of events may have been, a major effect of these tensions among the staff was to intensify the tendency of the Executive Office to become absorbed in its own affairs, to be largely inward-looking. Local jokes compared Caledonia House to the Lubyanka. Unhappiness among the staff must also have made it harder to deploy the resources of the Executive Office to full effect in the task of creating the new university.

In Summary

Under the guidance and leadership of the Executive Office, the UHI Project had made great strides, particularly in developing a coherent higher education curriculum and in providing the infrastructure of technology through which it could be delivered to all corners of the region. Nevertheless, it did not yet feel like a university and in some respects its progress towards that goal appeared to be slowing.

It seemed to have become bureaucratic, in spirit and structure. Discussion and debate were not encouraged. It might be concluded that it had so far failed to develop a university ethos because the questing spirit of university education had been stifled. Perhaps that was because those engaged in its governance were not primarily of a university frame of mind. In its business-like way the Board of Governors reflected a determination to succeed at all costs, but with no evidence of what that success should entail.

The enterprise seemed handicapped by the unstable and often uncomfortable relationship between the centre and the periphery, between the Executive Office and the partner institutions. The UHI partnership now had neither the mutual support of a federation nor the grim but effective driving force which a Vice Chancellor in waiting might have deployed.

Meanwhile, for most of the inhabitants of the Highlands and Islands, UHI had become a mystery, practically lost to view. The Executive Office appeared defensive and inward-looking. Effort was put into largely symbolic external links, but it seemed that no real attempt was being made to build a tangible university presence in its home region.

As to issues of management style and practice, other events would soon open up this aspect of the Executive Office for greater public scrutiny.

PART X

Crisis and Resolution

CHAPTER 33

The Struggle for Designation

Did the Dogs Bark?

During 1999 and 2000 the UHI Project was moving into crisis. Even those who were kept outside the gates could tell that all was not well. Yet there was no hint of problems in reports to the Foundation and no word of external criticism was accepted by those in charge.

At this point, before telling how the storm broke, it seems fair to pose the question whether the stakeholders in UHI had recognised the significance of the recent developments within the project and whether they should have seen the crisis coming. After all, the changes which had been introduced to the original blueprint (and to the assumptions underlying the current management's Strategic Plan of early 1998) were far from superficial, affecting the relationship with the partner colleges and with the wider community, radically altering the path to university status, abandoning the attempt to converge further and higher education and shifting the priorities within the market for students. In engineering terms, such radical alterations to a project costing £100 million should have been subject to a formal change management procedure in which the funders' consent would be essential. So did the funders – or their watchdogs – ever bark?

Even without internal evidence, it is still possible to make reasonable deductions about the attitude of some key players. Highlands and Islands Enterprise seems to have concluded that after 1996 the hard part of pulling together the UHI Project had been done. HIE's emphasis was now on monitoring the expenditure of its money on bricks and mortar – a proper priority, but not one which could guarantee the delivery of the distinctive university which had been the underlying goal. In policy terms HIE's focus had also shifted, away from the economic and business benefits UHI was intended to produce and towards conformity with a skills development agenda which had little to do with higher education. As to accepting the structural changes proposed by the Board in 1998, senior staff in HIE would have had little difficulty in going along with proposals which seemed designed to meet the requirements of the Scottish Office (HIE's own paymasters) and were being championed by HIE's own Chairman.

The other leading supporter of UHI from the start had been the Highland Council. However, apart from the monitoring of their own contribution to capital funding, they had steadily lost access to and influence over the project. They had been among the dissenters when the new constitution was proposed, but had been persuaded that outright opposition would damage the chances of ever securing a university for the region. Thereafter, they were as much in the dark about real progress as was the rest of the community.

And what of the Millennium Commission? As recorded earlier, the factor which had swayed them in favour of grant aid on such a large scale had been the social and community objectives of the UHI Project. They had only consented to contribute to the funding of a university on the grounds that it was to be a different kind of university. Like HIE, they had a fundamental duty to ensure that their money was spent properly on the creation of physical assets, but they also required evidence of progress towards the real purpose of their grant. Did they consent willingly to the radical redefinition of the project in 1998, or did they too feel under the pressure of force majeure? It must be relevant that these were unhappy days for the Commission itself, with increasing criticism of the cost and quality of the Millennium Dome in London. The last thing they needed was a public row about the way forward for one of their largest Scottish projects. The instinct to back the judgement of the Board and the Scottish Office must have been very strong.

The final watchdog, once the Foundation had been ousted from its role as the guardian of the UHI vision, was of course the Board of Governors of UHI Ltd. They had succeeded in making themselves constitutionally self-governing. Their responsibility for progress towards the goal of a distinctive university for the region was now unchallenged. They were in no doubt what should be done and they entrusted the Chief Executive and the Executive Office with the power and resources to do it.

It was in these circumstances that the leading players – HIE and the Millennium Commission, the Board of Governors and the Executive Office – now made common cause to ensure that nothing should stand in the way of the achievement of designated status.

The Scottish Office Asks Questions

It is necessary at this stage to speculate on what was the overall attitude of the Scottish Office towards UHI, notwithstanding the successive pats on the head the project had received from Ministers. Walls have ears and one senior official was heard to refer to UHI as "that ramshackle outfit". As time ticked on towards July 1999, bringing the establishment of the Scottish Parliament and the Scottish Executive which would serve it, the perception grew that the new university in the north was no longer a good news story.

There were signs of an internal debate on how to turn it round. Some officials were clearly attracted towards full rationalisation, going beyond the current constitutional compromise and ensuring that the "liquorice allsorts" partnership of colleges and research establishments was knocked into one organisation, with one head who, in Treasury terminology, would be the Accounting Officer. Those with a continuing interest in further education (which was coming under the aegis of a new Funding Council) remained keen to preserve the distinctive role of the FE colleges in rural Scotland. They were hearing stories about the attitude of the Executive Office to its academic partners which gave cause for concern at any further centralisation of power.

The issue of designation brought elements of this debate into the open. In December 1998 the Board of UHI Ltd wrote formally to notify the Scottish Office of its intentions to proceed down the path of designation. The response, not delivered until April 1999, was quite unexpected in content.

It was contained in an official letter, addressed to a wide range of bodies with a potential interest in the designation of UHI as a higher education institution. Views were sought "on the principle of designation of UHI as an institution eligible for funding by the Scottish Higher Education Funding Council". This might have been interpreted as an essentially formal gesture, a courtesy in advance of action already decided. The issues highlighted in the letter told a different story. Some serious questions had to be answered before the Scottish Office would give its consent to what the Board of Governors wanted.

The letter made it clear that the Board's request raised complex policy and practical concerns. Designated status for UHI was a step into the world of higher education, yet the colleges which were to deliver its courses would remain for the most part within the further education sector. Both Funding Councils would therefore require to be satisfied with the arrangements and with the formal relationships they reflected. Above all else, SHEFC required to know that when the Executive Office and the Board of Governors spoke and acted on matters of higher education, they did so as the single and agreed voice of all the separate partners.

Although the constitutional changes pushed through by the Board in 1998 had been defended as necessary to satisfy the requirements of the Scottish Office and its associated bodies, the letter suggested that there were fundamental uncertainties among just those bodies about the whole approach. In particular, views were sought on the suitability of structural and governance arrangements, on the relations between and respective responsibilities of UHI and the colleges, on arrangements for on-going provision of further education and training by local colleges, and on whether funding arrangements under SHEFC would secure continuing financial stability for UHI and the colleges.

Engineering a Response

All this was most unwelcome to the Board of Governors and their supportive stakeholders. Instead of speeding the project on its way, the politicians seemed to have decided it was time to sit down and think again. Why this sudden change of attitude? Suspicion fell rapidly on disaffected members of the partnership, who might have been telling tales in Edinburgh behind the backs of those responsible for managing the project.

Given the potential for at least one – and perhaps more – of the colleges to respond to the Scottish Office questions in a distinctly unhelpful manner, the Board of Governors sought to rally support. The reply they looked for would be a ringing endorsement of the new constitution and of all the consequential provisions that flowed from it. An attempt seems to have been made to dissuade the colleges from delivering separate responses, relying instead on expressing their – necessarily positive – views through the Board of Governors. When it became clear that this tactic would not fly, other means of persuasion were employed.

The FE colleges in particular were vulnerable to pressure at one point – in their wallets. Inverness was not alone in facing major deficits. Although the UHI Executive Office could not influence the level of FE funding, once designation was achieved it would be able to pay the colleges for their HE students at the rate appropriate to bodies funded by SHEFC. This was significantly higher than the rate they had received hitherto. It was therefore not difficult to present those who might be inclined to reply unhelpfully to the Scottish Office consultation as standing between their partners and a pot of gold.

Answers and More Questions

Thirty or so organisations and individuals responded to the Scottish Office consultation paper and its questions. Since only one response was confidential, the rest would be lodged in the Scottish Office Library and, after a decent interval, the responses would be summarised in the attachment to a published report on the exercise.

Among the matters to be highlighted were the following, all too familiar to those who had been following the project's progress with concern:

- UHI was developing in a manner that conflicted with the original federal concept.
- Arrangements for governance, management and academic regulation within UHI increasingly resembled those of a traditional higher education institution, rather than a university on a new model.
- The governance arrangements were incompatible with the incorporation of the constituent FE colleges and contravened sound management principles by separating authority from responsibility.
- Established HNC/HND provision, on which the university's portfolio of degrees was intended to be founded, was being eroded in favour of incongruent and non-synchronous degree courses.

The overriding sense of the collected responses from within the partnership was that notwithstanding the decisive manner in which the Executive Office and the Board of Governors were implementing the new constitution, the issues raised in the earlier debates had not gone away. As for the responses of those outside the UHI fold, the mutterings of the established universities were predictably a reminder of how closely guarded is the privilege of awarding degrees.

All this must have served as an unpleasant reminder to the Board of Governors that they were not really in sole charge of the experiment after all. It was their first setback in an otherwise easy ride to the frontier. But they were determined to make a further attempt to suppress any internal voices which continued to sing out of tune. Once the digest of responses to the consultation had been issued by the Scottish Executive (under the title "Matters for Concern"), the Board proposed that they should send back a point-by-point commentary and rebuttal which would have to be endorsed by a specific declaration from every partner, calling at the same time for UHI's designation to be granted. In spite of rumblings – particularly from Inverness and Moray

Colleges – the prevailing mood among the colleges was that all should sign regardless and that is what, in the end, they did. But this changed nothing of substance, for the Scottish Executive still kept asking awkward questions rather than agreeing to designate UHI.

Another Stand-off

By the Spring of 2000 the new regime of Scottish Parliament and Scottish Executive was well established. Tertiary education – and hence the control of UHI's future – was the responsibility of the Enterprise and Lifelong Learning Department, whose political head was Henry McLeish, later to be elevated to First Minister. Some 15 months had passed since the Board of Governors had made their confident application for designation. There had been encouraging news on the academic front, where the QAA had concluded after their inspection that "UHI Project structures and processes have met the threshold requirements for designation as a higher education institution", but designation as such was still denied.

A letter to Sir Fraser Morrison in early April 2000 – supposedly confidential but widely leaked – made it clear that officials and Ministers had recently met to discuss the way forward, but it contained little of comfort. It took account of the response made by the Board to the issues raised in the previous year's consultation, but it was apparent that the Board had failed to lay the various concerns to rest. For the letter's main purpose was to enumerate the "remaining issues which stand in the way of designation", set out as "an unambiguous agenda of the action necessary, though, it may, as a result, look a little stark."

The matters raised listed were once more those referred to in the response to the previous year's consultation. They included contractual matters, 'ownership' of students and federal collegiality. There was also a new and sharper tone of rebuke about the ambiguity of UHI's nomenclature and the apparent implication of a university title yet to be won.

The overall position on designation therefore remained a stand-off, between those responsible for managing the UHI Project (who had chosen to make the achievement of designated status their benchmark for success) and those in the Scottish Executive with the power to confirm that what was being proposed to them was a credible institution of higher education.

CHAPTER 34

A Very Public Crisis

Stall Warnings

For some time the UHI Project had slipped out of public consciousness in the Highlands and Islands. In these circumstances, most people make the charitable assumption that all is going well and that those in charge are just quietly getting on with their jobs. But the echoes of the internal disputes and of the outcome of the consultation over designation continued to spread. Questions began to be asked about the pace of progress and the manner of management.

Official enquiries seemed to get nowhere. The press began talking to anyone who might know part of the story. While no-one who knew it all seemed willing to speak, two and two could be put together. It seemed to point to the hypothesis that, in spite of having redrawn the blueprint in important respects, the current team of artisans were having great trouble finishing the building. This prompted yet more questions, especially about relationships within the Executive Office and between the centre and its academic partners.

The immediate outcome was a closing of ranks between the Scottish Executive and the Board of Governors. It was one thing to expose the management to the concerns of Ministers and officials in private correspondence. It was quite another to see charges levelled in the open, often by political opponents of the Labour/Liberal Democrat coalition which now ran the devolved Scottish administration. With the row about the costly and unloved Millennium Dome escalating in London, there may well have been fears that unless the Scottish Executive was seen to rally to the support of UHI and its management, the Millennium Commission might pull the plug on a troublesome Scottish project instead. But the task was about to become much harder.

Into the Papers

Within the press, the role of leading investigator was being played by the Highland correspondent of a respected Scottish daily paper, *The Herald*. He had begun to recognise the strains within the staff of the Executive Office as an important factor in the story.

It was said that relationships inside the office, perhaps exacerbated by external criticism, were already at breaking point. A trickle of resignations had begun, some voluntary, some assisted. Unknown to the outside world, a small number of staff members had felt driven to use the almost forgotten "whistle blowing" clauses in the staff regulations of UHI Ltd, in order to register a protest against their treatment. No action seemed to follow. Frustrated and hurt, somebody must have concluded that the only way forward was to take their complaints outside.

On 10 June 2000 – a Saturday – there was a front-page spread in the *Herald*, headlined "Staff strife amid university bid". It told two stories. One concerned the setback to hopes of early designation for UHI, quoting the Scottish Executive as saying also that it would be "some years before the institution will meet the criteria for university title". The other was about the breakdown of relations within the UHI Executive Office, setting out staff allegations which accused the Chief Executive of "mismanagement, intimidation, oppressive, autocratic and divisive leadership, resulting in a serious breakdown of staff morale". These charges were elaborated in the text, but it was made clear that those levelling them were not prepared to be identified "because they have no faith in the authorities to protect them".

Salt will have been rubbed in the wound by the appearance in the same issue of the *Herald* of a commissioned article in their occasional essay series, written by Graham Hills. Under the title "The dream of a University of the Highlands and Islands seems to be fading" this essay reiterated the earlier concept of UHI, with a particular emphasis on the arguments for a collegiate federation, and made a plea for more open discussion of where UHI was now heading.

It was perhaps to be expected that the main emphasis of rebuttal from the Board of Governors was reserved for the comments by Graham Hills. In a special press release, issued two days later in the Board's name, it was implied that the *Herald* essay had been no more than the outpourings of a disaffected elderly antagonist, whose views were now overtaken by events and no longer relevant. About the charges of mismanagement and intimidation within the Executive Office far less was said.

However, allegations about the management of a major publicly funded project have a way of circling back to the political establishment. What had been printed in the *Herald* offered Members of the Scottish Parliament ammunition they could hardly ignore.

On 6 July, at its closing session of Summer 2000, the Scottish Parliament held a debate on the UHI Project. It had been initiated by a cross-party group, responding to the allegations of mismanagement and the delay in achieving designation. It demonstrated renewed and widespread political support for the concept and substance of UHI, but speakers also had much to criticise about the way it was apparently being implemented. This embarrassing episode was turned on its head by the concluding remarks of the Minister who, whilst thought to be sympathetic to the critics, found it necessary to defend the actions complained of. Notes were flying round the chamber and, miraculously, the condemnatory motion was turned into one of resounding praise. Politicians may have hoped the concerns which had triggered the debate had been buried there and then, but too much was now in the open.

The Landslide

Although the Board had not commented directly on the allegations about the running of the Executive Office, one further comment from a UHI source had been quoted by the *Herald* on 10 June – and this proved to be the small stone that launched a landslide. UHI's company secretary, Eric Gibson, had issued a statement in which he said that: "UHI has not received any complaints of this nature from any member of staff and does not respond to unsubstantiated anonymous allegations. It takes these matters very seriously and has in place formal procedures for staff grievances which were agreed with the UHI staff association as well as a public interest disclosure policy and procedure to address any concerns raised through due process. No-one has taken recourse to these arrangements."

When this statement was queried at a subsequent encounter between the press and the Chief Executive, it was once more denied in front of the journalists that any formal complaints had been made by the staff of the Executive Office. But by now the press had written evidence to the contrary and they concluded that an attempt had been made to mislead the public. They decided to pursue the issue further with UHI's Chairman.

There was now no way back. The Chairman sought to limit the damage by asking the much respected 'ombudsman' of Highlands and Islands Enterprise, Kenneth McKay, to look into the matter.

At a special meeting of the UHI Foundation on 23 August 2000, where the McKay report was read out in full, the resignation of the Chief Executive was announced. In an exchange of letters with his Chairman the previous day, Brian Duffield had recorded his fundamental disagreement both with the way the McKay enquiry had been carried out and with the findings of the report, but he had recognised that "to contest these matters in the present climate would do serious damage to the UHI project and its public credibility". His departure was presented as the premature enactment of plans he had discussed with the Chairman for the appointment of a Principal designate for UHI once designation was achieved.

CHAPTER 35

Picking Up the Pieces

New Leadership

The UHI Project could not afford a hiatus in control at such a critical moment in its history. The new figure on the bridge, announced simultaneously with Brian Duffield's departure, was familiar to many as a staunch supporter of UHI and a respected academic in his own right. Professor Alistair MacFarlane had played a valuable role behind the scenes since relocating to the Highlands after his retirement from running Heriot-Watt University. As Chairman of the UHI Academic Advisory Board and a member of the Academic Council he had been influential in helping to prepare the UHI network for the trials of academic quality assurance. His agreement to serve as interim Chief Executive was seen as a very public-spirited gesture – and one which was clearly designed to reassure all the funders and supporters of the project that it would soon be back on course.

However, Alistair MacFarlane was not one to dive into muddy waters. Although it was known that he had been highly critical in private of aspects of the previous management's approach, he drew a veil across such matters and never referred in public to the issues which had led to his predecessor's resignation. All his energy went into restoring the confidence of both the Scottish Executive and the academic partners that this was indeed an institution fit for designation.

Sir Fraser Morrison and the other Governors remained in office. Apart from Brian Duffield, all the senior staff of the Executive Office stayed at their posts. The only addition to the team was Ralph Palmer, newly retired from HIE, who was recruited by Alistair MacFarlane as Vice Chief Executive to look after the non-academic side of the house. However, Alistair MacFarlane quickly made a more than symbolic change in the relationship between the Executive Office and the colleges. He established a new Executive Board, comprising all the principals and directors of the academic partners, to work with him in the implementation of his new plans and to participate directly in the management of the UHI venture. This inclusiveness won him valuable support at a critical moment.

Designation at Last

On 1 April 2001, exactly two years after the Scottish Office had launched its fateful consultation exercise, designation as a Higher Education Institution was formally declared by the Scottish Parliament. By now it almost seemed an anti-climax, though in reality it reflected a great deal of effort by Alistair MacFarlane and the academic partners to demonstrate that the collective commitment to quality higher education was now soundly based and underpinned with appropriate agreements and structures.

With the new status came a change of name – to the UHI Millennium Institute. Few saw this as a good choice. It was clumsy to say, even in abbreviation (as UHIMI). Only a year after the actual event, the word "millennium" already felt tired and dated, with uncomfortable overtones of hype. The new name was probably an attempt to shut up those in and around the Scottish Executive who had continued to object to the implication that UHI was the title of a university. This was a period of costly and unpopular changes of name in the corporate world, where the Post Office was being converted to Consignia, so the university project was in good – or bad – company. In the event, of course, everyone went on calling it UHI anyway.

And with the new name, inevitably, came a new logo. Not very new, and still recognisable in shape, but with colours changed from imperial gold and purple to a striking red. There was also a subtle change in the strap-line – from "Working towards the University of the Highlands and Islands" to "Creating the University of the Highlands and Islands". Of such things are marketing careers made.

An Extended Transition

Alistair MacFarlane's leadership had been intended as a brief interim phase. It heralded a steady outflow of staff from the Executive Office. Some had been closely identified with the previous Chief Executive. Others were seeking career moves elsewhere, like Patrick Dark who left the ICT hot seat to take an MBA at Cambridge. Although key senior posts – like the ICT one – were filled promptly, others were left vacant for the new Chief Executive to select. But finding the right substantive leader for the next phase of development was not proving easy.

It was to be another six months beyond the declaration of designation – October 2001 – before the new Director and Chief Executive (the full title of the post) took the helm. Professor Robert Cormack had previously spent many years at Queen's University in Belfast, but he had strong Scottish roots. His manner was calm but firm. He quickly went out of his way to build good relationships with the college principals and the heads of the other partner institutions. He seemed to have a clear idea of where UHI should be going and how it should get there, but he also showed a welcome readiness to listen.

In parallel, the Board of Governors gained a new Chairman. Sir Fraser Morrison resigned and was replaced by Colin MacKay, immediate past president of the Royal College of Physicians and Surgeons of Glasgow.

To complete the changes at the top, Alistair MacFarlane was persuaded not to break completely with the project to which he had already given so much. The UHI Foundation elected him as their Rector, replacing Donnie Munro (of Runrig fame) who had borne much of the stresses of the previous three years in a difficult and exposed role between the Foundation and the Board of Governors.

Alistair MacFarlane's knighthood, announced in the New Year's Honours List in January 2002, was warmly and widely welcomed. It was seen as the very proper recognition both of his own academic career and of the way he had coped with the heavy burden of picking up the pieces and achieving designation for UHI.

The Shattock Report

The new leadership inherited a commitment to review the constitution of UHI once designation had been achieved. There had been no early rush to return to this contentious territory, but in December 2001 Professor Bob Cormack took the bull by the horns. He commissioned a review of the management and governance of UHI from another of the UK's small number of experts in the field – this time Professor Michael Shattock, who had acquired a notable reputation within the higher education sector as Registrar of the University of Warwick, one of the most prominent research universities launched by the Robbins reforms of the 1960s.

Michael Shattock discussed aspects of the project and its governance with a wide range of contacts. He also visited the UHI Executive Office and three of the college campuses in March 2002. His report was delivered soon afterwards, in late April 2002. He was frank about the problems his discussions had revealed:

- That UHI was not a day-to-day priority for many of the partner colleges.
- That there was continuing resentment among the colleges against any sense of domination by the UHI Executive Office.
- That the current governance arrangements were not felt to reflect an appropriate balance of power among the partners.
- That only half of the staff questioned were confident of UHI's future, while less than half had confidence in the UHI organisation.
- That the powers of the Deans (supposedly responsible for UHI's Faculties) were in practice dependent on the hierarchies of the colleges in which they resided.
- That problems were more marked in the larger colleges than in the smaller (mostly island-based) colleges.
- That tensions had been heightened by the pressures of financial stringency and the vertical structures of the traditional FE college.
- That unless clear progress could be seen towards the goal of university status for UHI, there would be an increasing risk of colleges pursuing individual institutional goals at the expense of the success of the UHI project.

Shattock concluded that the first step back from this potential road to disaster should be "a reinforcement of the central ideas which made the UHI such an innovative development" – and in particular a return to the primacy of the regional economic development objectives for which the project had been launched. The second step should be to rebuild a sense of corporate responsibility for the future of UHI. This would mean taking practical steps in administration and governance, designed to eliminate the sense of "them" and "us" which he had detected among the partner colleges. At the same time, he made it clear that this was not to be a one-sided deal. He had concluded that the current constitution was unbalanced, binding UHI more closely than the individual partners, and in that sense inadequate both for accountability purposes and as a spur to close collaboration. He also endorsed strongly the concept that the core of UHI had to act as an active energiser of new activities for the whole partnership, rather than a passive servant of the short term interests of the colleges.

The detailed constitutional and governance recommendations of the Shattock report need not be spelt out at this stage in the narrative of UHI. What was most significant was Michael Shattock's renewed endorsement of the broad but radical principles which had guided the project in its early days and which had been in danger of vanishing from sight. Above all, he affirmed that UHI had to be different, no longer in thrall to some model of higher education designed for other times and circumstances. His bold conclusion was that "UHI should take every step to distance itself from the established Scottish and UK university model and emphasise its comparability with university institutions that have been created in economically peripheral areas in other parts of Northern Europe." UHI, it seemed, was at long last coming home.

The New Strategic Plan

This sense of a fresh start on the old road was reinforced by the publication of a revised Strategic Plan for UHI in August 2002, covering the period to 2006. In some respects it read as a cautious assessment of prospects, setting the aim of achieving university status a further five years away, in 2007 – that is, fifteen years after the delivery of the Hills report, rather than the nine or ten years originally hoped. However, this estimate was based on a sober and logical working through of the necessary (or at least conventionally necessary) steps towards proven academic quality within the QAA system.

But in other ways the new Strategic Plan was a bold defence of UHI as "a unique institution". It took up Michael Shattock's theme of strength through distinctiveness and set out a rallying cry for UHI's supporters which many had longed to hear again:

> UHI does not fit the traditional model of a higher education institution – and it is unlikely to do so in the future. We have the opportunity to create an institution that will not only be a credit to the region, but to Scotland and the United Kingdom. An institution that will provide an important and influential model to the world-wide further and higher education communities. The challenge to our supporters, funders and regulators is to assist us in achieving our potential.

Through this document, UHI could once more be recognised as an outward-looking institution, conscious and proud both of its challenging regional mission and of its ability to offer "distinctive education and research opportunities for local, national and international students in the magnificent settings of the campuses of the UHI Academic Partners".

Two Fellowships and a Lecture

Another of Michael Shattock's astute observations had concerned UHI's low – practically invisible – profile within its own community. As he put it: "If UHI is to achieve its objectives it needs to project itself much more effectively within the Highlands and to recapture the momentum it once had."

In line with this advice, an important opportunity to re-engage with the wider Highland community was created soon after the publication of the Strategic Plan, when UHI announced plans for an inaugural Annual Lecture on 6 September 2002, coupled with the award of the first UHI Honorary Fellowships. The event was originally planned for the Town House in Inverness, a relatively small venue, but with the well-known film-maker and educationalist Lord (David) Puttnam secured to deliver the Inaugural Lecture the decision was taken to book the far larger Eden Court Theatre. This was a gamble which paid off well, allowing large numbers of UHI's loyal supporters to join staff and students in an occasion with a distinctly celebratory tone.

The celebration was at two levels. First came a formal recognition of what two key personalities had achieved for UHI. The inaugural Honorary Fellowships were awarded to Graham Hills, as the founding father of the UHI concept, and to the Earl of Dalkeith, Scottish Millennium Commissioner, as the crucial enabler of its conversion into reality. The combination seemed ideally chosen and the tributes to the new Fellows were warmly received.

Next came the celebration of UHI itself, both in the reflective introductory contribution from Bob Cormack, in his most public appearance yet as the new face of the new university, and in Lord Puttnam's lecture, which lived up to its advance billing in every respect.

In a range of well-presented observations on the changing nature of education and on its central role in public policy, Lord Puttnam returned repeatedly to two imperatives for the future – the need to embrace new technology, so as to liberate learning from the burdens of past educational systems, and the need to use learning to strengthen both the economic and the social roots of the nation. In this supposedly peripheral corner of the UK, he said, the supporters and enablers of UHI had already spent ten years implementing a regional vision based on these two fundamental principles and now they were beginning to show the rest of the world how it should be done. This endorsement, from a declared supporter of New Labour, did much to reinforce the impression that the project was once more receiving the political attention it deserved.

Accelerated Progress

If UHI's own new Strategic Plan sounded conservative in assuming university title would not be secured until 2007, it seemed there were still those in positions of authority for whom no delay could be too long. The problem, it appeared, was with officials rather than Ministers, as it had been since the earliest days.

Somewhere in the system there remained a rooted objection to the establishment of a new university in Scotland – and especially to one which might be different from the norm. Whenever Ministers gave time to UHI and reiterated their support for it, the whisperings would cease for a while, only to start again once the politicians had turned back to other preoccupations. By October 2002 the only ploy left to the whisperers – but a dangerous one for UHI – was to put it about that realism would dictate a further twelve years in academic purgatory.

In 1996 Michael Forsyth had used a meeting of the Scottish Grand Committee to announce his support for the UHI Project, to the astonishment of his officials. Six years later, the slightly less grand platform of the Convention of the Highlands and Islands was being offered to Ministers for a further public endorsement of the new university – but what would they say this time?

The Convention – originally launched, ironically, as another Michael Forsyth initiative – was a twice yearly opportunity for Ministers to meet the convenors of local authorities, the heads of quangos and other representatives of the "great and good" from across the Highlands and Islands in order to give an airing to regional issues. Since devolution, this forum had also offered a means for Scotland's First Minister to demonstrate his personal concern for events outside the Central Belt. Prominent on the agenda for the meeting of the Convention to be held in Oban on 28 October 2002 was the future of UHI. The supportive attitude of local interests, led by HIE, was in no doubt. What was less certain was the line to be adopted in such a public setting by the Scottish Executive. The heavy guns had confirmed their attendance – including Scotland's First Minister, now Jack McConnell – but would the tone of their briefing succeed in muffling them? There was some tension in the UHI camp as the day of the Convention approached.

In the event it became clear that sound political instincts had once more won the day. UHI was reinstated, in the First Minister's own words, as "a flagship ambition for Scotland" and as a symbol of the importance of the Highlands and Islands not just in Scotland but across Europe. Ministers announced the establishment of a specialist task force, headed by SHEFC, whose role would be to deliver, within six months, a plan for the "accelerated progression" of UHI towards degree-awarding powers and university status.

Although there was some ambiguity whether the acceleration was to be merely from the whisperers' twelve years of purgatory to five, or whether it might now be possible by political pressure to achieve UHI's own plans earlier than 2007, the Scottish Executive's commitment and enthusiasm for a new university in Scotland was once more made unambiguous.

As the First Minister said: "I want to see a University of the Highlands and Islands – and I want to see it as soon as possible."

CHAPTER 36

Into the Second Decade

Although UHI is still en route to gaining full university status as we write, the commitment of all the key players to complete the job – and to do it properly – remains just as strong in 2003 as it was ten years earlier. It is therefore fitting to conclude the narrative part of this book with a short overview of UHI as it enters its second decade.

UHI in Action

In the academic year 2001/02 UHI had 5,610 higher education students on its books, representing just over 3,500 full time equivalents (FTE). While the majority were on sub-degree courses (HNC or HND), around 1,000 of the students were taking undergraduate degree courses, of which 24 were then on offer. A further 42 students were on taught post-graduate courses and there were in addition 30 research students. A total of 212 UHI students graduated with degrees at the end of 2001/02, thanks to the support and endorsement of the OU Validation Service. This was an increase of 27% on the previous year. UHI's first PhD was completed in December 2002 – appropriately enough at the North Atlantic Fisheries College in Shetland.

Even without degree-giving powers and university title, UHI is therefore already serving its region as a significant provider of higher education. While these results can be taken to vindicate the policy of building on the foundation of existing colleges, rather than creating a new institution entirely from scratch, they also represent a major success story for UHI itself, which has developed a coherent higher education curriculum for a region which had only scattered pockets of provision a decade earlier.

At another level, however, the figures for student numbers confirm the extent to which actual performance has lagged behind initial aspirations. Back in 1993 it seemed realistic to expect to meet the numerical targets then governing the award of university title within ten years. The key targets were to have at least 4,000 FTE higher education students, of whom at least 3,000 would be enrolled on degree courses. While UHI has now come close to the first of these, the number of students on degree courses remains significantly below the original target. How far this has been the effect of constrained resources, course design, market factors or the wider economic state of the region is unclear – and it would be unprofitable to probe further now. Perhaps the early aspirations were themselves lacking in realism.

In any case, UHI's real objective has always concerned people, not just numbers of students or courses. Through its ability to offer local provision and a flexible approach to learning through its partnership of 15 colleges and research institutes, each with their own local or specialist markets, the new institution has brought real benefit to the lives of its students across the Highlands and Islands. UHI's ICT networks and a range of local learning centres (some 50 in all) have been used, as was planned, to take the learning where it is needed. This flexible provision is reflected in the high proportion (61%) of UHI students over the age of 25 and in the almost exact balance between full-time and part-time study across the student body.

Distinctiveness and Quality

By 2002 UHI had also taken great strides towards that distinctiveness in its curriculum which had been a fundamental objective from the earliest days. While maintaining the strength it had inherited in subjects such as Gaelic (for which Sabhal Mòr Ostaig won a Queen's Anniversary Prize in November 2002), it had also acquired or developed a teaching and research capability in entirely new areas, such as Mountain Studies, Archaeology and Agronomy – and was even able to offer a BA in Golf Studies.

UHI's continuing mission to support the regional economy is typified by a recent initiative (led by North Highland College) to build on the opportunities presented by the run-down of nuclear activities at UKAEA Dounreay, through the establishment of a Decommissioning and Environmental Remediation Institute in Caithness. Elsewhere, UHI was active in plans to establish an Institute for Social and Public Policy for the Highlands and Islands. It has also given strong backing to community proposals for a Shetland Study Centre in Unst, Britain's most northerly island. Steps have also been taken to improve the process of transferring the benefits of UHI research into the local economy, by the appointment of a Research and Commercialisation Manager.

At the same time – and especially once UHI was under the scrutiny of the Scottish Executive's task force – the need to demonstrate appropriate levels of academic quality continued to occupy much of the time of senior management. During 2002 and the first half of 2003 the Quality Assurance Agency for Higher Education (QAA) were regular visitors both to Inverness and to individual colleges, undertaking formal reviews of academic standards in specific subjects and also appraising UHI as an institution.

The results of the QAA audits were most encouraging. The first seven subject reviews to be completed, ranging from Engineering to Theology, all provided confidence in academic standards and most gave "commendable" ratings for teaching and learning and for student progression. The FE tradition of student-centred learning, which was always intended to be a founding principle for UHI, could be seen in this way to be contributing directly to effectiveness in higher education.

The QAA's institutional review of UHI took place during March 2003. This was a particularly rigorous exercise, carried out over seven days and based on boxes of documentation which took up a full 20 metres of wall space. It was originally designed to assess the progress made since the earlier QAA review, which preceded UHI's designation as a Higher Education Institution, though it was now also to provide evidence for the SHEFC task force considering how to accelerate progress towards university status. While recommending a number of points for further attention (without which no quality audit would be complete), the review confirmed the considerable further progress made by UHI and concluded on a very positive note:

> UHI has made a considerable achievement in developing and sustaining a model of higher education provision which is providing learning and research opportunities for the communities in the areas it serves. Of particular note is the tremendous willingness and commitment from both staff and students to make this model a success.

By now, the management of UHI was hardly recognisable to those who had watched the unfolding of the crisis two or three years earlier. In addition to Bob Cormack (now formally designated as Principal of UHIMI) there were new faces in all the senior Executive Office posts, bringing with them to UHI substantial experience from the higher education sector elsewhere. Across the Executive Office some 30% of the staff had been appointed since mid-2001.

New managers with university experience were also filling the top posts in key colleges. Increasingly, this higher education institution was demonstrating the characteristics of a university – including a significant capability in research.

Having submitted a bid to the UK 2001 Research Assessment Exercise (RAE), generally seen as the preserve of well-established research universities, UHI was very proud to achieve a Grade 4 award for Environmental Sciences – the joint highest grade for that subject achieved in Scotland and the fifth highest in the UK as a whole. In February 2003 a further endorsement of UHI's progress in research was given by SHEFC, through a £700,000 grant towards research facilities.

Quietly and behind the scenes, a fresh strategic relationship had also been negotiated with HIE – itself under new management yet still recognising UHI as the single most important project in its portfolio. Towards the end of 2002 this led to the commitment of a further £800,000 by HIE to assist the progress towards university status.

Moving On

The prospect of a move from the "temporary" accommodation in Caledonia House was a further positive development for UHI as it entered its second decade. One vision for the longer term, often discussed but never acted on, had been to find a site for the university's central offices somewhere along the River Ness, one of the most attractive areas of the newly designated city of Inverness and already the location for the regional theatre and the cathedral. Thanks to further changes in the property needs of the Health Service in Inverness, the early 19th century Royal Northern Infirmary (RNI) became available for alternative uses in 2002 – in just the right place (with an elegant frontage on the River Ness) and at just the right time for UHI (when the Millennium Commission was seeking bids for a final distribution of its funds).

Designs for the conversion of the RNI as the new home for the UHI Executive Office, together with meeting and training facilities, were given formal planning permission in April 2003. In July 2003 it was confirmed that the project had secured Millennium Commission funding of £1.75 million, towards an estimated total cost of £3.5 million and that it was hoped to complete the move to the RNI by June of 2004. There was some quiet pleasure that this additional allocation from the Millennium Fund, together with £650,000 for a project at Perth College, confirmed UHI as the recipient of the largest amount of Millennium Commission funds in Scotland, overtaking the Falkirk Wheel.

And Then

There is never an ideal point at which to leave a still unfolding story. In the case of the UHI Project, we finish our narrative at a time when Ministers have yet to receive the task force report on how to accelerate progress towards university status. Although there seem to be clear indications that university title will be granted "sooner rather than later", in line with the intentions of the Scottish Executive as restated after the May 2003 elections, the how and the when remain for later historians to describe.

We can be confident that the life and times of UHI will continue to be a tale worth telling.

PART XI

In Perspective

CHAPTER 37

Lessons for Higher Education

Our narrative ends in the summer of 2003, with the leaders of the UHI Project (having overseen a significant and rapid regeneration from the darkest days) now awaiting the recommendations of a Scottish Executive task force on how best to secure accelerated progress towards university status. This is therefore a suitable time to stand back and consider what lessons may be drawn from the UHI experience.

When we decided to write this book, one of our objectives was to offer guidance and advice to others who might find themselves planning or implementing an innovative project in higher education. In the early days of the UHI Project we had found it helpful to be able to refer to the experiences set down by academic pioneers in British Columbia, in Sweden and elsewhere – though as often as not they provided warnings rather than reassurance. We hoped we might be able to offer the same service to those who came after us. Arguably, the bumpy road followed by the UHI Project in the five years since we first planned to record its history has made it all the more important to try to identify and spell out lessons for similar projects. Since UHI itself – partly as a result of those tribulations – is still work in progress rather than a finished product, its current managers may also be expected to have a direct interest in learning from the past. We trust that what follows will be of some value to them too.

The Unresolved Issues

The foundation of UHI coincided with a number of other developments affecting higher education world-wide. It was thought, perhaps immodestly, that this small-scale project on the northern periphery of Europe might provide at least partial answers to some of the important questions which were being raised in universities across the UK and beyond.

For instance:

- Can the theories of the New Learning Paradigm, which emphasise 'Mode 2 learning', be implemented in practice in a working university?
- Does the intensive use of ICT in higher education offer scope for reducing revenue costs?
- Is it desirable and possible to create a 'seamless robe' between further and higher education?
- Can a collegiate federation of like interests, spread across a large area, work as effectively as a single institution?"

In the event, these questions remained largely unanswered within the UHI Project. As has been recorded earlier, external forces have tried repeatedly to rein the whole enterprise back to an essentially conventional model of higher education, leaving the more progressive initiatives in pedagogy and technology under-resourced and without a strong champion. In recent years there has also been no great appetite within the Executive Office for full consideration – let alone implementation – of radical approaches to governance which might have bridged the FE/HE divide and tested the virtues of federation.

Yet these unresolved issues remain fundamental to UHI's mission to become a distinctive and innovative institution, serving its region in a manner tailored to a specific cultural and geographical context. They are also crucial factors in the continuing debate on the future shape and direction of higher education – but ones which the existing universities have proved no less reluctant to tackle over the past five years or so. The opportunity therefore remains open for UHI to play a pioneering role for the whole sector, in the manner Michael Forsyth foresaw when he first put the weight of government behind the project.

Two recent developments suggest that both within UHI and more generally within Scottish higher education the need to face up to some of these fundamental issues cannot be delayed much longer.

In terms of the development and distribution of curricular material, the academic world is on the cusp of a major change. Shortly, extensive course materials will be openly available from the leading research universities. In September 2002 MIT went live with its Open CourseWare (OCW) initiative, having decided that the best business solution was to make its courses and materials available over the Internet for free. At the launch of this initiative the President of MIT admitted that free access was perhaps counter-intuitive in a market-driven world, but he made it clear that it was in tune with the values at the core of MIT and its faculty – that the advancement of knowledge comes through the free distribution of that knowledge.

In a world where universities face the incentive to be market-driven, to try to sell learning materials and to slap a copyright on every innovative idea, this was revolutionary thinking, yet there seems every likelihood that other major universities will follow MIT's lead. Those who are fleet of foot – as UHI plans to be – will then be ideally placed to access the best globally available material to incorporate in their courses.

The other recent development was of less global significance, but nevertheless of great importance to UHI. In a largely unheralded paragraph in a report on Lifelong Learning, published in February 2003, the Scottish Executive gave notice of its intention to merge the functions of the two Funding Councils currently responsible for tertiary education in Scotland. Although suitable caveats were entered about the need to preserve the distinctive traditions of further and higher education, the prospective legislation will clearly offer an opportunity – if the enabling vision is sufficiently robust – to break down one of the educational barriers which has so far prevented the full flowering of the UHI concept, allowing delivery of the full range of tertiary education through a single institution.

Yet with this opportunity for UHI will come a major challenge. Its current constitution keeps it at arm's length from the FE business of the colleges, which have defended this part of their independence steadfastly and engage with UHI only for the purposes of higher education. The tricky question of defining relationships within a federal structure surely cannot be dodged any longer – and the very fact that such a crucial aspect of the project remains to be tackled teaches a lesson in itself.

In higher education, even more than in most walks of life, it is always tempting for those in leadership roles to avoid the difficult dialogue with colleagues and academic partners about contentious or complex longer term issues, opting instead to spend the time on the *minutiae* of committee work. Within UHI the need for those at the centre to engage the partner colleges in continuous dialogue about such questions – however unwelcome to the listeners – was neglected for too long.

So the first lesson to be learned from this educational experiment is that it is always a mistake to leave aside fundamental issues in the hope they might resolve themselves. They will not.

The Central Role of Politics

Academics tend to believe that the business of higher education can only be understood and pursued by its own initiates. However, it became clear to the UHI Project team early on that the fate of the various schemes to found new kinds of universities in other parts of the world had been determined chiefly by external factors. If one consistent message emerged, it was that the establishment of new universities is essentially a political matter, often involving both local and national politicians. Without their blessing, little is possible. With it, all is possible.

The narrative of UHI confirms this central truth. The cold hand of the Scottish Office would have continued to hold the door shut on this educational upstart, denying it both resources and approval, had not a Secretary of State seen it as ground-breaking venture which should be encouraged to the full. Labour Ministers in the next administration recognised the project's political appeal just as clearly, though from a different perspective. Most recently, Scotland's First Minister has stepped in to seek to accelerate progress again. In the face of what seems to have been entrenched opposition among a small number of officials, local and national politicians have taken the lead in keeping the vision alive.

But the lesson to be drawn from this aspect of the story is not the passive message of "Never mind, the politicians will save you whatever happens." On the contrary, there are some stark examples from other countries of politicians conspiring instead to cut an infant university's throat. Even within Scotland, it may never be known outside a very small circle how close the UHI Project came at times to being abandoned by fundamentally sympathetic Ministers.

Instead, the lesson is that those undertaking any major innovation in higher education need to be constantly vigilant in maintaining informal, behind the scenes contact both with politicians (Ministers and local authority elected members alike) and with those who most closely advise them. In the earliest days of UHI, when the political prospects were unpromising, these contacts were well developed. The irony is that they seem to have been neglected following the grant award from the Millennium Commission, when all appeared to be going UHI's way. As a result, it proved all too easy for the new university, for a time at least, to be forced back towards a conventional course of development by those with non-elected power.

Leadership and Authority

At all stages of its development, UHI has been a difficult and complex project to lead. Difficult, because its mission was to be different at a time when pressures for conformity were growing – and if it was not different it was nothing. Complex, because it sought to bring together in a single enterprise a large number of independent institutions at different stages along the academic continuum from further education to nationally significant scientific research. Indeed, one of the comments made in defence of the embattled management in the days of crisis was that "they had been asked to perform Mission Impossible." So should those now planning new universities be advised to take a more conventional course, based on simpler partnerships, or can other lessons be drawn?

Of course, every organisation has its share of the faint-hearted who seek security in normality and convention, but they need to be challenged if doubts are to be overcome and progress made. It is the role of leaders to counteract negative thinking by selecting and supporting those not afraid to break or least bend the rules. Therefore in a radical project like UHI, the centre's role is to be the most dynamic critic of the *status quo*.

Leadership is not for sheep but for continual engaging of the partners with ever more promising and demanding options. This should have amounted to a continuous revalidation of the mission and the vision of UHI, often assisted by outsiders coming unprejudiced to the argument.

As the narrative account of UHI has revealed, once the Board and Executive Office allowed themselves to be shunted down a conventional development path, the emphasis of their function changed from leadership to control. To deliver what was now wanted from them, they had to try to show that they could manage the conforming response of the independent academic partners. This was the surest indication that the core of UHI was looking earnestly backwards rather than bravely forward. It was also just the wrong way to try to run something which aspired to become a university.

Universities are, by definition, bottom-up organisations. It is the singular skill of a vice-chancellor or chief executive to challenge the orchestra of different talents to greater and greater deeds without in the least bludgeoning it into conformity. The basis of these assertions is simple. Universities are Socratic by nature. Dissent is their life blood. No one worthwhile joins a university to be told what to do.

In universities, the leader leads not by authority but by intelligence and consent. As long as he or she is intellectually out in front, he or she will stay there. At a critical point in the project's development, the attitude of the UHI management had grown antithetical to these sentiments and could only breed a climate of subservience or resentment. The centre became introspective, as centres always do. Constant dialogue between the partners, which is the basis of all successful federations, was no longer a priority.

Ironically, the reason why the whole project almost came unstuck at that point was not so much because of an excess of power at the centre but rather because leading figures both inside the UHI partnership and in the Scottish Executive concluded that the central authority was patently leading nowhere. Much was learnt from that unhappy experience which has informed the fresh start now being made by the new management.

Some general lessons can be drawn readily –

- That leadership of a project built around educational institutions should follow the bottom-up principles of university management rather than the power structures of business.
- That in partnerships (and especially in federations) authority comes from respect and consent, not from the accumulation of power.
- That constitutions matter and that time spent getting them right is never wasted.

On some other issues of leadership and authority, it may be harder to draw firm conclusions at this stage in UHI's development. In particular, during its first decade would the UHI Project have fared better if it had been led by a professional project manager (not an advantage it could ever boast) or by the kind of top flight academic leader Sir Robert Cowan had envisaged? Even if there were a consensus on that question, we are not confident that it could necessarily be read across to another new university in another country. Perhaps the only conclusion here is that the choice of leader for such projects is the most important deter-minant of future success and that going the extra mile and asking the additional question before an appointment is made will always be worth the effort.

University Partners

The experience of successful projects elsewhere suggests that a new university will flourish best with the support of existing institutions. To this end, the Hills Report of 1992 envisaged that the existing bilateral academic partnerships between some of the colleges and Scottish universities would be maintained and possibly extended during the development of UHI. This idyllic situation proved impossible to achieve in practice. The "zero-sum" mentality, fed by the fashion for competition in higher education, stood in the way of negotiating a multi-lateral agreement with the existing universities – though it was attempted. On the other side of the fence, doubts about the commitment of individual colleges to UHI were exacerbated by the continuation of bilateral links outside the region. Even at the more technical level of collaboration, the possibility of vice chancellors participating in the work of UHI's Academic Council was seen as a threat rather than a blessing.

There can be little doubt that the absence of nurturing support from existing universities (a problem encountered well before the management changes of 1997) contributed to the slower progress of UHI towards the maturity and the quality standards required for degree-giving status. The notable exception from the charge sheet is the Open University. The OU was true to its spirit, never saw the new university as a competitor and turned out to be ever helpful and supportive. It was the natural port-of-call for UHI after the demise of the Council of National Academic Awards (CNAA) and in its role as a validating body it did all that it was asked to do and more. But by using the OU primarily in a validating role, UHI appears to have denied itself wider opportunities for a new institution dedicated to distance learning – at least for part of its mission – to build on the expertise of the national leader in the field and to undertake joint initiatives in the use of new techniques and technology. Given the warmth of the initial relationship, it would not have been a large step to ask the OU to do much more, so that its university experience, its university ethos and even its university staff could permeate the new institution.

But it had been another of the founding principles of the UHI vision that an exclusive relationship with any existing university would carry the danger of being forced to adopt the parent's model of higher education. For all its differences from the higher education norm, a relationship with the OU alone would arguably have carried a similar risk.

External relationships are part of the unfinished story of UHI and there are those who believe that temporary adoption by one of Scotland's existing universities may yet prove to be a route favoured by politicians seeking to boost the new university into independent orbit. For the present, however, the lessons we would draw for others from the experience of UHI are that:

- Two or more academic god-fathers are better for an infant university than just one, though they need to be chosen carefully for their complementarity.
- Such critical relationships should be negotiated before getting too far down the development road and preferably before large sums are committed in investment.

- As in so many situations, don't rely on the goodwill of individuals or institutions. Get it in writing!

Individual Academics

UHI was designed to capitalise on a new world of learning in which the ownership of the knowledge base no longer determined the capability of the institution. What should have been spelt out more clearly in the design phase was that the same factors made a new approach to the ownership of staff both possible and desirable. The signs were there from the earliest days, but not sufficiently understood. When word of the plans for UHI reached the press, many highly distinguished academics from all over the UK wrote to find out more and to offer their experience as and when it could be used. Most had either worked in the region earlier in their careers or were regular visitors to carry out research in their professional field.

At the time, the UHI concept was still so far from being a funded reality that job offers were out of the question and most of the contacts were allowed to go cold. Yet with more boldness on the part of the Project Office it would have been possible to recruit from those contacts – well in advance of the wider build-up of higher education expertise across the staff of the colleges – the nucleus of a corps of visiting lecturers and professors, available to run short courses or summer schools and to support the development of the new faculties. Some might have come to stay, but the main benefit would have been the establishment of a tradition that UHI welcomes the scholarship of all those committed to the region, without wanting to own it full-time. The lesson for those who come after is – when building up a new university, never turn down offers of help from supportive academics, but don't feel you need to translate them into permanent posts.

Finance

When the UHI Project was launched, the financial prospects for a new university were distinctly unpromising. Public sector resources were drying up everywhere in the UK and the squeeze on FE and HE continued throughout the 90s. It constrained bold thoughts, generosity and risk-taking. Without the grant from the Millennium Commission, UHI would have remained a twinkle in the eye. With the grant and the other funding it levered – and thanks to explicit political support from the Scottish Office – UHI was able to acquire not just a clutch of new buildings worthy of a university but also the core of the learning infrastructure it would require to deliver a broad curriculum across the region.

However, having bypassed the general constraints on funding in its development days, UHI now has to face the common problems of securing sufficient recurrent income to keep running – and to maintain its classy real estate. At a time when all UK universities are seeking to reduce their dependence on public funding, UHI has to look elsewhere too.

Some traditional routes are less immediately promising for a small regional institution, though they still have to be pursued with determination. Commercialisation of the in-house science base, through licence arrangements and spin-out companies, will be a gradual process if the volume of research is still fairly low and the reputation rests on a few points of excellence. Private sector donations are harder to secure in a region where the industrial base consists mostly of small firms.

From the beginning, it seemed that the most obvious source of external funding for UHI was the cohorts of overseas students accustomed to paying economic fees for their education. Provided the new university was prepared to meet their every reasonable request – including housing them in halls of residence of a standard which would allow the university to compete for conferences outside term time – there was no limit to the additional income their presence could generate. This seemed the only way of raising surpluses for further investment, particularly in new staff. It was also a direct way of fulfilling the original vision of using higher education to augment the income, prosperity and confidence of the Highlands and Islands.

The reasons why this clear aim disappeared from the objectives of UHI at a critical juncture have been touched on in the course of the narrative and do not need to be elaborated here. They were linked to the development of an insecure, inward-looking philosophy within the management. New managers have now reinstated the priority to recruit from abroad and although valuable time has been lost there seems no reason to doubt its ultimate success, trading on the strong appeal of the "Highlands and Islands experience" to young people from across the world.

The last lesson to be passed on to others is therefore to base financial projections from the earliest days of a new university on the need to recruit fee-paying students from outside the UK, including the provision of courses and buildings designed for them.

CHAPTER 38

Lessons for Regional Policy

In parallel with its educational objectives, the UHI Project was designed to achieve a range of economic and social benefits for the whole of the Highlands and Islands region. It is now rare to find a new university project across the world that does not share some of these regional policy objectives. What lessons can the story of UHI so far provide for those engaged in regional development?

Achieving the Benefits

As recorded earlier (in Chapter 18), the economic arguments by which Highlands and Islands Enterprise justified its support for UHI were based chiefly on the additional employment which the new university was expected to generate over a period of years, both through its building programmes and through the staff recruitment it would need to undertake in order to deliver its higher education mission. By applying the multiplier effect, assumptions of direct employment were then converted into a forecast of spending in the regional economy which – boosted further by the spending of students drawn into the region to follow UHI courses – would lead indirectly to further employment benefits. In addition, longer term but unquantified industrial benefits were expected to arise from the establishment of a high quality research base within the region and from the local availability of a "feedstock" of new graduates across a range of disciplines. From a regional perspective the social and community benefits were expected to be just as significant, ranging from a stimulus to cultural activities at the local level to an overall growth in self-confidence among the region's inhabitants.

In practice, however, the impact of the UHI Project on employment, economic development or social cohesion has so far lagged behind these original hopes and expectations, both regionally and at the local level. It is to be hoped that this is mainly a problem of timing, reflecting the fact that the number of additional staff – both academic and support staff – recruited by the colleges and by UHI itself is still well below the levels forecast in the Millennium bid. Similarly, although overall higher education student numbers continue to rise at the UHI colleges, all but a handful of them have been drawn from within the region. In turn, these shortfalls imply that additional spending in the region, through the multiplier effect, will also have fallen significantly below the original estimates.

But was it ever clear whose responsibility it was it to monitor progress towards these objectives and to sound the alarm if targets were being missed? While regional development was clearly the top priority for HIE in backing the UHI Project (as it was, in the broadest sense, for the Millennium Commission), for the colleges and the UHI Executive Office the perspective and priorities were understandably different. Economic aims were always acknowledged, but the chief preoccupation of management remained – and indeed remains – the pursuit of academic goals. Yet the way those goals were interpreted would also affect the economic outcome – for instance, through the policies adopted towards external recruitment of staff or the low priority accorded to attracting students from outside the region.

If the external monitoring of the project's progress was largely confined to the oversight of capital expenditure, as seems to have been the case, it is perhaps not surprising that the failure to meet wider aims was not picked up by HIE for some years. Here again, recent developments point to a deliberate realignment of UHI and HIE objectives, which should serve to bring these important aspects of the venture back on course. Yet the shortfall from original plans is not only apparent in the hard indicators such as employment. The social benefits of having a developing university within the region were intended to include a boost to culture, together with all the invigorating effect on local communities that a student population brings. Had UHI achieved that kind of impact by now, the chances of Inverness competing successfully in its recent bid for European Capital of Culture status would surely have been greatly increased.

The first lesson we would suggest other regions and nations might draw from this aspect of the UHI story is that those with the most direct interest in the economic and social benefits of a new university project should never assume that the academic managers will deliver the goods for them. Through monitoring and governance arrangements, mutually acceptable ways have to be found to ensure that the ends of regional development are achieved in parallel with educational objectives.

But this alone may imply too negative a role for regional development agencies. After all, they have a well developed expertise in using financial and other incentives to support their existing industries and to attract new ones. Yet they too rarely recognise education as an industry in its own right – indeed, one of the world's biggest growth industries.

HIE's consistent and generous financial support for the UHI Project does it great credit, but it is only comparatively recently that HIE and its network of Local Enterprise Companies have begun to adopt the perspective that this amounts to a long term investment in one of the key drivers of the new global economy.

A further lesson we would suggest to others would therefore be that regional planners should play their part in securing the desired economic objectives by treating a new university as a prime candidate for industrial investment, not just in the launch phase but through its successive stages of development.

The Community and the Driving Seat

It is in the nature of projects to create new regional universities that the initial driving force behind them is the community in which they are to be based. The origins of the UHI Project, as recorded earlier, owe a great deal to the sheer persistence of the region's local authorities in refusing to accept that a university was not for the likes of them. Their continued practical and moral support for UHI was a determining factor in persuading the Millennium Commission that the project met the criteria of being rooted in its community.

Yet there was always resistance to letting them edge too far on to the driving seat. HIE had traditionally been reluctant to allow the Highland Council too great a say in the running of any flag-ship project. In some quarters, elected councillors were considered incapable of taking a sufficiently business-like view and thus could not be entrusted with a major role in key decisions about the new university. At some of the colleges, memories of being kept on a tight rein by their local authority were still too vivid for comfort

Inhibitions about involving the wider community with the project appeared less marked. The establishment of the UHI Foundation, linked – by a process of nomination – to the governing body itself, was presented as a deliberate gesture to formalise that relationship. A more cynical conclusion might be that individual representatives of the community were thought less likely to be able to offer a coherent threat to the power structure.

In the event, both the Foundation and the local authorities found themselves largely disenfranchised by the constitutional changes of 1998. The deliberate reduction of community involvement with UHI, which became especially marked at that point in the project's development, had consequences which might have been foreseen and avoided. As noted elsewhere, the project virtually disappeared from the community's radar screens – the community in this case including young people, parents, teachers and local businesses, as well as representative bodies. When troubled times came and support (especially political support) was needed, it was hard to reactivate. Once more it is reassuring to report that positive and urgent moves are being made under the new management to re-engage with the community across the Highlands and Islands, though at the time of writing there is still no local authority representative on the UHI Board of Governors.

We would certainly not wish to argue that a complex and costly project like the establishment of a new university should be entrusted to local authority committees or to small community groups. Yet unless governance arrangements permit and encourage the wider community to maintain a real and appropriate influence over the direction in which such a project develops, it will be next to impossible to retain the essential popular commitment to it as "our university". Without that counter-balance it can be all too easy for those in charge to forget that what they are managing is indeed a project, an institution still in development, and that they are doing so in the name of their region.

From all of this two simple lessons might be drawn:

- That local politicians and community representatives should be treated as an essential and positive element of governance throughout the development of a new university.
- That constitutions matter and that time spent getting them right is never wasted (a lesson already proposed to the higher education sector).

Distinctiveness

Much of regional policy turns on trying to resolve the tension between a centralist pressure to conform or standardise and a regional belief in the virtues of distinctiveness and diversity. Those arguing the case for new regional universities encounter a special and potent version of this tension, where the standardising pressure comes from a higher education establishment certain of its own superiority and reluctant to admit newcomers who will not recognise or conform to it.

As a region, the Highlands and Islands of Scotland can only thrive by being "different but better". The UHI Project has always made fastest progress when it and its backers adopt the same formula. It is on this basis that UHI can plan to attract to the region students from other parts of the UK and fee-paying students from the rest of the world. So the lessons which other regions might wish to consider are:

- That a new regional university is most likely to thrive if it reflects the distinctiveness and special qualities which already define its region.
- That these are also the characteristics which will give it a competitive edge in seeking to attract students from beyond its own boundaries.
- That making a reality of the vision for a new university will require no less tenacity than the political defence of the region against centralism.
- That no region confident of its own strengths should make do with a second-best university.

PART XII
Afterword

CHAPTER 39

Universities in the Future

This book has concentrated on describing and reflecting on the efforts to found a specific university for the Highlands and Islands of Scotland. It did so against a background of universities in general, old and new, well aware that universities world-wide were under pressure to change, reform, economise and grow. This made the project all the more interesting because whilst this ferment was throwing up all kinds of new ideas that might be incorporated into UHI, it was likely that the inertial response from the existing universities would still be formidable. Universities are, by and large, ancient institutions with deep-seated traditions, most of them hostile to change. Nothing is so resistant to novelty as a university senate, the members of which are elected on the basis of being masters of the art of defending the *status quo*.

The Hills Report of June 1992, which provided the launch-pad for UHI, was written in full knowledge of this institutional inertia, tempered with the hope that a new foundation, blessed with technology and nurtured by its community, would succeed in overcoming the forces of conservatism. A decade later, it is possible to see more clearly that the essential ground on which to challenge the deep-seated traditions of higher education is a new understanding of the nature of knowledge, scholarship and learning.

Reference has been made earlier (Chapter 10) to the important theories set out in 1994 in the book *The New Production of Knowledge*, which distinguished between the universities' traditional preoccupation with codified knowledge (called Mode 1 by the authors) and the potential benefits of the more contextualised and more skills-based knowledge which they called Mode 2. The book implied that the old authoritarian world of Mode 1 scholarship would and should give way inexorably to the more relaxed approach of Mode

2, which would utilise information technology to the full and emphasise personal skills.

It is now possible to set this insight into the wider framework of global developments in higher education and to speculate on what the future may hold for scholarship and for universities in general. To complement and balance Graham Hills' original report (at Appendix 1), he has therefore used this theme as the basis for an essay which appears as Appendix 2 to this book, under the title "The Future of Universities in a Global Context".

The Future for UHI

But to tie this work once more back to the particular, in the years ahead when UHI has attained its university title how might it seize the opportunities offered by a new understanding of higher learning?

Against the backdrop of thousands of big universities set in their ways and with cohorts of academics whose professional lifestyles are largely Mode 1, it might be hard to identify such a small new recruit to the ranks of the great and the good. But change has to start somewhere and UHI might yet be a pathfinder. None of the experience of the past ten years suggests that the original vision was fundamentally flawed, though it is now possible to see more clearly how it might be refined.

In general terms this means that the new university should be avowedly Mode 2 in its thinking and in its behaviour. That accommodates almost immediately its cherished desire to fuse FE and HE into a continuum. Because it comes late, UHI can afford to build a new regime of tertiary education without destroying older established regimes. Because Mode 2 is general and open in concept, UHI does not require to own and manage large numbers of gifted academics as permanent fixtures. Rather it could decide to hire the best of brains as and when they are needed. This is surely the educational equivalent of Aesop's fable of the sparrow and the eagle. Furthermore, there is nothing expensive or unattainable in the customisation of the New Learning Paradigm for the Highlands and Islands. The mentors and tutors are already there, many of them in scattered communities where their professional skills are currently under-used.

The UHI of the future might therefore have two specific remits:

1) to create Mode 2 undergraduate schools likely to attract significant numbers of students from outwith the region; and
2) to identify a number of credible specialisms on which to build Mode 1 centres of expertise.

The likely subject areas of specialisation suggest themselves. They embrace subjects already flourishing in the Highlands & Islands even if their research outputs are as yet quite small. They include:

- the ecology and management of the environment
- estate management, forestry and agronomy.
- renewable energy systems.
- marine science and biotechnology.
- archaeology
- Celtic and Gaelic history and culture.
- eco-tourism and 'green' leisure industries.

The level of indigenous expertise need not be large. Modern methods of communication can be supplemented by study visits and sabbatical leave. The output of researches and postgraduate qualifications will be subject to normal requirements of quality. There is no need for the second best.

The subject areas of the undergraduate curriculum are not limited. They should be closely related to the global curriculum increasingly defined by the Bologna Declaration and in accord with the general studies advocated in the precious chapter. The standardisation of these curricula is wholly acceptable because, as we have seen, the contents of the knowledge bases are largely arbitrary and a matter of choice. The crucial factor determining whether the new university will attract its share of gifted students will be the intellectual climate it generates and excels in. This is the biggest challenge and will be met by ensuring a distinctive role for UHI.

That role has to be the creation of an educational experience second to none. It will owe something to PPE, the undergraduate course in politics, philosophy and economics which has made Oxford University famous. That, of course, was the brain-child of Alexander Lindsay, one-time Master of Balliol College and, as a Scot, a life-long advocate, as was noted earlier, of the general first degree, the elements of which he sought to inculcate into Keele University of which he was its first vice-chancellor. It would therefore be proper and rewarding for this kind of degree to be transplanted back from whence it came, even after a century or more 'on hold' in North America.

Moreover, because everywhere the educational content is now less important than the learning regime in which it is lovingly clothed, the first-order characteristic of the new university has to be the quality of teaching staff who see themselves as the dons of the future.

Their personalities and their knowledge and experience of the world outside academia will be as important as their academic specialisation. It will be essential to their success. They may be full-time or part-time. They may be occasional visitors. They will nevertheless be the trend-setters, the role models and the inspiration of the young. The success of UHI as a university depends on them and on nothing else.

Given this level of academic opportunity it is then a simple matter to complement it with a range of experiences of a distinctive kind designed primarily to enlarge the characters of the students. These experiences will be those appropriate to the Highlands and Islands. They are mountaineering, orienteering, sailing, husbandry, fishing, sports, art and music. A successful independent school – Gordonstoun – long ago built its reputation on these foundations. UHI would not be the first to pioneer this holistic form of higher education. Alverno College, Milwaukee, and Acadia University in Nova Scotia are already well established examples of new university colleges wedded to the ideals of a broad education and the development of the individual. Both are agreeably small and pleasantly situated. To walk out of Acadia University is to walk out of any of the colleges of UHI and into the Highlands.

To cap these New World developments, 2002 has seen the launch of an Old World initiative, taken on behalf of higher education in Scotland as a whole and designed to secure a better future for its universities. It is called simply "The Interactive University". It is an add-on, largely virtual supplement available to all institutions of higher education, centred on Heriot-Watt University and sponsored by Scottish Enterprise. It is part of a general movement towards e-education and offers, on a not-for-profit basis, help with "developing and supporting partnerships for delivery of accredited post-compulsory educational programmes". It is intended to underpin a parallel movement of fundamentally re-engineering education at all appropriate levels, making educational provision more flexible whilst at the same time raising standards. It offers in hard copy and software BA, BSc and MSc programmes as well as The Scholar Science Foundation Programme. It is already net-worked to 25 international partners in 15 countries. It is another big step towards the globalisation of HE and FE. It is over-the-counter and invitingly easy to use. UHI could well absorb what is on offer as part of its acceleration towards university status.

Conformity and Distinctiveness

If there is a sting in the tail, it is because the university world itself has not stood still during the unfolding of UHI. In less than a decade momentous events have surfaced to shake the character and confidence of universities in general. The explosive growth in undergraduate student numbers has propelled universities and colleges into the centre of national arguments for greater economy, increased utility and better technology. The universities' centuries-old independence from government has been further eroded.

Whereas once there was a respectful rivalry between the different kinds of universities, there is now intense competition. Inevitably this leads to antagonisms and, worse still, to conformity in values and uniformity in style. The consequential loss of diversity is an obstacle to evolution. Distinctiveness, once a blessing, can readily become a curse. The pressures on UHI to be conventional will continue to grow.

On the positive side, the rise in the comparative importance of skills *vis-à-vis* esoteric knowledge (Mode 2 *vis-à-vis* Mode 1) has led to the beginning of a merger between higher education and further education, as advocated by the UHI project from the start. The coming together of the separate funding councils in Scotland, as well as in England and Wales, is a good start, though creation of "the seamless robe between HE and FE" will take longer. Attitudes of mind are difficult to shift and none more so than in academia. Scotland's universities have already reacted with scandalised indignation to the floating of ideas for a common title for all tertiary institutions.

It has been rather arrogantly predicted in this book that UHI might well be a template for universities of the future. Some of these recent developments seem to confirm the prediction, though others could still undermine it. For those who launched and have nurtured this academic and social venture and now see the attainment of university status so close at hand, the priority must be for UHI to hold fast to its own distinctiveness through the turbulence of shifting policy. As long as the Highlands and Islands remains the distinctive, attractive region it undoubtedly is, this goal at least should be attainable.

It seems fitting to end on this note. A partnership of the local and the global seems the best recipe for all universities. By holding to its founding principles and adopting the best of new practice, UHI still has the opportunity to become truly a university of its region, yet with relevance for the rest of the world.

Appendix 1

University of the Highlands and Islands Project

Report to the Advisory Steering Group

Co-ordinated by Highland Regional Council
and Highlands and Islands Enterprise

Graham Hills, June 1992

1. *Executive summary*

A wide range of interests has been canvassed from which it is evident that there is considerable support for the systematic extension of higher education within the Highlands and Islands region. The cultural and economic value of further and higher education and of training is widely recognised and held to be a key factor in sustaining cultural values and in regenerating the economy.

The educational and financial climate is ripe for the further extension of higher education. Demand at all levels and ages is high and unlikely to diminish. The opportunity to create a new university is seen to be attractive, especially if the new university can embrace the most modern educational attitudes, procedures and technologies.

The model most favoured is that of a distributed network of independent colleges linked to a small administrative hub. The new university would then be a federal, collegiate university, not unlike Oxbridge, but in distance terms more like the much larger University of California.

Separate colleges of the university might exist in:

Argyll;
Elgin;
Fort William;
Inverness;
Orkney;
Shetland;
Skye;
Stornoway;
Thurso.

The word 'might' is used to emphasise that successful federations are invariably voluntary in nature. The separate further education colleges will soon enjoy a new form of independence under the Scottish Office Education Department. In becoming part of the new collegiate university, the separate colleges will want to be convinced that it is in their interest to do so. An early challenge to the new university will be to elicit their enthusiastic support.

The main authority of the new university, especially its central administrative and academic authority, would then derive from the collective will of the constituent university colleges, in the form of a committee or senate of their individual Principals.

The academic programmes of the new university will make great use of recent developments in educational practice, namely open learning, distance learning, modularisation, course credit transfer and course credit accumulation. The vehicle for much of the knowledge transfer will be the new Integrated Systems Data Network, ISDN. The quality of education and training can thereby be as high as we wish it to be. It would be a deliberate policy of the new university to blur the present distinction between education and training. It would therefore seek to provide courses offering coherent mixtures of vocational and non-vocational studies and at levels ranging from foundation studies to the honours degree.

In its steady state the new university could aspire to a student population of 5,000 full-time equivalent students, at least a half being part-time mature students, many from outwith the Highlands. The direct economic benefit of such a student population would annually be £20 million.

2. *The background to the new university*

The history of successive efforts to create a university institution in the Highlands goes back at least to the 1920's and is well documented. The attempt to be part of the Robbins expansion in the early 60's failed but narrowly so. The reinstating of the aspiration for a university presence in the Highlands and Islands, during this second surge in the growth of national higher education, would therefore be timely.

The reasons for a region and a community to become a centre for higher education have themselves widened during the 80's. An indigenous culture needs self-expression at the highest levels if it is to survive and prosper. At all times the tenor of local life has to be not too far out of step with that experienced worldwide, for example, as seen on television. Moreover, the looked-for level of intellectual and practical skills continues to rise. These skills are essential components of the modern economy whether it be rural or urban. Economic regeneration is therefore particularly dependent on the ready understanding and easy assimilation of new technologies, ranging from genetic engineering to software design. There is also a growing demand for education in its wider sense. It needs to be offered in a range of settings and in a range of communities from which students can acquire life-long attitudes and understandings. It might be thought that the Highlands and Islands have a special contribution to make to this new appreciation of the value of further and higher education.

The desire for a University of the Highlands and Islands led to concerted efforts to persuade the country at large and the educational authorities in particular that such a university was feasible. The 1960's, the 1970's, and the 1980's saw the publication of cogent and convincing analyses and proposals which nevertheless failed to reach that critical momentum required for any new project to take off. The present study, begun in Autumn 1991, is the latest and possibly the most advantageously placed in time and context to succeed.

Unlike previous studies, the present study produced a near unanimity of view that the new university should not be a replica of an existing traditional university, i.e. located at a single centre on a conventional campus. Rather, it should endeavour to take the form of a dispersed network of near-autonomous satellites, each reflecting local needs and local interests and each inputting into the network as well as receiving course components from it. The imminence of the new BT ISDN system was seen as a great opportunity to enhance the distance-learning modes of teaching and academic study. The now ready accceptance of flexible course structures and course contents, of credit transfer and of credit accumulation pointed towards a looser federation of interests that earlier would not have been possible or acceptable. The model of the new university that rapidly emerged from the discussions was seen to have the advantages of adaptability, of easy interactions with other universities and of economies of operation. As such, it might emerge not just as a new university of its time and circumstances but as a model of universities to come. This heroic view was not thought unrealistic but rather a natural expression of a community dedicated to excellence in education at all levels.

In discussion with the Principals of other universities and colleges in Scotland, there emerged an acceptance of the idea of a new institution of higher education more deliberately focussed towards the people and the interests of the Highlands and Islands. All were willing to enter into varying degrees of cooperation and collaboration. All accepted that the time would come when the developed colleges would collectively seek independent status, under the umbrella of the new university.

Several of the colleges involved, such as those at Inverness, Thurso and Elgin, already have formal links with existing universities. At least two have launched joint degree programmes so that the emergence of higher education (and the university label that goes with it) has already made its appearance in the Highlands. These links should be encouraged since they represent the natural, organic growth of existing institutions. They are the surest foundations on which the new university can build.

Two other connections with existing universities need to be highlighted, one already in being and the second still in embryo. The first is that with the Open University. This university already has an impressive presence in Scotland and especially in the Highlands and Islands which, it has observed, are its most fertile territory. Its pioneering experience with distance-learning procedures means that it will always have much to offer the new university, by way of available courses, the management of such courses and its willingness to validate courses and degrees offered under its aegis. The second connection, yet to be made, will be with a continental university, probably in France, such as to impart from the outset a proper European outlook to the new university. The range of inter-university connection at present envisaged is shown in **Appendix 1.3**.

The process of building on and building up existing colleges is recognised as being different from that employed in the 1960's when entirely new universities were created *ab initio*, often on green-field sites. In the particularly generous financial climate of those times, 'instant' universities were created over periods of five years or so, the ensuing 20 years then being given to building up student numbers and academic reputations. Some of those new universities have remained small but most have arrived at acceptable positions in the hierarchy of higher education. One or two have done exceptionally well and demonstrate what can be achieved with clear vision and firm purpose.

It could therefore be argued that it would be easier to start with a 'clean slate' than to carry the burden of existing organisations and their structures and attitudes. This option for the University of the Highlands and Islands was ruled out, if only on the basis of cost. In any case there is no evidence that the final outcome of other universities developed incrementally has been unduly affected by their sometimes modest origins. The transformation of existing arrangements will nevertheless remain a challenge to those responsible for creating the new university. As remarked earlier, what the present times lack in terms of financial resourcing, they more than make up for in the availability of new educational attitudes and possibilities.

3. The structure and operation of the new university

The model of the university will be that of a hub and spokes. The hub will be the administrative centre responsible for the conduct of the university as a corporate entity. As such it will seek to mediate and harmonise the activities of the separate university colleges, especially those of delivering distance-learning material in the most cost-effective way. It might also be the natural meeting place of trans-college departments, schools and faculties seeking the advantages of corporate size in sustaining smaller scale activities of the colleges themselves. The hub would speak for the university itself. It is nevertheless intended that it be small and determined to use its resources largely to further the aims and objectives of the separate colleges.

It is proposed that each of the separate colleges, irrespective of size, should offer a vertically integrated set of educational and training options as represented in **Appendix 1.4**. Each rung of this ladder of opportunity signifies courses and modules corresponding to the level of attainment of the certificates, diplomas or degrees denoted, largely irrespective of the route or time taken to arrive there. Each of the rungs of the ladder is therefore both a point of entry and a point of exit. They are also intended to be separated by the same degree of effort, roughly equivalent to one year's full-time study.

An ambitious school-leaver might expect to climb the ladder in 4 or 5 years. The in-service trainee, having been awarded a higher national diploma, might proceed to the first degree by the equivalent of one further year of full-time study. An adult with, say, an honours degree in philosophy might well step onto the ladder (again) at the HNC level in order to begin a course in public sector management. Entry to and exit from this gradation of steps would be unconstrained. Wherever possible, bridges would be built across to other ladders in other colleges or other universities. The transverse links between the colleges (as opposed to the administrative hub) will be pathways for sharing knowledge, skills, staff and students. Each will define a plane of horizontal integration and it is fortunate that modern methods information technology are able to handle any degree of complexity of the final matrix of relationships.

The course materials might be originated locally but many will be 'bought in' from the other colleges or from other universities. The idea of 'owning' a knowledge base is losing ground as the advantages of sharing it or leasing it become ever more obvious. It follows that the local provision of knowledge can be based on the best course materials available anywhere and often originated at the highest levels. As the Open University has shown, the quality of the information and knowledge transferred needs in no way to be inferior because it is delivered at a distance and from some other source. Across the whole range of vocational and non-vocational education and training the new university will be free to access immediately and efficiently the material it requires for educational, training and community purposes.

As noted earlier, during the period of debate about the new university, there has been a comprehensive reconsideration of thepurposes and practices of the training programmes of the United Kingdom. Training has been a late comer to the educational scene. Once seen as something inferior, desirable only when desperately needed and certainly beyond the pale of academic instruction, it is now seen as a vital component of the provision of skills of all kinds, from those software skills of the service sector of management, marketing, computation and design to corresponding hardware skills of the manufacturing sector, e.g. instrumentation, computing, technology and catering.

Given that knowledge only becomes useful when it is applied, then appropriate application skills are now seen as a valuable, some would say an essential adjunct to the knowledge itself. Skills awareness and skills training can therefore expect to become an integral part of most university degree programmes, as they have always been in the teaching of medicine, dentistry, law, music and other such non-academic pursuits.

Recognition from the outset that the once rigid divisions between education and training no longer serve a useful purpose might therefore be one of the principal statements of conceptual beliefs on which the new university is to be founded.

Another fundamental change in attitude likely to affect and to distinguish the new university is that concerning the basic approach to education itself. Although the thought of 'filling up' the student (as one might an empty vessel) would have been derided as a parody of what actually takes place, it is still not too far from the truth. Mass education of all kinds has invited a standardised industrial approach to what is a sensitive personal matter for individuals. New phrases such as 'student-centred learning' have therefore taken root as part of the rejection of the chalk-and-talk method of didactic teaching nevertheless still practised widely in schools and universities.

Given the availability of excellent learning and teaching material in the form of written texts (books and notes), audio-visual aids, video recordings of academic star performances and of on-line tutorial procedures, it seems sensible to. make full use of this range of material, as has the Open University in its study programmes for adults. Of course, such departures from the conventional ways of educating young students would need to be used carefully and monitored for their effectiveness. The transition from school to college and to university has not to be too abrupt or too demanding, although it looks likely that schools themselves will be encouraged to develop their own open-learning techniques.

Given the almost total accessibility of course materials at all levels, then it will be for the separate colleges to decide what particular courses leading to what particular qualifications they will want to offer. They will be guided by their strengths and inclinations and also by the perceived needs of their student customers, young and not-so-young, many of whom will have firm views on the matter.

The more specialist subjects will inevitably be based on local strengths and needs. Examples would be Gaelic studies, fishery technologies, forestry and rural environment studies. Most students, however, especially the younger ones, would benefit from coherent assemblies of enabling technologies leading to diplomas and degrees in the areas of Service Sector Management, Information Technology and Environmental Management. These latter degrees would be broad based and lead to an unclassified degree, equivalent to the American first degree or the older Scottish M.A. degree.

The range of possible courses is wide. A list of largely vocational courses offered under the SCOTVEC Advanced Course Development Programme is given in **Appendix 1.1**. It may be compared with what is at present on offer in the Highlands and Islands, as listed in **Appendix 1.2**. There is clearly much scope for further provision in the region even at this level. Beyond this level lies the more advanced work leading to first degrees, honours degrees and beyond. For the Highlands and Islands to reap the benefit of a comprehensive university presence a much wider range of options will need to be provided, many of them in conventional university subjects. This will be done in association with neighbouring universities in Scotland, with the Open University and with universities even further afield. There, are no limits to the range of subjects to be studied in this way, except where large laboratories and other special facilities are required. Here also, close collaboration with the other participating university colleges or with other universities will obviate the need to acquire extensive and expensive facilities to be used only sparingly by the new university. With these exceptions, the range of university subjects to be studied can be at least as wide as in other universities. Access to effective tutoring in these subjects will then be a crucial requirement for the hew university.

So far no mention has been made of research. In Britain, it *is a sine qua non* that, by definition, universities carry out research. The better the research, the better the university. Every member of the academic staff is expected, in his or her terms of appointment, to carry out fundamental research of one kind or another. It is said that the best researchers make the best teachers, although there is abundant anecdotal evidence that that is not so. In relation to this new university and in the context the emergence of tens of new universities, we must therefore ask the questions, "Do these criteria still apply?" and "Will the credibility of the new university depend on a substantial research effort?"

Given the rate of expansion of higher education, and within a tightly controlled national budget, it seems unlikely that all universities could or would want to insist that all staff in all departments carry out research. In the United States some of the most prestigious universities are Liberal Studies Universities which pretend to no graduate schools and therefore no significant research except by individual scholarship. This may become the pattern in Britain, as the only affordable basis for the establishment of mass higher education. It would be an entirely credible (and salutary) development if the new university were to see itself as a forerunner in the provision of university-level Liberal Studies in Britain.

Nevertheless, all institutions of higher education will want to foster research and scholarship whenever they can. In the new university, this is likely to take two forms (i) the bottom-up pursuit of scholarship and research developed out of existing interests and strengths at undergraduate and postgraduate levels and (ii) a top-down development of research including or embracing the efforts of existing research centres in the region.

There is certainly scope for sustained scholarship and research in the fields of human endeavour already prized in the Highland and Islands. These include the many aspects of rural communities, their histories, their languages, their attitudes and their industries. None of these are scaled-down versions of the larger interests of urban communities. At the same time, specific researches into the effectiveness and efficiency of rural industries such as fishing, agriculture and renewable energy resources are likely to be of universal significance.

In general terms, the students of the new university are likely to be of two kinds, (i) school leavers and (ii) adults seeking retraining, a first qualification or simply continuing education. The second category may predominate until the new university begins to attract large numbers of young undergraduates from ouiside the region.

Although the new university will oversee a large land mass, it will not seek territorial rights. Other colleges and universities will be free to operate in the High lands and Islands just as they do now. Indeed, in its open stance, the new university will seek partnerships wherever it can. In this context of relationships and comparisons with other universities it is important to reiterate that to make its mark upon the university scene in Britain, the new university must be unashamedly novel and confident in adopting the newer procedures of shared knowledge bases and open learning. From a practical viewpoint, it is only in this way that it could expect to be able to offer the wide range of looked-for courses and subjects in a thoroughly efficient and economic way. At the same time and in going down this path, it will be pioneering the emergence of this kind of university, heavily committed to open and distance-learning techniques whilst maintaining the closest interest in the individual student by effective tutorial and mentoring procedures. This will be its most distinctive feature, setting it apart from many other universities and therefore not inviting competition from them.

The educational bedrock of the new university will be the wide-band information network made possible by ISDN. All the separate colleges will be permanently linked together in real time and, via the hub, to all the other universities on the national and international networks. In this way, not only can the knowledge base be delivered efficiently but can be repackaged at will. Moreover, by means of permanent computer conferencing the colleges will be able to simulate much of the academic ethos and ambience of conventional higher education. Computer managed learning will emerge as an enabling factor for every student and will be the forerunner of interactive computer-assisted learning. Scotland is already well ahead in these areas and there is much for the new university to build on.

In this regard, and especially for its younger students, it will be going beyond the present scope (though not the aspirations) of the Open University. The follow-up procedures of digesting and consolidating the newly acquired knowledge will be at least of equal importance as the business of knowledge transfer. It will be in the face-to-face tutorial and mentoring sessions that the students will develop their understandings and the personal confidence and learning skills to last them a life-time. This is another major contribution the new university will make to the higher education scene in Britain.

If these two separate academic and vocational activities can be regarded as taking up two-thirds of the students' time, then the remaining third can be given to sport, recreation, music and other such extra-curricula, student-centred activities likely to bring out the best in the young. It might well be in this area that the Highlands and Islands can make their biggest contribution to the development of the University's students and especially so for those coming from outwith the region. In this regard, there is always a need for good quality, community-based residential accommodation. There is ample evidence that custom-built student residences can be provided on a self-financing basis. Their integration into existing, holiday accommodation would be an important matter for the smaller centres.

4. *The nature and status of the new university*

In operational terms, the ethos of the new university might therefore be defined in terms of the time and effort given by its students to the three separate kinds of activity outlined above, i.e. (1) the transfer of knowledge and skills which would progressively move onto a basis of open learning, (2) the enrichment and consolidation of the transferred knowledge and skills, involving extensive tutoring and mentoring of individual students, and (3) non-academic pursuits, such as sport, music, travel and community living. Each kind of activity would enjoy equivalent status or weight. Together they would provide a considerable foundation for the good citizenship looked for in all our people.

In what follows, the steady state of the new university is now described as it might be in the year 2000, having been launched in 1993 and formally inaugurated in 1998. The university will be based at six or seven locations:

Inverness;
Thurso;
Moray;
Sabhal Mòr Ostaig;
Lews Castle;
Kirkwall and Stromnes;
Lerwick and Scalloway;
Fort William and Argyll.

Each college will have one or more principal teaching centres, together with residential accommodation and other facilities. The scope of the facilities will depend on the nature and size of each college. The larger colleges will continue to grow and develop as any other higher education institution, with libraries, common rooms, lecture theatres and laboratories. The smaller colleges will have closer knit accommodation comprising seminar rooms, computer terminals and residential facilities on offer to the whole range of community activities. As noted above, all will be linked together on the ISDN network and to the hub. They will also be on-line to the worldwide data networks already available to all UK universities. In particular, they would be linked to the Open University and to neighbouring universities such as Aberdeen and Robert Gordon's.

4.1 *Programmes and courses*

The kinds of courses and students at the separate university colleges might be broken down into five categories.

1. Vocational and non-vocational foundation courses for school leavers or other new students. Largely full-time, they would normally progress to the level of the first, unclassified, degree but will often go further, to the honours degree and beyond.

2. Non-vocational courses for senior students, adults or returners, largely part-time and perhaps in association with the Open University or the Continuing Education Department of Aberdeen University.

3. Specialised full-time courses in the humanities, in the sciences or in technology, following on the foundation courses or in parallel with them.

4. *Ab initio* honours degree courses. The number of such subject areas to be offered is unlikely to be large. Some would be taken in association with other universities. Home-grown Honours courses might include Gaelic Language, Gaelic Studies, Rural Economy, Rural Communities Development, Environmental Studies, Archaeology, Tourism, and Leisure Management.

5. Courses based on the culture of the Highlands and Islands. Given the distinctive life style of the region, there is much to be said for making available experience of that life style as such or as a background to more formal studies, the combination of both being likely to attract many students from outwith the Highlands and Islands.

Students coming from Lowland Scotland or further afield to take the foundation degree courses described above would quickly appreciate the special environment of the Highlands and Islands. It might well be the reason for them choosing to study here. Clear evidence for this is to be had from Heriot-Watt University's experience at their postgraduate centre in Stromness. For students coming from distant countries, a substantial part of their educational experience in the Highlands and Islands might be that of appreciating its culture and its history, of coming close to the community, to crofting and fishing and to the open spaces. This could be a major feature of well organised summer schools, either in Community Studies or in Ecological, Environmental, Archaeological and other subjects likely to attract summer school undergraduate students.

The cultivation of this kind of student incomer will be an important aspect of the marketing of the new university. Given the beauty and distinctiveness of the Highlands and Islands, one must be optimistic about the ability of the new university to attract a wide range of students.

Many of the courses (full-time, part-time or summer school) will lead to qualifications ranging from certificates to degrees. Some will be informal and taken for personal satisfaction. The novelty of the proposals is that no attempt will be made to categorise or segregate the different levels of study or to separate those studying at different levels and those teaching at different levels. The same high standards of tuition, of provision and of accommodation would apply to all.

4.2 Staff

The staff of the new university will largely be those of the separate colleges. As these grow into their university college status and begin to give degree courses of their own, they will recruit lecturers and professors as circumstances dictate. Many of these staff will be subject specialists and offer academic leadership at the highest levels. This will be especially true of the larger centres at Inverness, Thurso and Elgin.

However, most of the subject specialisms will be supplied by part-time or visiting staff, recruited from other universities. The new university will differ sharply from others in deliberately not seeking to own its knowledge base but rather to use it or to lease it as required. In striving for excellence, the new university will seek to acquire the best academic leadership wherever it is available. In time it will acquire its own special brand of leadership but that will come later.

Instead, and again as a distinctive feature, it will wish to recruit another kind of gifted teacher, i.e. those imbued with the personal skills required for them to become outstanding tutors and mentors. These staff will be the backbone of the open learning system whereby students are encouraged to acquire the many professional skills they will need in their lives, not least the skills of learning readily and confidently. Trained staff of this kind are, as yet, uncommon and will need to be found or retrained. The new university will be recognised as being a pioneering institution in this burgeoning field of student-centred education and training.

A complex, distributed organisation of the kind envisaged will also need to be well managed. The sign of success will be the obviously reliable procedures for delivering excellent course material at the right time in the right place to a widely dispersed clientele. Information technology has a major part to play in ensuring efficient delivery of all material. The managers will need to be proficient in this area.

4.3 Finance

The resourcing of the new university will be based almost entirely on the income from student fees. Under the newly established funding regimes, the money follows the students. The resourcing of the university will be of two kinds, that required to create new colleges and to build up existing colleges, and that required to run them in their steady state. In previous times obtaining those resources would have been the major hurdle. Whilst, in general terms, the present financial climate is even less propitious, there are two factors in favour of the new university.

The first is that the government is committed to the expansion of further and higher education. Even the ambitious targets it has set itself will hardly match the performances of our competitors. There is, therefore, scope for growing all the existing colleges and the smaller centres with aspirations to become colleges.

The second factor is that-under the new Education Act, the funding of higher education, and almost certainly of further education, will be formula-driven and to a good approximation in direct proportion to student numbers. This means that the constituent colleges in their further education mode can expect to be funded at present levels by the Scottish Office Education Department or a Further Education Funding Council, if one should be formed. Accordingly their income will grow as they grow and develop. They will also be able to bid for capital developments in the usual way.

As the colleges increasingly enter the realms of higher education, they can also expect to be funded by the Scottish Office Education Department for their advanced work. If their students spend a year or more in a higher education college or university then the college of the incipient University of the Highlands and Islands may benefit indirectly from the Scottish Higher Education Funding Council in terms of the full-time equivalents generated in that sector. In brief, therefore, the basic cost of translating from further education status to higher education status will not fall on the new university itself.

Given the present financial outlook, it might be supposed that the transition of the individual colleges from further education status to that of higher education will be slow. Given also the number of new universities now coming into being, the transition might be thought to be less than certain. It will therefore be a principal role of the new university-in-embryo to ensure that the transition does take place and at an acceptable rate. From the beginning therefore it will be the job of the hub and its Project Task Force to promote and accelerate the growth of the colleges to university status, principally by raising additional support and funding on their behalf. The corporate leverage of the hub, acting on behalf of the whole region, has to be a significant factor in the winning of university status for the Highlands and Islands. Its constituent colleges will, we believe, wish to be partners in that endeavour. An outline of a possible implementation schedule is given in **Appendix 1.5.**

The expenditure entailed in establishing and running the Project Task Force at the hub will be the first cost to fall on the budget of the new university. The annual running costs are unlikely to be less than £250k. The Project Task Force will nevertheless more than earn its keep. It will be instrumental in accessing European Community funding much of which will continue to be directed towards the more distant and therefore less well placed members of the Community.

It may be that Highland Regional Council and Highlands and Islands Enterprise will wish to play a larger part in the process of enhancing the opportunities for education and training in the region They could raise investment capital for new buildings and new residences on the strength of the predicted income from increased numbers of students. For example, given that each student residential place will involve capital expenditure of not less than £10k per student place, then self-financing residences with a pay-back period of, say, twenty years, will need to be planned in association with local developers. The cost of creating new teaching accommodation and of enhancing existing accommodation may also have to be met by investment funding with the help, it is hoped, of the Scottish Office and the European Community. If the new university is to be created within a decade, then strenuous efforts will need to be made to raise capital for buildings and equipment over and above that to be expected from the Scottish Office Education Department and the funding councils.

In brief, the recurrent costs of staff, services, maintenance and depreciation of the new university in its steady state will eventually be met out of the normal further education or higher education funding councils. In other words, the full cost of the university will fall upon the 'fee income' of the students, at present provided by the government, and not on the region. However, the costs of accelerating the growth of the University will depend on the rate of that acceleration, i.e. on the ability to raise additional funds over and above those for maintaining the secretariat.

5. *The next steps*

If this more detailed description of the new university is accepted as satisfactory or at least as a sufficient basis on which to proceed further, then it is suggested that the following steps be taken with the aim of presenting a complete academic programme, a corresponding business plan and a five year implementation schedule by the summer of 1993 in time to inaugurate formally the framework of the new university. Discussions with the Scottish Office and the funding councils will need to be finalised by September 1993 so that the build-up of the corporate university can begin.

In the meantime four groups of people need to be constituted to oversee this continuing planning process and to begin the business of fund-raising and friend-raising If the present momentum is to be maintained, two of these groups need to be set up without delay, i.e. by this summer. These four groups are as follows.

5.1 *The Academic Advisory Committee*

This should consist of the Principals of each of the constituted colleges and two independent senior academics from outwith the region. It will be their task to see the university-in-embryo through to its fully chartered state. It should be chaired by an independent, part-time chairman, preferably a senior academic with wide experience of universities and their management, i.e. someone of the kind described in the brief for the academic consultant appointed to carry out the feasibility study. Two universities, Aberdeen and Napier, have offered to assist the new university during its formation period.

5.2 *The Project Task Force*

The Academic Advisory Committee would need to be served by a second group of people, namely the Project Task Force. This would consist of 3 to 5 experienced administrators closely associated with the idea of a new university. They might eventually be the nucleus of the hub of the new university but since their task is essentially for a five year period in the first instance it would be best if they were seconded from HIE and/or HRC, full-time or part-time, to ensure the continuity and refinement of the present arrangements.

The Project Task Force would be advised by the Chairman of the Academic Advisory Committee and the Chairman of the Advisory Steering Group to which this report is addressed.

5.3 *The New University Steering Group*

The existing Advisory Steering Group would therefore stay in being, augmented or otherwise, and constitute the third of the groups to oversee the launch and growth of the new university.

5.4 *The Group of Patrons*

The fourth group, to be created gradually and with some care, would be the patrons of the new university, being 'the great and the good' born in or attracted to the Highlands and Islands. Described earlier and light heartedly as a 'Supporters Club' it would have the immensely important task of 'crediting' the new university, of lending it some of their distinction until it could repay them with its own. This group of friends and supporters, perhaps one day to be the first Fellows of the new university, could be formed and activated towards the end of 1993 when the way ahead was clear and agreed.

As noted above, the costs of these first steps need not be large. Only the Project Task Force is likely to involve significant expenditure. The costs of the growing hub will also not be large because of the determination to keep it very small. The main costs will be those of the separate colleges and they will be met one way or another, by the Scottish Office Education Department, by the funding councils, aided and abetted by HIE, HRC, the Project Task Force and the patrons.

6. Conclusions

On the basis of widespread discussions amongst many interested parties, there is a strong belief that the new university is a feasible and inviting proposition. The time could hardly be more ripe for its foundation. With vision and determination it could carve out a niche for itself in the history books and be seen as a significant contributor to the regeneration of higher education as well as of the Highlands and Islands themselves.

There is a world-wide movement towards greater educational opportunity. In Britain, this is taking the form of seeking to fulfil the recommendations of the Robbins Report, one of which is that all UK citizens should enjoy the right to be educated to the limit of their ability. However, what was once an altruistic response to social needs has now become an economic imperative. A successful trading nation will increasingly rely on a skilled and educated work force. The demand for places in higher education from both school leavers and adults continues to grow, notwithstanding the demographic downturn. That downturn will, of course, soon be over and as the number of school leavers rises again, the demand will be commensurately greater.

The purpose of a University of the Highlands and Islands would be to bring the benefits of higher and further education directly to this particular part of Scotland rather than to offer it at arms length. An additional value of such a university would be that of strengthening the economic basis of the Highlands and Islands, and in so doing of reinforcing the culture, confidence and competence of the region. This is not simply an optimistic assertion. It is happening worldwide and not least in the emerging countries as all subscribe to the values of an educated liberal democracy.

In its final form, the University will have seven impressive campuses, differing widely in size and style. The larger centres will want to grow into high quality buildings and surroundings, lending substance and inspiration to their localities. The smaller centres will be content with smaller campuses, relying more on their surroundings than themselves to define what they have to offer. Each will need to be in character and some of the existing ugliness will have to go. Because the new university will be a late arrival it can be more modern than most, in its buildings as well as in its attitudes and its methodologies. It will certainly be a university of the twenty-first century.

The potential connections of the new university with the business community are as yet unformed. However, it is certain that the Local Enterprise Companies and their business constituencies will welcome more and better facilities for education and training. The separate colleges and their sophisticated terminals will be of at least as great a value to the trainers as to the educators. There is room therefore for effective and efficient collaboration between these two sectors. The general benefits to the local economies will be those of a livelier, more-in-touch and confident workforce, including the managers. Specific benefits will derive from groups and facilities dedicated to focussed improvements in performance in, say, agriculture, tourism and retailing. The further benefits from identifying and promoting specific business opportunities are likely to come from well informed people automatically connected to the proposed information and knowledge networks.

Corresponding improvements can be looked for in the public sector e.g. in administrative performance. Business skills allied to enabling technologies provide a powerful combination, stimulating to teach and satisfying to learn. They are the basis of the education of the new generalists and the new managers, as much at home in the private as in the public sector.

The arguments for the enhancement of educational opportunities in the Highlands and Islands therefore remains strong. The model and the vision presented here are not so different from those advanced in previous proposals. Indeed, the framework proposed here is almost identical with that argued in 1975. However, twenty years on, the implementation of those earlier proposals now looks much more feasible, if only because of the progress of technology and the liberalisation of educational thought. As also then foreseen, in its full flowering the new university will patronise and stimulate the life of the region, reaching into every cultural corner and the remotest glen and croft. It will make the region that much more satisfying to its inhabitants and that much more attractive to the inward investment of the resources to keep it so. It would be a further guarantee of the region's ability to control its own destiny.

That being said, it remains a fact that all new ideas and proposals eventually meet resistance from the other establishments who will see the new university as unnecessary or simply as a rival. The implementation of these proposals will therefore require vision, skills and determination of a high order. These qualities are undoubtedly on hand to see that the new university at last succeeds.

Appendix 1.1 SCOTVEC Advanced Courses Not Available

A representative selection of subjects from the Advanced Course Development Programme of SCOTVEC (1991) mostly not available in the Highlands and Islands.

Advertising, Marketing and Public Relations
Agriculture
Agriculture Science
Animal Technology
Applied Biological Sciences
Architectural Technology
Arts Administration
Arts Management
Biotechnology
Business Administration with Langauges
Business Administration with Tourism and Leisure
Business Information Systems
Communications
Community Broadcasting
Computing
Consumer Business Studies
Countryside Recreation and Conservation Management
Design for Printing
Drama and Theatre Skills
Environmental Sciences
Exhibition Management
Food Product Development
Food & Beverage Management
Food Science
Furniture Design
Graphic Design
Horticulture
Information Media Technology
Journalism Studies

Knitware Manufacture
Legal Studies
Leisure Management
Manufacturing Engineering Systems
Marketing
Modern Musicianship
Office Administration with Languages
Photography & Audio Visual Technology
Professional Culinary Arts
Promotion and Events Management
Radio Broadcasting
Rural Resources
Textiles
Tourism
Video Production

Appendix 1.2 SCOTVEC Advanced Courses Available

A list of SCOTVEC Advanced Courses at present available in the Highlands and Islands.

Accounting
Automatic & Technology Management
Building Management
Business Administration
Business Studies with Gaidhealtochd Studies
Business Studies and Information Technology
Business Studies with Office Technology
Chemical Engineering
Chemistry
Computing
Construction Studies
Electronic and Electrical Engineering
Engineering
Fabrication and Welding Design
Forestry
Gaelic Broadcasting
Hairdressing and Salon Organisation
Hospitality Management
Information and Office Management
Management
Mechanical Engineering
Social Care
Higher Certificate / Diploma in Gaelic Broadcasting

Appendix 1.3 The Inter-university relationships during the formation period

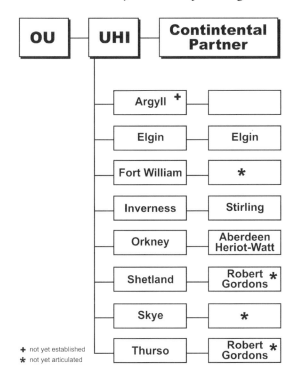

Appendix 1.4 The ladder of entry and exit qualifications

Appendix 1.5 The The original development schedule

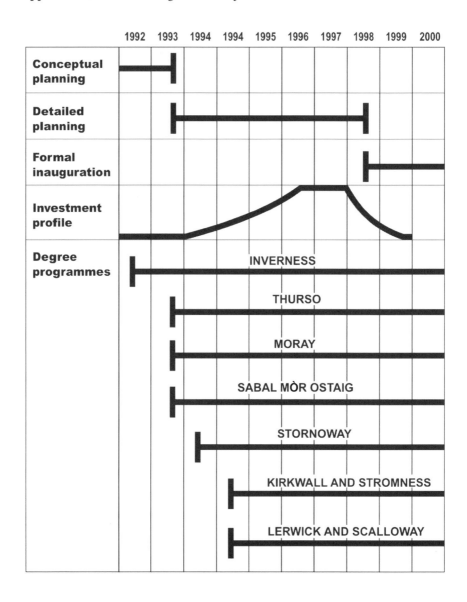

Appendix 2

The Future of Universities in a Global Context

A New Kind of University

The tug-of-war between the old and the new in higher education policy has been elaborated at various points in the main text of this book. However, defensive and conservative attitudes are not restricted to universities. They are universal and immortalised in the words of Machiavelli in his book *The Prince:*

> It must be considered that there is nothing more difficult to carry out, nor more doubtful to success, than to initiate a new order of things. For the reformer has enemies in all those who profit by the old order, and only lukewarm defenders in all those who profit by the new order, this lukewarmness arising partly from fear of their adversaries …; and partly from the incredulity of mankind, who do not truly believe in anything new until they have actual experience of it.

The excitement attached to the University of the Highlands and Islands Project was therefore that although it would be obliged to take note of established university customs, it was nevertheless free to think 'outside the box'. It carried no baggage from the past and, as noted earlier, the clean sheet of paper in front of the founders was regarded by them as a good place to start. It is a welcome fact of life that in changing times coming late is always an advantage. Other people's shoulders invariably offer an inviting prospect.

Nevertheless, once formed, universities quickly revert to the stereotype of a bastion of culture. As a result they are the great survivors. They can boast nearly a millennium of uninterrupted existence in Europe such that the prime mover, Bologna, is to a first approximation the same institution as when it was founded. Over that period almost all other public and private institutions withered away. A potential rival for longevity, the church, is still hanging on – but only just. In Europe the monasteries came and went, their lands and possessions being seized by greedy kings. Frontiers moved, ideologies blossomed and faded but universities remained intact and untouched until the present day. The very idea of a new kind of university might therefore seem a contradiction in terms.

The Purpose of a University

If the university scene changed at all, it was as the result of growth of knowledge and the growth of numbers. Thus the universities, as one-time religious academic institutions, survived the Reformation by bending under the pressure of the scientific revolution ushered in by Galileo and Newton. To satisfy those with less patience, a number of new universities emerged in the early 1800's devoted to the new knowledge, to new skills and to new world views. Four types of university dominated the nineteenth century. They are described in outline in *Table A* and represent different historic views of the purpose of a university.

Table A – Four types of University

Napoleonic Model	**Napoleonic Model**
Formal status – state dominated	**Formal status** – subject dominated
Purpose – the training and education of administrative elites	**Purpose** – production of research based knowledge, research dominated professor dominated, PhD important
Knowledge business – seperate research centres	**Knowledge business** – non-utilitarian
Places – Grandes Écoles, Écoles polytechniques	**Places** – global, international
Ethos – efficiency	**Ethos** – knowledge
Historic character – Paris Model	**Historic character** – know what

English, Oxford Newman Model	**Scottish American Model**
Formal status – collegiate life	**Formal status** – democratic and global
Purpose – tutorial learning, development of the whole person	**Purpose** – useful knowledge, utilitarian, market driven, industrially focussed, non-elitist, pluralistic emphasis on independence, innovation and technology transfer
Places – small colleges	**Places** – anywhere
Ethos – efficiency	**Ethos** – non-elitist, pluralistic
Historic character – Bologna Model	**Historic character** – know-how

The Napoleonic model reflects the ambitions of the nation state to organise and govern the essential requirements of modern armies, modern empires and modern industries. The very strength of French government and its largely state-owned industries remains a testament to its Écoles and their output of a well educated and well trained administrative elite.

A cynic might observe that France simply exchanged one kind of central university authority, the Roman Catholic Church, for its secular equivalent, the state, and that the new model was only new in its embracing of science and technology. The German Model, however, represented a fundamental change which is still continuing. Essentially, the then still extant mediaeval universities were challenged into subjection by the growing body of scientific knowledge. The University of Berlin, founded in 1808 by the Humboldt brothers, was devoted to rational thought and the unfettered accumulation of systematic knowledge. The Humboldt model was quickly copied throughout the Western world. The central theme was of independent thought, curiosity-driven research and the teaching of research-based knowledge by a new community of researchers and scholars. This was the triumphal academic ethos of the 19th and 20th centuries which, in one form or another, is likely to continue.

The Oxford model in *Table A* is a variant of the Humboldt model. Its thesis, the value of knowledge for its own sake, was extolled by John Henry Newman in his influential book,

The Idea of a University. Whilst his aim was knowledge in general, it was mainly that of the humanities, of ancient languages and moralities. It was redeemed by its insistence on the centrality of the student.

The soft-pedalling of the volume of knowledge in favour of the quality of the experience led to a supremely satisfying (but expensive) model of higher education, the ideal of the Oxbridge system hardly affordable anywhere else. In some famous words, Newman wrote:

> I consider then that I am charged with no paradox, when I speak of a knowledge which is its own end, when I call literal knowledge or a gentlemen's knowledge.

Those kinds of sentiments went down badly with industrialists in Scotland, North America and elsewhere. Neither in the Oxford model nor in the other two models referred to was there much interest in utility, but a more utilitarian model emerged to promote useful knowledge, such as technology. It is the fourth option in *Table A* and Germany, Switzerland, Japan, the USA and tiny Scotland established outstanding centres of technology which would be the engines of their industrial supremacy. But even these retained their traditional university structures, their methods of teaching, their faculties, their senates, their gowns and their degrees. In that sense, the traditional university was alive and well in all of them. Up till the late 1900's, the universities therefore seemed settled, teaching the same subjects in the same way as did their forebears a century earlier.

More Means What?

But then radical change erupted, resisted of course – but in the end adopted as the result of *force majeure*. The first big development was the massification of higher education. What had, in England at least, once been until, say, 1950 a cottage industry of educating a tiny elite of carefully selected and appropriately groomed young people (mainly male) was, in a generation or so, transformed into another, bigger business for educating and training a large fraction of the age group from, say, 18 to 22, at least 50% of them female. Many of them were necessarily from families and schools not used to producing undergraduates of any kind. For them, the factory methods which had earlier made schooling available to all would find their way into universities. The pessimists who cried "More means worse" were (just) confounded and the champion of mass higher education, Sir Christopher Ball, was able to retort that "More means different". For certain, this new future of mass higher education had come to stay.

In Britain this good news was unfortunately bought at a price and that price was the seemingly thoughtless acceptance that the expansion of the age participation rate from 10 to 50% could best be effected simply by the linear extrapolation of the old, elitist system of higher education. The down-sides of this mischievous naivety were many, excessive cost (the highest unit cost in the world), the consolidation of all the old subjects, all the old methods and all the old attitudes. When, later, the otherwise separate, polytechnic sector was merged with the then fifty or so existing universities, the UK system of higher education was formally doubled in size, but not in resources. The budgets of both HE and FE were simply added together thereby achieving the cosmetic outcome of a greatly reduced average unit cost.

This still incomprehensible step effectively halved the appropriate costs of teaching and research. Amidst the clamour for all of these universities, old and new, to reach for the highest of standards, the whole university sector would now be driven if not to bankruptcy at least to penury. As a result, a frozen, zero-sum mentality descended on all involved and at a time when boldness and innovation were the self-evident keys to national progress and prosperity. It was a dispiriting time to be a British academic and it was a sharp lesson for those contemplating a new future for HE.

Exercising Choice

The qualitative results of mass higher education were no less dramatic. There would be seismic shifts of academic interest. The immediate post-war years had seen an explosive growth in conventional subjects, especially those allied to science and technology. The standard route for first-generation, erstwhile working class students was engineering. Science was a close second. Families without prior experience of being related to medics, lawyers, academics and philosophers stuck to their utilitarian lasts, leaving the middle classes to fill out the more genteel professions. But the succeeding, second generation, changed all that and, by the year 2000, faculties of engineering and science were hard put to find enough able undergraduates.

This was also because deliciously new subjects had caught the eye of the young. Media studies and business studies were among the earliest of new subject areas, immediately greeted with derision by the university authorities, especially those of the older universities. But the flood was unstoppable and soon identified as a necessary source of income. Even Oxford University eventually boasted a business school.

Given the chance, the undergraduates of the late twentieth century would exercise choice to the full. All that kept the barbarians from the gate was the apparently immovable structure of existing subjects and their professors whose livelihood depended on them. Ultimately, complete departments, many of them famous, even faculties, closed for the want of undergraduate numbers.

There was now in train a quiet revolution in which academic emphasis was being replaced by more vocational considerations. The old elitist model of scholarship and explicit knowledge, soon to be referred to as Mode 1, was giving way to another model of implicit knowledge – contextual and useful – now known as Mode 2. Although it was not recognised as such, the one-time students of Mode 1 were flocking to become the students of Mode 2. The context of education had overtaken its content.

An Age of Uncertainty

Another, less benign change occurred everywhere as the result of the near explosion of student numbers. Big expenditure on higher education soon became very big expenditure. Governments which had hitherto accepted the expenditure on universities as a marginal necessity now began to query the costs of higher education and the benefits supposedly flowing from it. Perpetual students, drop-outs and failure rates became matters of serious concern. The current mania for accountability quickly spread to the university sector. League tables of performance sprouted everywhere and for everything. The conformity which these competitive pressures inevitably required was another dispiriting feature of UK universities.

To this misery was added another, namely underfunding. Government funding is always deficiency funding and, by definition, inadequate. Salaries were pegged and the best of professors and students, however defined, no longer queued up for academic careers. The universities became resentful places. Their students also deserted their traditional protesting role of supporting lost causes and threatening overweening government. The only cause they espoused, and that only feebly, was to protect their privileges and personal incomes and to march against modest fees and fox hunting. As far as the great issues of our time were concerned, university students in Britain were no longer anywhere to be seen.

The end of the 20th century therefore saw universities unsure of their role and united only in defence of a *status quo* dreamily based on their supposedly glorious past. This was no basis for sparkling and daring visions of any future whatsoever.

Of one thing they could be certain and that was the ever more inviting consequences of the advent of the Internet some ten years earlier. This, the most remarkable of learning tools, was poised to change entirely our view of knowledge and the role of the universities. Although it was the invention and child of industry and almost wholly Mode 2 in character, it had to be the starting point of any new future universities.

The New Starting Point

The automation of the organisation of knowledge content by the Internet inevitably throws light on the context of that knowledge. One of the obvious consequences of that contextualisation is its universal exposure to the continued growth of knowledge, which is global and not confined to universities. There is only one Internet and there will be only one, with a global language, global software and eventually global values. It is ironic that notwithstanding the ramifications of history, religion, politics and race the world would be eventually united by two machines, the terrestrial television set and the personal computer; the latter responsible for the democratisation of knowledge itself.

Such a volcanic eruption was bound to have profound effects on education but inevitably, given their conservative character, universities sailed on regardless, more concerned than anything with the question of whether hand-calculators should be allowed in the examination room. In spite of acres of personal computers their attitude to knowledge, to learning, to examinations and to performance remained and largely remains unchanged.

One particularly stark outcome of the Internet was to undermine the privileged position of the universities as a whole whose very existence was predicated on their owning and guarding the keys to knowledge. The rational response to this has to be the New Learning Paradigm which switches attention away from the value of explicit knowledge to the value of the implicit, personal knowledge defined by Michael Polanyi. The new role of universities is then the revival of their earliest role of the development of the individual by rhetorically exchanging current wisdom and its associated skills in the Socratic manner.

One of the surest signposts emanating from this reflection on the likely future of universities is that whereas until roughly the year 2000 skills of all kinds were incidental to the knowledge base, the knowledge itself is now incidental to the skills base. This 180 degrees turn in educational values has yet to sink in, but sink in it will.

The Future of Universities

Given that the new instrumentation and the new emphasis on intellectual and other skills are here to stay, then the future of universities for some time to come is clear. They will remain the focal points of congenial gatherings of undergraduate students, not unlike the older academies. The need for massive libraries, massive laboratories and massive populations of students will evaporate to make way for more intimate experiences built on personal contacts between students and dons and between students and students, the Oxford model no less. The word 'don' is revived to remind us of that tradition and deliberately to break with the arid customary vocabulary of teacher, lecturer and professor and their didactic implications. Words like guide, mentor and councillor are also too linked to the present arrangements to be the signal of new procedures and new values.

The aims of the undergraduate university are then threefold:

(1)   to come to terms with the growing and shifting explicit knowledge base, the Internet;

(2)   to use the Internet and all the other sources of information to address topical problems and projects (problem-based learning); and

(3)   to defend these case studies in written and verbal exchanges with the resident dons and other experienced practitioners.

The success of education, and especially of higher education, has been and always will be dependent on an intimate, emotional experience of the discovery of the self. It has less to do with the passive acquisition of knowledge *per se* and everything to do with the development of the personality and character. It is perhaps surprising that it required machines to 'clear the deck' and make this human activity once again possible.

A question that might be asked is whether the absence of formal laboratories would make everyone an armchair theorist? Since most undergraduate technical laboratories are already of the museum variety, the answer has to be that, in addition to the skills of music, the arts and sport, the skills of observation and measurement are readily attainable from the widespread instrumentation already available in non-traditional unspecialised learning laboratories.

The General and the Particular

The real business of acquiring the vital, professional skills of science, engineering, medicine, dentistry and research can then be safely left to the professional graduate schools linked to or as part of professional practice in hospitals and research laboratories. This sequential separation of the learning process into the general and the particular is the expected natural bifurcation of knowledge resulting from excessive pressure on an otherwise monolithic system of one kind of knowledge. It is also the practice of the United States, where perhaps 90% of all undergraduate students terminate their formal studies at the level of the first degree.

This degree will become the universal bench mark of graduateness, the point at which the 21-year-old will be qualified to enter the work place or future studies. And because of the breadth of their education and training they will be qualified to enter almost all work places.

They will bring with them a confident awareness of the global knowledge base, its languages, its procedures and the verbal and written skills to communicate them. Their education will have been not to fill them with knowledge but to infuse them with curiosity, with personal skills and with a knowledge of themselves. The rest is up to them.

Bologna and After

This possible resurgence of the older Scottish system of general education at both the secondary and tertiary levels, now firmly rooted in the USA, coincides with the emergence in Europe of the Foundation Degree now promoted by most governments including that of Britain. The initiative to promote a common general degree throughout Europe is one of several efforts aimed at binding the countries of the European Federation more closely together. The Bologna Declaration of June 1999 was the natural successor to the earlier Erasmus Programme of interchanges of undergraduate students between different member states.

It was thought, rightly so, that serious undergraduate experiences of other countries would, in time, reduce historic animosities based on cultural prejudices. If it could not start with the open-minded young, where could this fraternising start? The Erasmus programme was a success as long as it lasted – which turned out to be as long as it was subsidised by participating countries. When pump-priming support dried up, so did the programme. In any event, even fully subsidised it required a greater flexibility and homogeneity of courses, terms and assessments than was normally the case.

The Bologna Declaration therefore decided to go one stage further and press for a common first degree sufficiently in harmony with the wishes and practices of most member states. It Such a development would open the doors to all undergraduates for them to spend one or more semesters in another country, perhaps continuing their studies there, perhaps working, perhaps both. Nothing would so raise the quality of the university experience and so inexpensively.

It would probably be true to say several of the governments that signed the Treaty did not seriously consider the full implications of so doing. The British Government has not consulted widely and is quoted as stated that the new arrangements are close enough to the British way to be acceptable. Unless the British Government is prepared to support the idea of an 'intermediate' undergraduate course *for all* then the Bologna ideal will have been lost. Indeed, there is every indication that the Government's desired outcome would be the re-instatement in England of a 2-year, sub-degree qualification not too far from the earlier Higher National Diploma and even earlier Diploma of Higher Education.

It is extraordinary how a notion, however mistaken, once entrenched into Government lore remains there forever awaiting its opportunity.

In Scotland, this is not a problem. There is already and there always has been a first degree of the kind envisaged by the Bologna Declaration. It is called the Ordinary Degree and once was the only degree. It was then the (old) Scottish MA and it was upon the character of that degree that Scotland's international reputation as an educated nation rested. Notwithstanding the devolution of responsibility for education at all levels for the Scottish Parliament, it is unlikely that Scotland will be allowed to go it alone. The opportunity for it to adopt European standards before its big sister England is nowhere to be seen in the documents describing the future of HE in Britain. It therefore seems that a Scottish baccalaureate and a Scottish Bologna degree will remain attractive but unattainable ideals.

These uncertainties, together with attendant problems of funding and fees, make the future of higher education and universities in the UK far from clear. Happily the French, the German, the Dutch and the Italian and Spanish governments have warmly welcomed the Bologna proposals and indicated their willingness to press ahead.

Whatever the outcome of Bologna, the rampant costs of traditional higher education for all will require a rethink of the work of universities. Their direct value to society will continue to be as the major source of professional studies, such as medicine, law, accountancy and, it is hoped, engineering. The cost of such courses will continue to escalate as instrumental sophistication drives on change and development.

The need for all academic professionals to work closely and usefully with their hospital, business or industrial counterparts suggests more focused research schools, with numbers severely constrained by costs. The organisation of research schools in many countries is a haphazard affair reflecting historic interests and personal inclinations. The pressure of the context of research and development will continue to grow, forcing the most expensive researches to be conducted in separate, free-standing institutions (such as CERN) and forcing the rest to transfer their science into technology.

The main imports into those special centres will be from a restricted number of smaller research units attached to the larger universities, just as it is in the United States. The remainder of the universities, perhaps three quarters of them, will find their new roles as the bed rock of undergraduate studies, equally excellent, equally expensive and equally revered. Again, just as in the United States. As noted above, the descriptive term for this kind of university college in the USA is 'Liberal Arts' but the rest of the world might better settle just for *university* and allow the proliferation and diversification of all universities to match the needs of their circumstances.

The threat to both kinds of universities and especially to the specialist research centres is that the more specialist and successful they become, the more likely they are to be outmoded. As Ziman reminds us, science in the steady state requires the constant pruning of existing interests to allow the birth of the new. Universities are not good at doing that and their tendency to sanctify the present and cling to the past has been their undoing.

The Globalisation of Higher Education

The globalisation of these 'undergraduate universities' and the competition between them will lead quickly to the harmonisation of their courses and practices. Whether or not the Bologna Declaration is put into practice, this harmonisation would open the door to the migration of undergraduates throughout the civilised world. There is no good reason (and there never was) for them to be sequestered in a single institution for three or more years. Perhaps it will become the norm for two or more semesters to be spent in other seats of learning. As noted above, familiarity with other countries and other customs is, for most students, a large and beneficial experience. As a prop of world unity and global peace there could be no better foundation.

The practices to be globalised in this way include the modularisation of all courses, the credit accumulation of all assessments, continuous or otherwise, and a uniform pass-fail gradation, hopefully not too high. Even so, for many traditional institutions these simple reforms will remain in the unthinkable category. In the end, no organisation should be obliged to adopt any of the new practices. The choice of being global or not is theirs and, it is hoped, will remain so.

In spite of the growing good will towards harmonisation, there remains one formidable obstacle to its widespread adoption – who pays? When fees were small, even negligible, this question did not arise. At most, students paid for their own travel and their own living expenses and that was that. Such open-handed behaviour was sustainable because numbers were small. Now neither numbers nor fees are small.

It is possible to imagine that UNESCO or some other global organisation could manage the intensity and the complexity of the financial exchanges, but only just. The more likely outcome is that financial exigency will force governments to identify the economic costs of undergraduate education and to seek to recover part or all of those costs from student fees, which might or might not be means-tested or otherwise subsidised. This would, in effect, sever the direct link between national governments and universities and thereby free the students to move and take their certificates, scholarships or vouchers with them. A happier outcome still would be for the first, foundation degree to be seen as an extension of general 'compulsory' education and therefore free. At the same time the costs of professional education at graduate schools would also need to be at economic levels and would be that much greater because of its high value. It is unlikely that such complex procedures could be switched on easily but, as the price of global understanding and global peace, they would be good value for money.

There is an important principle at stake in these considerations. As long as students are directly funded by national governments, their capacity to move and to choose will be limited. Under these circumstances the full flowering of the international opportunities to university students and to universities themselves will be inhibited. Evolution depends on diversity and it is already the case that within nation states competition *between* universities encourages conformity and thereby discourages change and reform. It might be that inside the European Union, as in the United States, that the free flow of students could become possible. The Erasmus ideal would then be reinstated and at no great cost to government.

New Learning in Practice

The future of universities is therefore predicated on the basis that they will take up the opportunities presented by the hardware and software of the personal computer and the Internet. They will do so out of a mixture of beliefs that the new procedures would be more effective and student-friendly and that they would be economically more efficient.

Thus the effective deployment of the New Learning Paradigm does not require the constant attention or the constant presence of large numbers of full-time distinguished academics. For the mentoring and tutoring of the case studies, part-time professional practitioners would be as competent as any. For the 'star' lectures and seminars to stimulate and motivate the undergraduates, charismatic professors, living or recorded, are essential. For both kinds of student supervision, the personalities of the new dons will be crucial.

This emphasis on face-to-face teaching and tutoring is at the heart of the new university. As noted before, such engagement is essentially an intimate, small-scale activity. That being so, it is questionable whether increased institutional size offers any advantages. For most of their existence universities have been small affairs with student numbers less than 1,000. The mega university is a new phenomenon justified only by supposed economies of scale. This short-term view of life conveniently overlooks the down-sides of size. Evidence of long-term benefits of unlimited growth has yet to surface, but common sense suggests they will be small or negative. Learning remains, as it has always been, an emotional engagement between small numbers of people and their abiding interests. The days of the packed auditorium and other factory methods are surely limited.

The re-humanisation of higher education is not just a pedagogical response to the increasingly arid transfer of explicit and therefore objective knowledge as information. It puts the human being at the centre of the knowledge business.

The Two Modes Revisited

That it could be elsewhere is plain from the epistemological study of the flood of scientific knowledge which dominated the culture of the eighteenth and nineteenth centuries. The Age of Enlightenment was an age of open-minded inquiry of the kind harking back to classical times. Its success led on to what Ziman called the scientific or academic ethos in which explicit knowledge would come to dominate all other forms of knowledge. Its essentials are set out in *Table B*. They describe the educational thinking and the educational practice of most people today. The academic ethos is a triumph of the human intellect and as humans we can be proud of this pinnacle of observation and rational thought.

In their seminal book, *The New Production of Knowledge*, Gibbons and his colleagues refer to this body of knowledge as Mode 1. It is authoritative and linear in its thinking. One of its greatest fruits is the Internet, the new repository of exact, objective scientific knowledge in words and images.

But this extraordinary achievement is not without its defects. An obvious feature (of its success) is its now near infinite size. Another is its tendency continuously to fragment into an ever greater number of knowledge sub-sets, each subject representing a homogeneous island of knowledge in a sea of other such islands. The management of the new knowledge requires

Table B – The Mode 1 World of Higher Education

The Academic Ethos

Social Practice	*Epistemic principle*
subject specialisation	fragementation of knowledge
specialist publications	homogenous knowledge bases
impersonal attitudes, open publication and argument	objectivity, empiricism and realism
Systematic criticism, orderly controversy, peer review	Consistency, reliability, refutations but also estgablishment-minded, internally referenced
open to novelty, personal autonomy	progress, conjecture
universality, transcultural	general laws, comon unified abstractions
decisive criterion	Is it right?

Table C – The Mode 2 World of Higher Education

The contextualisation of knowledge; the world of technology

Holistic, not reductionist

Context driven, not subject driven

Mission-oriented research, not blue skies

Team work, not individual scholar

Multi-authored publications, heterogeneous knowledge bases

Divergent not convergent thinking

Reflexive philosophy rather than objective statements

Decisive criterion: does it work?

This is the world outside academia

constant organisation, regulation and verification. The need for local homogeneity of meaning and practice inevitably ends as a new Tower of Babel. The old adage of knowing more and more about less and less has come into its own.

And since the golden rule of Mode 1 is that all of its knowledge should be explicit and therefore objective, it follows that whenever possible the human element is kept at bay, always to the detriment of its human interest.

The designation of this scientific knowledge as Mode 1 was no doubt driven on by the emergence of another class of knowledge conveniently called Mode 2. This encompassed all the rump of the other knowledge, all of it implicit and therefore human in character and in context. It is described in *Table C.* It is the world we live in. It is the world of work. All of the knowledge of Mode 2 is contextual and therein lies its anchor to reality. In higher education, it is best manifested in the case study involving the novel collection of facts, circumstances, values and judgements. Its knowledge bases are largely heterogeneous and therefore open to easy engagement with other such knowledge bases. It is the home of innovation, design and technology. It is a proper intellectual environment for all undergraduates whether they intend to specialise further or not.

For the specialist, the brain surgeon, the concert pianist and the particle physicist the way beyond these foundation years is clear, namely practice and further practice under the eye of the best practitioners available and in what is essentially a Mode 1 experience. For the undergraduate it is enough to study in a Mode 2 intellectual environment. It can be made an heroic adventure appropriate to students of the twenty first century. They care for their world in a way that their antecedents could not and almost certainly because they know more about it.

The Greenpeace movement, the anti-capitalist demonstrations, and the GAP year point to a greater degree of idealism not easily nurtured on a global scale before the advent of television and the World Wide Web. These emotional issues will increasingly require appropriate responses from the providers of education and only the old systems stand in the way of a landslide of student preference for better things.

Graham Hills
July 2003

Index